ADULT PSYCHIATRY IN FAMILY AND CHILD LAW

ADULT PSYCHIATRY IN FAMILY AND CHILD LAW

B Mahendra

 **Family Law**

Published by

Jordan Publishing Limited
21 St Thomas Street
Bristol BS1 6JS

British Library Cataloguing-in-Publication Data

A catalogue record for this book is available from the British Library.

ISBN 1 84661 025 7

Typeset by Etica Press Ltd, Malvern, Worcestershire

Printed in Great Britain by Antony Rowe Ltd, Chippenham

CONTENTS

TABLE OF CASES

TABLE OF STATUTES

References are to paragraph numbers.

CODES OF GUIDANCE

References are to paragraph numbers.

GLOSSARY

Abnormal Outside of the norm in a statistical sense. Not necessarily pathological.

Aetiology Cause(s) of a disorder.

Affect Mood.

Affective disorder Mood disorder, especially where mood is pathologically elevated or lowered as in mania or depressive illness.

Agoraphobia A phobic anxiety disorder in which the patient has a pathological fear of venturing into situations where crowds of people may be met.

Alzheimer's disease A dementing disorder due to degenerative processes taking place in the brain. Believed to be the commonest cause of both senile and pre-senile dementia.

Anorexia nervosa An eating disorder, suffered predominantly by females, due to a distortion of body image leading to fear of weight gain.

Anxiety state A disorder in which there is a pathological and disproportionate sense of fear in the presence of trivial or no stimuli. Usually divided as between generalised anxiety disorders and phobic anxiety disorders.

Asperger's syndrome A disorder placed within the higher end of autistic spectrum disorders due to a pervasive developmental disorder. It is characterised by mild autistic features involving impaired social functioning and stereotypical repetitive behaviour. There is no impairment of intelligence.

Attention-deficit hyperactivity disorder (ADHD) A disorder of childhood involving overactivity, distractibility and impulsive behaviour.

Autism A pervasive developmental disorder of childhood within the severe end of the spectrum of autistic disorders. Intellectual impairment is usual.

Benzodiazepines A group of drugs used as anxiety reducing (anxiolytic) agents. They are depressants of the central nervous system but a paradoxical effect may cause disinhibition and aggression. Highly addictive.

Bipolar affective disorder A disorder of mood where episodes of mania and/or depressive illness may occur.

Brain scans Imaging techniques including computerised tomography (CT) and magnetic resonance imaging (MRI) allowing brain structure to be studied.

Bulimia nervosa An eating disorder in which patients, usually women, display binge eating and preoccupation with weight which is regulated by vomiting, abuse of diuretics and laxatives and excessive dieting.

Cardiovascular Relating to arterial blood vessels supplying the heart. Impairment of function may lead to ischaemic heart disease and heart attacks.

Catatonia A collection of behaviours involving disorders of speech, movement and posture. May be seen in schizophrenia, depressive illness and neurological states.

Cerebrovascular Relating to arterial blood vessels supplying the brain. Impairment of function may lead to strokes.

Cognitive behaviour therapy A form of psychological treatment used in dealing with maladaptive behaviours and abnormal mood states by attempting to change negative thought patterns of the patient.

Compulsion The motor counterpart of obsessional thinking.

Confusion A symptom resulting from an impairment in consciousness as may be found in acute organic states such as delirium. To be distinguished from disorientation.

Conversion symptoms A feature of hysterical states. In avoiding inner conflict there is produced psychological energy which is converted into physical symptoms such as paralysis or blindness. There is primary gain for the patient through relief from anxiety.

Creutzfeldt-Jakob disease The classical illness (and its more recent variant) are rare causes of pre-senile dementia. A viral cause is suspected.

Delirium An acute organic disorder involving disturbance of consciousness commonly seen in states of alcohol withdrawal (delirium tremens) and infections, especially in the elderly.

Delusion A false belief unshakeably held despite evidence to the contrary, and out of keeping with the individual's social and cultural background.

Dementia An acquired global condition which leads to an impairment in functioning of the intellect, memory, personality and social behaviour. The term is entirely descriptive and the causes may be various, for example, degenerative brain disease, endocrine disease, etc.

Depot injection A drug, usually an anti-psychotic agent, which is given periodically by intramuscular injection. Obviates the need for daily ingestion of medication and thereby improves compliance.

Depression A pathological lowering of mood.

Depressive illness A disorder in which the central feature is a pathologically diminished mood.

Dissociative disorders Formerly hysterical reactions. A disorder in which the integrity in the relationship between memory, identity, sensory perception and motor control appears lost as a result of unconscious mechanisms. Common manifestations include amnesia, fugue (wandering), stupor and motor disorders. An extreme variant is trance or possession states.

Down's syndrome A disorder with (usually) severe intellectual impairment which is a common cause of mental handicap or learning disabilities. Due to a chromosomal abnormality.

Electroconvulsive treatment (ECT) A procedure by which seizures are induced by the passage of electricity through the brain. An effective treatment for severe depressive illness.

Epidemiology The study of the distribution and possible causes of disorders in a population.

Functional disorder A disorder in which no obvious adverse change in the structure and function of the brain can be discerned in the present state of knowledge.

General paralysis of the insane (GPI) A condition due to tertiary (ie untreated or incompletely treated) syphilis. In the past a severe untreatable dementia used to be a feature.

Hallucination An abnormal perception arising in the absence of an external stimulus (cf illusion). May involve any of the senses, for example, auditory, visual, etc. Could be true or pseudo hallucination. Their significance depends on the entirety of the clinical picture.

Huntington's chorea A cause of pre-senile dementia characterised by abnormal movements and mental disorder including dementia. It is a genetic condition.

Hypomania A less severe form of mania.

Hysteria The older term for conversion/dissociative disorders.

Illusion A misperception due to misinterpretation of stimuli. Usually normal phenomena occurring in such situations as believing a shadow conceals a person.

Incidence Number of new cases of a disorder occurring within a defined population over a defined period of time, for example, 12 months (cf prevalence).

Insight The awareness a patient possesses in regard to a condition he suffers from. There are gradations through full, partial and no insight.

Life events Potentially stressful events such as bereavement, divorce, a house move, loss of employment, etc, which may have a bearing on the onset of psychiatric disorders, in particular depressive illness.

Mania A form of affective disorder in which the central feature usually is an elevation of mood, for instance, elation. It is associated with increased energy, overactivity, disinhibited behaviour, pressure of speech and grandiose ideas or delusions.

Maternity blues Transient mood changes involving depression and anxiety occurring in over half of mothers with a newborn baby.

Mental disorder A compendious term including mental illness, learning disabilities, personality and psychopathic disorders and addiction and other disorders not amounting to formal illness.

Morbid jealousy A psychotic disorder presenting in its own right or as a symptom of another psychosis such as schizophrenia or alcohol abuse characterised by a false belief in the infidelity of spouse or partner.

Munchausen syndrome A disorder involving persistent simulation of illness associated with pathological lying, exaggeration of symptoms and the making of importunate demands on hospitals and medical staff. A variant is the controversial, possibly discredited, disorder by proxy in which a carer involves (usually) a child in the simulation or exaggeration of illness. Best understood as a severe personality disorder.

Negative symptoms (of schizophrenia) Include lack of motivation, apathy, poverty of speech, social withdrawal, emotional unresponsiveness and self-neglect. May respond poorly to standard forms of treatment.

Neuroses Minor psychiatric disorders in which insight and a sense of reality are preserved and there is a discernible contribution of the personality to the disorder. Neurotic conditions include minor depressive illness, anxiety states, obsessive-compulsive disorder and hysterical reactions (dissociative/conversion disorders).

Obsessive-compulsive disorder. A neurotic disorder in which is found ideas and thoughts which are persistent, intrusive, unwelcome and subject to resistance without success on the part of the patient. The motor counterparts are called compulsions.

Organic Refers to disorders where there is demonstrable structural or functional (ie pathophysiological) disturbance of brain function.

Orientation An individual's awareness of time, place and person. Disturbed in the dementias.

Parasuicide Deliberate self-harm in which the element of intention is absent from the behaviour leading to self-harm. Usually associated with reckless behaviour.

Personality disorder Involves an abnormal personality whose behaviour is at odds with the norms and standards applying in his culture. The disorder is enduring and is separate from any formal illness which may from time to time come to overlie it. The diagnosis is made at presumed maturity but the onset is invariably in childhood as behaviour disturbance. There are problems usually in the personal, social and occupational spheres. Many categories are described (see text).

Phobic anxiety state An anxiety disorder which is situation-specific such as claustrophobia or social phobia.

Positive symptoms (of schizophrenia) These include symptoms such as delusions, hallucinations and speech disorder which are features of acute illness and usually respond to standard treatment.

Post-traumatic stress disorder (PTSD) A delayed and/or protracted response to a stressful event of an exceptionally threatening nature likely to cause distress. Probably overdiagnosed. Clinical utility suspect as features may be subsumed within depressive illness and anxiety states.

Pre-morbid Antedating illness, especially in the case of personality before onset of illness.

Prevalence Total number of cases of a disorder in a defined population at any given time (cf incidence).

Pseudohallucination A hallucination, usually auditory, arising from within an individual's mind and not relating to the world outside. May be seen in states of grief and is less significant than true hallucinations.

Psychopathology A study of abnormal mental states either in terms of their description (also called phenomenology) or as mode of causation (psychodynamic psychopathology).

Psychosis A mental disorder which leads to loss of contact with reality and insight along with the presence of symptoms such as delusions and hallucinations.

Psychosurgery A specialised and controversial form of brain surgery for modifying behaviour and emotions.

Rehabilitation Procedures aimed at minimising or preventing secondary social disability due to mental disorder by restoring previous levels of functioning.

Schizoaffective disorder A disorder in which the symptoms of a schizophrenic illness and an affective illness are both present.

Schizophrenia A psychotic disorder in which pathological changes occur in thinking, behaviour, perception and, occasionally, mood.

Schizophreniform Schizophrenia-like. A symptomatic form of schizophrenia akin to true illness. May be seen in cases involving drug abuse.

Selective serotonin reuptake inhibitors (SSRIs) A group of antidepressant drugs including fluoxetine (Prozac) and paroxetine (Seroxat).

Senile dementia Dementias occurring at the age of 65 or after. Pre-senile dementias occur before that age.

Somatic symptoms Usually seen in cases of depressive illness. Involves symptoms such as sleep disturbance and changes in appetite, bowel habits, menstrual regularity and libido.

Somatoform disorders Disorders in which the patient makes persistent complaint of physical symptoms (for which no obvious cause can be found) and refuses to accept the assurances of his doctors.

Suicidal behaviour Deliberate self-harming behaviour which involves an element of intent.

Tricyclic antidepressants Older generation of antidepressant drugs including such agents as amitryptiline and dothiepin. Now out of favour on account of adverse side effects and potential for a lethal outcome on overdose.

INTRODUCTION

As everyone will now agree, the practice of family and child law has come to play an increasingly significant part in legal proceedings. It is also plain that psychiatric assessments of the adult parties involved in these proceedings are now increasingly common. This book was prompted by the perceived need to bridge the gap – in knowledge as well as in attitudes – that still appears to exist between the family and child law practitioner on the one hand and the adult psychiatric expert on the other.

There has been no attempt made to produce yet another textbook on psychiatry. Several outstanding works already exist for study by those specialising in this field and for consultation by any interested person. Rather, an attempt has been made in this book to provide a readable and yet reasonably comprehensive outline of the salient features of adult psychiatric disorders for lawyers and other professionals involved in family and child law practice. Child lawyers, especially, need a comprehensive yet manageable and portable source of psychiatric information. Many decisions in respect of psychiatric evidence – the need for it, the appropriate expert to instruct for the purpose, the terms of the instructions to be given – are often made in the environs of a courtroom. Further, much negotiation in respect of the terms of the instructions to be given to the expert is usually undertaken by lawyers from their offices. During hearings matters of psychiatric import come up frequently. There is a clear need for a source of basic psychiatric information to be readily available to these non-medical professionals. Fairly substantial detail is therefore made available in respect of the common psychiatric disorders and some which are not so common but are of interest for a variety of reasons. But the emphasis has not been on detail but – being mindful that this work is directed primarily at a non-medical readership – on understanding. Therefore, no references, let alone any footnotes, are given. It is easy enough to acquire and build up additional knowledge when the essential structure has first been put in place. Any practitioner who desires greater depth of understanding could seek access to standard textbooks such as the *Oxford Textbook of Psychiatry* for this purpose.

The purpose has also been practical, not academic. At all points the author has borne in mind the particular and practical requirements of the practitioner in family and child law and has utilised his own knowledge of and experience in this branch of law and medico-legal practice to inform the work.

Another particular interest for the legal practitioner is in the interaction between himself and the psychiatric expert. This process normally begins with the formulation of instructions for the expert to act on. It has been the experience of the author that there is much variation in the quality of these instructions. Some sets of instructions are complete as well as being succinct, covering all the relevant points with an economy of expression, while others are vague, sometimes verbose and prone to cause confusion. In an effort to improve the standard of drafting of instructions some specimen sets of instructions are given in Appendix A. These are based on fictional case histories which nevertheless bring in the facts of real cases that have been encountered. These are by no means model sets of instructions, merely an attempt to stimulate and inform the thought processes of legal practitioners.

Two preliminary points need to be made about the nature of adult psychiatric evidence set before a court. First, the adult psychiatrist is an expert in the nature of mental disorders. He is not usually an expert on parenting or any other relevant issue that comes up for decision before the family courts. He should not, therefore, step outside his field of expertise by commenting on, say, aspects of childcare which are outside his field of expertise and the court and the professionals involved in the proceedings should not expect him to do so. Secondly, the nature and limitation of diagnoses in psychiatry – and, for that matter, in medical practice – should always be borne in mind. Occasionally, one observes seemingly endless arguments in court on some disputed diagnosis – usually involving the personality disorders – when what should be of interest to the court is the behaviour on the part of a spouse, partner or parent that led to the diagnosis being considered. For this reason fair detail is given in the book to the process leading up to a diagnosis being given and the unreliability that may attend it.

In the account on the substantive disorders in Part II of this book a general outline of treatment for the conditions is also included. There is much misunderstanding of the nature and scope of treatment available in psychiatric practice. Drug treatment apart, therapy in psychiatry needs substantial time in order to make any worthwhile impact on the mental state of any patient. This investment of time is not normally envisaged in family and child proceedings where an outcome is desired in a matter of weeks, occasionally months. There is far too much confidence placed on 'counselling' and 'therapy' for the parties – spouses, partners or parents – who may be involved in these proceedings. It is unlikely any change is to be noted in weeks or months in the average case given the complexity of human behaviour and the all too well-known impact on human beings of their social circumstances, some of which may well be beyond their control. It is also quite easily forgotten that any worthwhile treatment has its own side effects, some of which are adverse, and any psychiatrist needs to run his own risk/benefit assessment before offering treatment to any patient, whether this involves drug treatment or any psychological form of treatment. Intuition in these matters can turn out to be wrong, as witnessed by some recent studies on post-traumatic situations of stress. For a considerable time it was believed that all survivors of any significant traumatic event should be offered, as soon as possible after the event, and persuaded and encouraged even to accept, 'debriefing', to 'open up' and 'get it off their chest'. Now, an increasing body of work casts doubt on whether this form of therapy should be indiscriminately offered to all survivors. Rather, it is the carefully selected victims who seem to show most benefit. Some victims may, in fact, come to suffer harm from being thoughtlessly pursued by therapists when all they want is time and peace to collect and reorder their rudely disturbed thoughts. Similar confidence is sometimes placed in the treatment of alcohol and/or illicit substance misuse when the single most important factor in any positive result being obtained is the motivation shown by the patient; an attribute over which the therapist has limited control.

Fair detail is given also in the discussion of some concepts which are commonly misunderstood. One such concept is capacity. There appears to be two apparent difficulties concerning an understanding of capacity. First, there is the unwarranted assumption that mental disorder equates with loss of capacity and another, that capacity is always to be found in its absence. Secondly, it is not always appreciated how the courts have approached the subject and what tests the expert is required to use for assessing capacity. The opportunity is taken to deal with the subject at fuller length than is usual in a medical book and the Mental Capacity Act 2005, while it is not likely to have a direct bearing on the average case in family and child proceedings when it comes into force, will nevertheless act as a powerful reminder of the importance the law now attaches to issues of decision-making capacity and the questions regarding the autonomy of the individual that underpin it.

Readers may find some repetition in the issues discussed. This is deliberate. It is expected that most users of this book will dip into it as the need takes them. Therefore, various discussions on such matters as the interaction between genetic and environmental factors in the causation of disorders, cultural influences on pathology and behaviour, the principles to be utilised in deciding on treatment and so on are repeated wherever appropriate in the book so that the reader does not need to go back to consult the more general treatment of the subject.

Family and, in particular, child proceedings attract a wide range of professionals who each contributes his particular expertise. These professionals include judges, lawyers, social workers, psychologists, those assessing parenting skills and children's guardians. Medical professionals such as paediatricians and child and adolescent psychiatrists are also commonly involved. These latter professionals will have access to specialist medical works and may only need to update their knowledge, while others, it is felt, will benefit from having access to a straightforward account of issues arising in adult psychiatric practice. It is hoped these professionals will find this work of use to them in their activities in the field of family and child law.

B Mahendra
London, Summer 2006

mahen@supanet.com

PART I

GENERAL CONSIDERATIONS

Chapter 1

THE PSYCHIATRIC EXPERT IN FAMILY AND CHILD LAW

It must be obvious that psychiatric and psychological problems can affect individuals and have a significant bearing on the issues in any area of life including, of course, the subject matter involving the practice of family and child law. This book concerns itself with adult psychiatry and the accounts and discussion of the subject matter involving assessments of the parties will only concern those who are the spouse, partner, parent or, on occasion, an individual, usually a family member, applying to be a carer of a child or otherwise involved in the proceedings. It follows that there is usually ample scope also to deal in these proceedings with child and adolescent psychiatry in respect of child subjects and also in respect of adult and child psychological assessments. These disciplines are well-recognised specialities in their own right and their subject matter is obviously beyond the scope of this work.

The rules generally applicable to expert evidence in the law also find application in family and child law proceedings. Those features that are specific to family and child cases will be dealt with in detail in the rest of this chapter. The general rules – which, according to the judicial strictures applied regularly in case-law, show no signs of slowing down in their frequent reiteration, thus demonstrating that these rules are not yet fully appreciated by those concerned – demand of the expert witness that he be independent, unbiased and have as his overriding duty the rendering of assistance to the court through his evidence. He is not to be guided in his pronouncements by whoever might have instructed him and is responsible for his fees. He must be competent and be recognised as an expert in his field. The court itself must have acknowledged before directing the appointment of the expert that the subject matter on which enlightenment is being sought in respect of the proceedings is beyond its own lay knowledge and that expertise is required in assisting it with its deliberations. These matters are expanded in the rules of the court and the guidance offered to expert witnesses in family proceedings.

These rules come within the *Code of Guidance for Expert Witnesses in Family Proceedings* ('the Code') and form part of the *Protocol for Judicial Case Management in Public Law Children Act Cases* ('the Protocol') (see Appendix C). There is no material difference, as far as the expert is concerned, between public and private law proceedings involving children for the expert witness's duties are now recognised to be universally applicable. With suitable adaptation they also find application in all other family law proceedings.

As specialist lawyers are familiar with these rules, they are convenient to take up here from the psychiatric expert's point of view. The court at the outset has to identify, narrow and, where possible, agree the issues between the parties. The court then has to decide whether it requires opinions from expert witnesses about the questions which are not within its skills and experience. Having done that, the early identification of the questions that need to be put to the expert and answered by him is encouraged by the court.

1.1 DUTIES AND THE LIMIT OF EXPERTISE

The Code – mirroring the general law on expert evidence – expressly states that an expert witness in family proceedings has an overriding duty to the court that takes precedence over any obligation he may owe to the person from whom he has received instructions or by whom he is paid. Therefore, reports furnished should be entirely independent regardless of which party gave the instructions and must be the fruit of the expert's own labour alone.

The next requirement is a crucial one for much controversy has raged recently as to what an expert's field of expertise might be. The Code demands that opinions are confined to matters which are material to the issues between the parties and are in relation only to questions that are within the expert's expertise (that is, knowledge, skill and experience). If a question is put which falls outside that expertise, the expert must say so. This is a far more significant point than when it appears in print. It appears from reported cases – and also from unreported cases and anecdotal evidence – that the two principal causes of problematical expert evidence are not in respect of any lack of skill or competence but are due to bias and/or the expert stepping beyond the confines of his subject. With psychiatric practice there is an ever-present temptation to wander away from one's subject. The confines of the subject are poorly defined.

On first impression almost any human concern could become a part of psychiatric practice. Virtually the whole of medicine and surgery have implications for psychiatry as any systemic illness may give rise to mental health symptoms as part of the disease condition itself or as a complication of treatment. At the other end of the scale are the psychological factors which may also have an impact on disease conditions. Therefore, all human behaviour has the scope to come within psychiatry's ambit.

In practice, an attempt is made to distinguish between normal and abnormal psychology, the latter being a legitimate concern of psychiatry but, then, one may well ask where does normality end and abnormality begin? To the lay observer, psychiatry appears to be constantly adding to its bag of tricks even where the evidence for the presence of any mental disorder may be tenuous or tangential at best. To take one example, pathological gambling is now considered by some professionals to be a legitimate concern of psychiatry on the basis that addictive/dependency-inducing behaviours may have, at least in part, a common foundation. However, it may not be obviously apparent to a reasonable layman why this should be so, for cultural and social factors, not to mention legislative initiatives, may have a more potent bearing on problem gambling. The retort to that from a psychiatrist could be that social and cultural considerations are part and parcel of everyday psychiatric practice and the psychiatrist is at least as well equipped as any professional to comment on this or any analogous phenomenon.

One can better appreciate the risks involved in this alleged attempt at psychiatric expansionism when moving on to consider, say, violent behaviour which, as is plain, has numerous causes beyond the purely psychiatric. One could also include matters concerning statistical analysis and their interpretation in areas in which the average adult psychiatrist has limited, if any, expertise. Further, it is the case that the involvement of the adult psychiatrist in family and child proceedings is usually a limited one, important though it may be. There are usually so many other factors essential to the final determination of the issues. It is tempting, in those circumstances, for the psychiatrist to try to move beyond his own somewhat circumscribed role and try to play a part on the bigger stage. Whatever the reasons for the impulses for this temptation, the psychiatrist – assisted by the lawyers instructing him and the court – must eschew it and stick to what one might call the views of a 'reasonable, representative and responsible' body of the psychiatric profession in characterising what is to be considered as being the legitimate subject matter of adult psychiatric practice today.

1.2 OPINIONS AND THE UNDERLYING MATERIAL

The expert is also required, when expressing an opinion, to take into consideration all of the material facts including any relevant factors arising from diverse cultural contexts, indicating the facts, the literature and any other material the expert has relied upon in forming an opinion. This appears to be self-evident and will become even more obvious to the reader when the substantive psychiatric disorders are discussed in the next part of this work.

The information available to the adult psychiatrist is often limited at the time of the examination. The medical records, for example, may be tardy in arriving. Any report made in the absence of these records must be qualified as being preliminary. The Code emphasises this by saying that the expert should indicate whether his opinion is provisional (or qualified, as the case may be) and the reasons for the qualification, identifying what further information is required to give a definitive opinion without qualification. If such further information becomes available, and the expert then needs to change his opinion, he is required to inform those instructing him, without delay, of any change of opinion and the reasons for the changes.

1.3 LEAD SOLICITOR'S PRELIMINARY ROLE VIS-À-VIS THE EXPERT

The lead solicitor bears the responsibility of informing the expert of the following:

1. the nature of the proceedings and the issues likely to require determination by the court;

2. the questions about which the expert is to be asked to give an opinion (including any cultural or religious contexts);

3. when the court is to be asked to give permission for the instructions or whether leave has already been given;

4. whether permission is sought of the court for the instruction of another expert in the same or any related field;

5. the volume of reading which the expert will need to undertake;

6. whether or not (this will be exceptional where an adult psychiatrist is involved) permission has been applied for or given for the expert to examine the child;

7. the likely timetable of legal and social work steps;

8. when the expert's opinion is likely to be required; and

9. whether and, if so, what date has been fixed by the courts for any hearing at which the expert may be required to give evidence. (This is a most important practical point. The expert's diary can become festooned with dates on which his attendance at court may possibly be required without any further information forthcoming as to whether he is actually going to be summoned. This may occasionally lead to double booking and the expert may well find himself needing to appear in two places on the same day or having to choose where he will appear, with inconvenience all round. In any event, it is relatively uncommon nowadays for the adult psychiatrist to be summoned to court to give oral evidence and he always is grateful for up-to-date and clear information on this point.)

1.4 THE EXPERT'S PRELIMINARY RESPONSE

These preliminary obligations are reciprocal and the expert must make his own response. Among the preliminary requirements are that:

1. the expert must confirm that the work requiring to be undertaken is within his expertise;

2. the expert is available to do the relevant work within the suggested timescales and also the dates and/or times to avoid. This is crucial as the expert may have a waiting list for appointments, and there may be a delay, which may not be at all compatible with the prompt determination of issues which, in childcare proceedings in particular, are deemed essential;

3. the costs of the report must be settled giving the hourly and global rates and specifying what the fee suggested is for. It is usual to charge separately for attendance at experts'/professionals' meetings and for court attendance. Disputes about fees form an unedifying, and not truly professional, spectacle involving solicitors and experts. One does not wish to see satellite litigation commence in an attempt to recover fees due.

1.5 SEEKING LEAVE OF THE COURT

The solicitor then has to seek the leave of the court to instruct the expert by giving, among other matters, the following details:

1. the details of the expert (discipline, qualifications and expertise, usually by way of a curriculum vitae);

2. the expert's availability;

3. the relevance of the expert evidence sought to be adduced to the issues in the proceedings and the specific questions on which it is proposed the expert should give an opinion;

4. the timetable for the report;

5. the responsibility for giving instructions;

6. whether or not the expert evidence can properly be obtained by the joint instruction of the expert by two or more of the parties. This matter has no small interest for the expert. While it does not usually matter who gives the instructions, and the expert will be more concerned with the substance of the instructions, agreed joint instructions take time to prepare. An expert who might have undertaken to provide a report within a certain timescale may find it difficult, sometimes impossible, to do the work involved if solicitors cannot agree instructions and their transmission to the expert;

7. other matters of concern to the solicitor applying for leave are to say whether or not the expert evidence can be obtained by one party only, whether it is necessary for more than one expert in the same discipline to be instructed by more than one party, why the expert evidence proposed cannot be obtained from other sources (the social worker or the

guardian), the costs and their apportionment. These matters do not usually concern the expert.

1.6 DIRECTIONS OF THE COURT

The court may be required to give further directions among which the following may be of relevance to the expert:

1. The disclosure of the report to the parties and to any other expert. The normal rule is for the report to be disclosed to all relevant persons including the parties on whom the examination has been conducted. There may, however, be exceptional reasons for denying or delaying disclosure and thereby sight of the report. A case illustrates this. An examination was done on a grossly mentally disturbed mother (she was diagnosed to have severe conversion/dissociative disorder; see Part II for the substantive details). Reports had been sought from an adult psychiatrist, a psychologist and a child and adolescent psychiatrist (on the child involved) and the adult psychiatric report on the mother became the first available. In the circumstances – applying the rule that the welfare of the child was the paramount consideration in these proceedings – it was agreed with the mother's solicitors that the psychiatric report on her would not be revealed to her until all the reports became available. It was believed that if she had caught sight of one, essentially negative, opinion on her she might have taken offence and possibly withdrawn from the pending assessments and the proceedings themselves causing inconvenience all round. If she had chosen to withdraw once all the reports had been filed much less disruption would have been caused. It is hard to imagine circumstances – except possibly in cases of extreme vulnerability on account of mental disorder involving a party – in which an expert report is not disclosed at all to a subject of an examination.

2. Directions may be given for the conduct of an experts' discussion on the relevant issues. This is a valuable device which brings together diverse experts, each of whom has usually been working in isolation, who can at such a meeting have a frank discussion of their concerns in a case. Properly handled and planned it can be a very edifying source of relevant information.

3. There may also arise disagreements – real or imagined by the professionals – as between experts. Directions may be given for the involved experts to meet or speak or otherwise communicate (a physical meeting is not always required) to see if the disagreement between themselves can be narrowed. A statement of agreement and disagreement can be prepared at the end of this discussion. It is obviously beneficial to narrow down the issues in this way and to save court time later. It is very occasionally the case that an expert, so sure of his findings and conclusions, refuses to co-operate with other experts

and may even come to defy the court, but that situation, fortunately, is a rare occurrence.

Another hazard was illustrated recently in *Denton Hall Legal Services v Fifield* [2006] EWCA Civ 169 which involved a work-related personal injury case. Two experts had been required to discuss and narrow down their disagreement. They issued a jointly agreed statement, but when one expert was later questioned on the details of the agreed statement by his instructing solicitors he retracted his agreement. He said he had been mistaken in agreeing with the other expert; he regretted he had not properly checked the wording of the document before signing it; he had been the subject of a 'pressured telephone discussion' with the other expert; and in all the circumstances he wished to retract his statement. The Court of Appeal dealt harshly with him.

1.7 LETTER OF INSTRUCTIONS

This important document deserves to be considered in a section of its own. It is, of course, the basis on which an expert works. It is surprisingly often forgotten that the expert does not simply provide any psychiatric report; he writes one on the basis of the instructions he has received. As with most other matters in these proceedings, there is much variation in the quality and detail of the instructions. In Appendix A at the end of the book we give a few specimen letters of instructions so as to assist the process of comprehension of those drafting letters of instructions in respect of what could be sensibly required of an adult psychiatric expert. These specimen instructions are based on some brief fictional case histories where, however, the facts are obtained from real cases. The solicitor (or solicitors) involved in drafting the instructions is required to pay attention to, among other matters, the following points:

1. to set out the context in which the expert's opinion is sought (including any diverse ethnic, cultural, religious or linguistic contexts involved);

2. to define carefully the specific questions the expert is required to answer ensuring:

    (a) that they are within the ambit of the expert's area of expertise; and

    (b) that they do not contain unnecessary or irrelevant detail;

    (c) that the questions addressed to the expert are kept to a manageable number and are clear, focused and direct; and

    (d) that the questions reflect what the expert has been requested to do by the court;

3. to list the documentation provided or to be provided for the expert as an indexed and paginated bundle which shall include:

    (a) a copy of the order which gives permission for the instructions of the expert;

    (b) an agreed list of essential reading;

    (c) all new documentation when it is filed;

    (d) a copy of the Code and of the Protocol;

4.   to identify the relevant and professional people concerned with the proceedings (eg the treating clinicians) and inform the expert of his right to talk to other professionals provided an accurate record is made of the discussion. Busy professionals habitually talk to all and sundry – ordinary psychiatric practice involves communication with a vast array of individuals and agencies – and it is not always apparent in those situations that one needs to minute the ensuing conversation and only a brief clinical entry in the records is usually made (hardly an accurate or detailed account). The expert must be reminded that the rules governing family proceedings are very different and informal chats as between the professionals involved or anyone else are not permitted;

5.   similar considerations apply to other experts in the proceedings. The expert has a right to talk to other experts – having sought permission from those instructing – but a detailed record of any conversation undertaken should be made;

6.   cost factors must be identified including how much will be paid to the expert, when the expert will be paid and what limitations to the fee there will be. Disputes are to be avoided as far as possible;

7.   in default of agreement on the format of the letter of instructions, the court will determine the issue.

1.8 THE EXPERT'S REPORT

This is, of course, the key element in terms of the expert's involvement and the rest of the proceedings may well come to turn on the findings and conclusions arrived at in that document. The precise format is left to the expert but many ancillary matters are dealt with in the Code. There is no material difference between what is required from the expert in this respect in family proceedings as opposed to other proceedings. Some of the relevant requirements are as follows:

1.   The Report is addressed to the court, reminding the expert once again of his overriding duty to the court, a duty that goes beyond any he may owe to any party in the proceedings.

2.   It is self-evident that the details of the expert's qualifications and experience are given. As far as adult psychiatry is concerned, the courts in England and Wales (and also Scotland and Northern Ireland) will normally accept specialist accreditation with the GMC as proof of

expertise. If the adult psychiatrist wishes to claim additional expertise, for example, in child and adolescent work, psychology, etc, the onus is on him to show evidence of his qualifications and experience in these fields.

3. It is a requirement that the substance of all material instructions given to the expert is set out. From what has been said already, this must seem to be an obvious requirement. Any psychiatric report can only be read and its sense apprehended in terms of what has been required of it. It sometimes happens that further questions are put to the expert which, as we shall see, is a perfectly legitimate exercise. What is unacceptable is to ask the expert – especially at a hearing – about matters that did not feature in the instructions and will generally not appear in the findings or conclusions of any psychiatric report. Thus, while it is usual for the expert to review, with the help of the individual examined, his previous criminal record, unless specific instructions are given as regards relevant past offences, for example, assaults in the course of domestic violence or the expert has been prompted by the inclusion of a record of convictions among the papers, it is unreasonable to expect the expert to focus on such specific matters especially when faced by denials on the part of the individual examined.

4. The expert must refer to the facts as found in the letter of instructions, in the relevant papers or as established by him on examination. Obviously his findings and conclusions are based on the facts as established.

5. Details of the literature or other research material upon which the expert has relied in giving his opinion must be given. This is especially true when an unusual or controversial opinion is being given. An unintended by-product is that the literature can also assist in helping to quell uninformed lay opinion as regards (usually) some fashionable illness. At present Asperger's syndrome is a disorder catching the public eye. A 20-year-old girl, mother of a young baby, had had several episodes of schizophreniform illness which required hospitalisation and, on occasion, compulsory detention. She gave a long history of illicit drug use and non-compliance with prescribed medication. There was also considerable family conflict and childhood behavioural problems. She had, in fact, been assessed by child and adolescent psychiatrists when she was younger and family tensions were noted as being strong pathogenic elements. She also had a half-brother who was severely disabled by childhood autistic disorder. In childcare proceedings there was persistent interest expressed in whether she might have Asperger's syndrome. For what it was worth, the diagnostic criteria for Asperger's disorder which includes the requirement, 'Criteria are not met for another specific Pervasive Development Disorder or Schizophrenia', were handed out.

6. While it is not usual in Psychiatric Reports for any extensive testing to be undertaken, details of any test conducted by the expert have to be given. In family proceedings it is not uncommon to have the results of

DNA analysis, liver function tests and the results of hair strand analysis of illicit drugs discussed in the Report. These test results (apart from liver function tests which form part of the medical record) come in the form of statements made by those technical experts who have undertaken the analysis and the psychiatric expert can refer to them in the usual way.

7. Especially in psychiatric practice, it is not at all unusual to have alternative possibilities where diagnosis is concerned. In clinical practice there is differential diagnosis among possibly conflicting alternatives. As in the case described above, it is by no means always certain with a 20-year-old who has a history of drug use and has also developed a schizophreniform illness whether he has true schizophrenia of the usual kind or whether the psychotic features he has shown have arisen as a result of the impact of illicit drug use in a person who is genetically susceptible to schizophrenia. This is a matter of some clinical importance for the prognosis to be given in each case will differ. A schizophrenic illness (see later the account in Part II) may require prolonged drug treatment as prophylaxis. A drug-induced psychosis can be expected to resolve upon the cessation of misuse and with a relatively short period of symptomatic drug treatment. At present there is no certain way of being sure – hence the provisional diagnosis of a schizophreniform or schizophrenia-like illness – and a Psychiatric Report dealing with such a case must consider both possibilities, summarise the range of opinion and give reasons for the opinions expressed.

8. The expert's Report should end with a statement proving that the expert understands his duty to the court and has complied with that duty and that he verifies this by a statement of truth.

1.9 SUPPLEMENTARY QUESTIONS

A surprisingly little-used device is that any party, having read the Report, may pose questions on it to the other parties with a view to putting an agreed form of questions to the expert for his answers. It is obvious that this is a most useful method of clarifying any doubts or uncertainties, hence the surprise it is not more often used. In the absence of the agreement of the parties, the court may intervene to approve the questions to be posed.

1.10 EXPERTS' MEETINGS

These meetings, under the direction of the court, are also most valuable methods of seeking further insights which might not have been apparent when reading the reports by themselves. It is also an opportunity for experts in diverse specialities, usually working in isolation, to meet and compare notes, so to speak, on what is, after all, a common enterprise, namely to assist the court with the knowledge it otherwise will not have. Understandably, it is not always convenient to assemble a group of busy professionals in one location, although salvation has arrived in the form of telephone conferences and video links. The experts are usually asked to:

1. identify and narrow the issues in the case;

2. reach agreement wherever that is feasible;

3. identify the reasons for disagreement and identify what action may need to be taken to resolve any outstanding areas of disagreement;

4. obtain elucidation or amplification of relevant evidence in order to assist the court; and

5. limit, wherever possible, the need for experts to attend court to give oral evidence.

The proceedings of an experts' meeting – usually chaired by one of the solicitors participating in the proceedings – are minuted and a statement of agreement and disagreement, signed by each of the participating experts, must be prepared and filed.

1.11 FINAL HEARING

The Code and the Protocol give specific instructions for the management of the expert who has been called to give oral evidence but, sadly, this element of the Code usually appears to be more honoured in the breach. There is probably no part of the entire proceedings which is potentially more often wasteful of an expert's time than the preparation (or the lack of it) that is made in respect of the expert and the hearing. The process starts with the expert being notified early – usually at the time of receiving instructions – of the dates of the trial and asked to give his preferences. This could, in fact, be several months into the future but the responsible expert will mark the dates in his diary and usually no other appointments can be made for that day. It sometimes happens that the final hearing is postponed and the expert is not informed of this. This may mean the waste of a day or two if the expert is not also required on the subsequent date as well. In fact, the Code says that if the expert's oral evidence is not required he should be notified as soon as possible. Experience suggests this may or may not happen.

If the expert is, in fact, required to attend, confirmation should be made to him not less than 2 weeks before the hearing. There is also supposed to be a 'witness template' which should state how long the expert is likely to be giving evidence and it should be possible to indicate in which session of the day the court is likely to accommodate the expert. These matters are all very well in theory but, often, the expert may not conclude his evidence on the day allotted and may have to return on another date which, depending on his commitments and the availability of court time, may be many weeks ahead, thereby also prolonging the trial which, in cases involving children, may not be conducive at all to their well-being. The Children Act 1989 (CA 1989), s 1(2) states:

> 'In any proceedings in which any question with respect to the upbringing of a child arises, the court shall have regard to the general principle any delay in determining the question is likely to prejudice the welfare of the child.'

1.12 POST-HEARING ACTION

This, too, is a rare occurrence where the expert is concerned. The Code says that within 10 days of the final hearing the solicitor instructing the expert should provide feedback to the expert by way of a letter informing the expert of the outcome of the case, and the use made by the court of the expert's opinion. This does not happen with any regularity. It is now accepted that an expert benefits considerably by being informed about his evidence and some judges in the Family Division have started to do this on their own initiative.

1.13 SOME GENERAL CONSIDERATIONS

At this stage in our consideration of the involvement of the psychiatric expert it is well worth reminding ourselves of some general principles which find application in childcare proceedings.

1. The welfare of the child is the court's paramount consideration (see CA 1989, s 1). This principle is well established and well accepted even in lay circles – 'the child must come first' – but is not always adhered to by the psychiatric expert and, as we shall shortly see, some courts. This is, on the whole, understandable, if not acceptable. The focus of attention of any doctor in normal clinical practice is his patient, whether adult or child. Usual forensic practice does not change this focus. In childcare proceedings the emphasis shifts, of course, to the child and some experts find the necessary adjustment difficult to make. This may reflect itself in considering treatment for a parent who may be a subject – under the directions of a court – of a psychiatric assessment. As we shall later see in Part II of this book, there are available a wide range of treatments for mental disorders but a feature common to all of these is that they take time to work, even when they work at all. Even antidepressant drug treatment, probably the most common form of psychiatric treatment employed in practice, may require 8 to 12 weeks to show a full functional effect. By this is it is meant that, while symptoms may show fairly rapid amelioration, the behaviour relevant to childcare and which might have raised questions in proceedings, namely parenting abilities, may need a much longer timescale to show necessary improvement. Where psychological treatment is concerned, measurement of time

required for improvement in weeks or even months is optimistic; as we shall see later, several months or even years may be needed to bring about worthwhile improvement. This kind of delay is not usually compatible with s 1(2) of CA 1989, cited above. Much psychiatric treatment of a nature fundamental to the modification of behaviour is simply not realistic within the timescales normally envisaged in these proceedings.

2. One, therefore, needs to take a realistic view of what treatment is feasible for a mentally disordered parent. The question arises as to what extent resources – both of time and money – should be expended in attempting to treat the parent within childcare proceedings. The House of Lords recently pronounced on this matter in the case of *In re G (a child) (Interim care order: Residential assessment)* [2005] UKHL 68. The case turned on the interpretation of s 38(6) of CA 1989 where the relevant provision reads:

> 'Where the court makes an interim care order, or interim supervision order, it may give such directions (if any) as it considers appropriate with regard to the medical or psychiatric examination or other assessment of the child.'

While the words are plain enough, a child's assessment or examination may – usually will – require the involvement of the parent. The mother in these childcare proceedings had a troubled history in regard to childcare before she gave birth to child E. A few days after the birth the local authority commenced care proceedings in respect of this child and the care plan had been to place E for adoption. The local authority was, however, persuaded to agree to a period of residential assessment of the family at Cassel Hospital, a well-known establishment which offers specialised assessment and treatment for severely disturbed adults and families. On the basis of s 38(6) of CA 1989, the judge at first instance had directed a 6- to 8-week period of residential assessment at the hospital. That period was subsequently extended, but when the hospital recommended a further period of residential stay in the hospital the local authority refused further funding. The Family Division refused to extend the family's stay as in-patients at the hospital but the Court of Appeal allowed the family's appeal.

The House of Lords came to disagree with the court below. Their Lordships pointed out that it was common ground that the main purpose of residential assessment was to ascertain whether, by a course of intensive psychotherapy, the mother could be sufficiently improved so as to be brought into a state in which it would be safe for her to have care of the child E. They said the view of the Court of Appeal, that the essential question arising under s 38(6) of CA 1989 was whether the assessment enabled the court to obtain the information necessary for its own decision, was wrong. While there was no doubt the proposed therapeutic regime the mother was to receive and an assessment of her was likely to be valuable evidence informing the court's final decision, that was not the true purpose of the exercise of the statutory power. Section 38(6) of CA 1989 was contemplating an assessment of the child. While any meaningful assessment of the child may need to include an assessment of the child with its parents, to come within s 38(6), the proposed assessment must be an assessment of the child. The main focus had to be on the child. In this case the main focus had not been on E; it had been on the mother. What was to be assessed was the mother's capacity for beneficial response to the psychotherapeutic treatment she was to receive. Such an assessment, no matter how valuable the information might be for the purposes of the eventual final care order decision, could not be brought within s 38(6).

3. It is an essential part of childcare proceedings, as we have said, that the expert should not have informal, unrecorded discussions or undisclosed correspondence with any of the professionals or lay parties involved in the case. This may be a self-evident proposition for legal practitioners but it does go against the grain of ordinary clinical psychiatric practice. Very little of importance will happen in ordinary clinical practice if the psychiatrist does not speak informally not only with professional colleagues but also with a patient's family, friends, neighbours, the housing manager, the police, almost anyone you could name. In fact, it is an essential part of any complete assessment of a violent patient who may be predisposed to suicidal or homicidal behaviour. The expert in childcare proceedings will need to unlearn these habits and stick to the rules applying in these cases. A useful habit to develop is not to speak, write or participate in any activity involving these proceedings except on the express instructions of the solicitor with whom one is involved. Not only will this rule keep the expert protected and within bounds but it will also save him valuable time, for any number of persons – including occasionally representatives of the media – appear to be keenly desirous of having a word with experts on these matters.

4. This brings us conveniently to the question of obtaining confidentiality in family and child proceedings. There may be an arguable case for the proposition that the rules of a normal doctor-patient relationship do not apply when the individual being examined is technically perhaps not a patient. However, this point does not appear to have been tested in the courts, presumably because there is an express statement of rules already available concerning CA 1989 proceedings. The papers, including the substance of the papers, are confidential and cannot be disclosed without the leave of the court. Any discussion involving these papers (or the substance in them) is only possible with the agreement of the parties and the leave of the court. Even the seemingly innocent activity of passing a copy of a report one has written to those treating the patient so that management can be informed and commenced without undue delay is forbidden, the leave of the court being required before this can be done. As is also well known, these proceedings take place out of sight of the general public (although there are steps now being taken to see if there

should be less secrecy in the future) and the names of the parties and the participants are suitably anonymised when legitimate publication of proceedings, for example, in the law reports, is permitted. There is, therefore, no scope for any campaigning expert – sometimes very desirable of protecting children against abuse or asserting the rights of parents or exposing the iniquities of the system – to have a quiet word with any unauthorised person. Contempt of court proceedings and the disciplinary sanctions of the professional body concerned with the expert may follow, as we recently had cause to observe in a high-profile case involving a solicitor.

5.   The expert is sometimes in a dilemma as to what view is to be taken of a factual dispute, for example, whether one spouse has been assaulted by the other, or a child has been abused. The resolution of these factual disputes resides in the province of the court. Occasionally, the court, as a preliminary, may make findings of fact, namely the spouse has indeed been assaulted or the child has suffered abuse. These findings of fact should make the expert's task easier – he simply needs to accept the court's holding. If, however, the factual dispute is still in play and is likely to be contested at the final hearing the expert could face some difficulty. This situation is not novel for the expert as it is routine in expert assessments in criminal proceedings, for example, where well before a tribunal of fact – the magistrates or jury – has pronounced on an issue the expert may be required to carry out an evaluation as to whether the facts of the alleged offence could be related to the probable mental state of the defendant at the time the facts took place. The expert can take the same approach when assessing a parent in childcare proceedings. The expert does not, of course, always need to know the precise truth in these matters. One can work on alternative possibilities. More to the point, the examining psychiatrist need only concern himself with the likelihood or the probability of an event having taken place – bearing in mind that not all mentally disordered individuals commit assaults or abuse and a normal mental state does not preclude violent behaviour – and that his primary task is to try to establish the probable mental state at the time of the alleged offence or incident. As will be discussed later, in pronouncing on the future likelihood of the recurrence of past behaviour, the papers, including the record of convictions when available, are more useful sources of information on this point than the examination of any current mental state or the circumstances of a disputed incident.

Chapter 2

PSYCHIATRIC DISORDERS AND THEIR CLASSIFICATION

2.1 PSYCHIATRY AS A MEDICAL DISCIPLINE

Mental illness and disorder still remain much of a mystery to the lay public, and even those who have studied and practised in the field for many years are constantly surprised by what psychiatry can still throw up. Part of the problem lies in the fact that the structure and function of the brain and its dysfunctions are still not mapped out with any great accuracy. Considerable progress might have been made in those respects but we still do not know for sure what happens where in the brain and how and why things go wrong and, when things do go awry, what exactly it amounts to. Neurological treatment, perhaps with the possible exceptions of the management of epilepsy and the handful of other conditions, remains rudimentary by the standards achieved elsewhere in medicine, for example, the treatment and control of infectious diseases. To give but one example of this, which will be very familiar to lay persons, paralysis, either of two limbs or all four, is irremediable in terms of the cures much of the rest of medicine takes for granted. Those paralysed following a stroke or trauma or for whatever reason, learn to adjust to their disabilities through the processes of rehabilitation and do not expect root and branch treatment to make them whole. Despite the promise carried by stem cell research, relevant treatment is probably many years away. Degenerative brain disease leads sooner or later to death, the life expectancy usually curtailed by the disorder.

If progress has been so small in our understanding of the brain in sickness and in health, is it any wonder, one may ask, there is so much to be done when it comes to comprehending the processes of the mind? That we continue to use such archaic terms as the 'mind' for the 'mind-body' distinction, derived from medieval philosophy, has placed a fell hand on the progress in psychiatric thought. From the last century this distinction dominated the classification of neurological and psychiatric disorder and, hence, their study. Rigid boundaries came to be placed and two kinds of specialist physicians – the neurologist dealing with the brain, the psychiatrist taking up what was left behind in the form of mind disorders – emerged. In fact, before the nineteenth century, so sparse was knowledge, there was no rigid distinction except that the alienist came to deal with madness, which usually meant those psychotic conditions requiring treatment in a lunatic asylum. The neurologists themselves made valuable contributions to our understanding of what are now considered psychiatric disorders through the study of conditions such as schizophrenia, dementia (Alzheimer's name is honoured by attachment to the commonest cause of dementia) and hysteria, among other disorders. Freud himself started professional life as a neuropathologist. The separation of neurology and psychiatry was an aberration of a century and it is certainly conceivable that the two branches will meet again in the future.

The reason for giving this prognostication with some confidence is that scientific research has now shown that almost all, perhaps even all, psychiatric disorders to be discussed in this book are due ultimately to brain malfunction. The rub is that we are far from achieving an understanding of the precise mechanisms involved in the aetiology, the pathogenesis and the symptomatology of mental disorders. At present this presumed involvement of the brain has to remain an article of faith, for knowledge, while growing and now amounting to a substantial body, still does not answer many practical questions. A legitimate view that can at present be taken of psychiatry is that it mostly encompasses those neurological conditions which have not yet been fully described or understood as definitely being due to brain disorder.

However, even when the time comes for the mental disorders to be fully classified within the disorders of the brain, psychiatry will continue to be exposed to the environment for, as we shall see in Part II of this book, social, cultural and environmental factors abound in psychiatry to an extent that they do not with conventional neurological disorders (although that statement, too, may need to be qualified when the knowledge of the causes of brain disorders – still pitifully meagre in practical terms whatever the increase in basic knowledge – is expanded to take in pathological viruses and environmental toxins among other causative pathogens). In the meanwhile, psychiatry, *par excellence*, attempts to see the patient as a product of his environment. To an extent all medicine should be subject to this holistic approach – can one sensibly deal with and advise a victim of a heart attack whose condition has been contributed to by his lifestyle without considering his environment? – but, in practice, it does not. Most physicians in other branches of medicine have neither the time nor the inclination to deal with the wider social aspects of illness. Psychiatry simply cannot afford this lapse as its significant participation in family and child legal practice shows. If he did ignore social concerns and influences, the psychiatrist will have remarkably little to do apart from listing signs and symptoms and making a stab at diagnosis. Prognosis will be uninformed and any advice or recommendation to the court most likely valueless.

2.2 GENETICS AND THE ENVIRONMENT

A study of the possible causes of mental disorder reveals why this holistic or universal approach is essential to the practice of psychiatry. In the present state of knowledge, the aetiology of most psychiatric disorders, like that of most conventional neurological disorders, remains largely unknown. Where neurology can turn to neuropathology – a respectable subspeciality over a considerable period of time – psychopathology still means only descriptive study from which conclusions have to be drawn.

The genetic basis for psychiatric disorders is becoming clearer – as in all medicine – but is still far from having been fully elucidated. All we can say for now is that in close or first-degree relationships (as between parents and children and siblings) the chances of 'inheriting' a condition is greater than with more distant relationships. Much of this knowledge has accrued from twin and adoption studies.

Identical (monozygotic) twins share a similar genetic make-up. Therefore, any disorder with a genetic basis should show itself in both individuals when they have been brought up in the same environment and thereby they should have a higher incidence of most psychiatric disorders than when the twins are not identical (dizygotic) or are merely ordinary siblings. This has, indeed, been proved to be the case with many psychiatric disorders. It has been shown that even when one of the identical pair of twins has been given away for adoption the increased risk of disorder still persists. This risk also increases when a child from a family with a known history of mental disorder is adopted by a family with no history of mental disorder, when there is still an increased risk but not to the same extent if the child had remained within its biological family. What all this leads to is the expected conclusion that in causing disorder both genetic factors and environmental influences have a part to play.

It is usual to say there is an interaction between genetic and environmental factors in precipitating disorder. How these factors may influence one another is still largely unknown, but recent studies have been focusing on what has been called the 'nature of nurture', by which it is meant that one must also consider genetic factors when evaluating environmental influences. Stress is a well-known cause of mental disorder but the way an individual may react to stress – indeed, the way he might have been drawn to situations involving stress – could well be genetically determined.

Work undertaken at the Institute of Psychiatry has helped to illuminate the complex relationships between genetics and the environment. One finding has been to show that children growing up within one family may be as different as those growing up in widely different families. Another of the findings is that genetic factors influence the way we experience our environment. Thus, some measures, ostensibly of pure environmental risk – such as life events and psychosocial stress – may show genetic influence.

Similarly, association between environmental risks and disorders may often be substantially mediated by genetic factors. This is not at all a surprising finding which finds replication in the rest of medicine. An individual may have a heavily loaded family history, say, for ischaemic heart disease but it is by no means the case he will suffer a heart attack and possibly an early death for, as is now well known, adjustments to lifestyle can provide an important protective cushion in even the most inauspicious of genetic circumstances. This finding has also found reflection in epidemiological studies.

In the late 1960s medical students were taught that Finland led the world in ischaemic heart disease. It would appear that in the poverty that followed the war the Finns – who inhabited a largely agricultural society – had a primarily dairy-based diet. Now, Finland is one of the most prosperous lands on earth, the diet of its population is altogether better balanced and the rates of ischaemic heart disease have shown a corresponding fall. The dubious honour of leading the developed world in ischaemic heart disease appears now to have passed to the western regions of Scotland.

This issue – genetic v environment – is far from academic, as is to be observed in cases involving potential adoptive parents of a child who might have been born into a family where one or both of its biological parents might have suffered from mental disorder (whose effects could well have been the reason for seeking an adoptive placement). One is often called upon to advise on the genetic element in any future risk of the child suffering from similar, or any, mental disorder without any reference being made to the environmental influences which may increase or diminish the chances of the adopted child suffering from mental disorder. In fact, there seems at times to be a preoccupation, indeed an obsession, with the genetic inheritance of such a child. It must now be accepted that many, perhaps most, disorders – whether in or out of psychiatry – are dependent on a complex interplay of multifactorial elements before the disorder can manifest itself. It is wholly prejudicial – an accusation that has also been levelled at some insurance companies – if one takes to 'visiting the iniquity of the fathers upon the children unto the third and fourth generation'. Except in regard to some rare genetic disorders, it is virtually impossible in the average case to predict with any respectable certainty that an individual, free of disorder at the time of examination, may or may not come in time to suffer a mental disorder.

How genes play a part in inducing mental disorder is far from clear. Also, the issue arises that if a full complement of genes is required to produce illness what less than a full house of genes may do. It is feasible that a less severe illness or disorder will be the result, and it has been suggested that the varying types and severity involving depressive illness may be a measure of this variation in number of the relevant genes. There is also the possibility that fewer than the full complement of genes required for the emergence of disorder may not cause actual symptoms but may instead give rise to an increased vulnerability or susceptibility to illness. In the face of overwhelming psychological stress or some other assault on well-being (eg illicit drugs, infections, etc) this may be sufficient provocation to tip a susceptible patient over the edge. Stress-related conditions often show this feature and the concept of an 'egg shell' personality is applicable well beyond the bounds of tort law. There is also a further intriguing observation, made over many years, especially concerning cases of schizophrenia. It has been noted that close relations of a patient with the full-blown condition may be especially gifted, successful or creative individuals. The reason often given for this is that the less than the full complement of the genes required to produce real illness may carry some advantages to the individual and society. If true, this may account for the continuing presence of disorders which may otherwise be deemed disadvantageous in evolutionary terms. Schizophrenic patients traditionally have had low fertility and relatively few offspring, which is a disadvantage for the evolution of the species.

The environmental factors involved in the causation of disease are suspected to be many and various. Some of these are discussed in the substantive sections on disorders in Part II of this book. A few have been recognised for a long time. The treponemic infection causing syphilis, for instance, if left untreated, can lead to tertiary syphilis including the condition of general paralysis of the insane (GPI), which is of historical notoriety. This has become rare now, although syphilis itself is said to be showing a renewed rise in incidence. It is believed that it was not so much the specific treatment of the infection that controlled the complications of syphilis as the continuing sensitivity of the responsible microorganism to penicillin and related antibiotics (unlike the gonococcus causing gonorrhoea) which meant that the widespread use of antibiotics in the treatment of infections generally eliminated the treponeme whenever it was present and although it was unrecognised. This little digression is made so as to be alert to the possibility that if the microorganism, as is the case with many bacteria, were to become resistant to antibiotics, perhaps through mutation, history may well come to repeat itself. It is well worth reminding ourselves of the mutability of illness; some go away but may return.

Viruses causing or contributing to mental disorder still occupy a book that is closed to us at present, although snippets of information reach us from time to time suggesting they could play a pathogenic role. Viruses, as is well known, mutate rapidly and the changing features and severity of any disorder may plausibly be attributed to this propensity of viruses to transform themselves.

Other environmental toxins are manifold and although the part some of them have played in human disease is well known – elements such as lead, arsenic and mercury have long been known to produce physical and mental symptoms – and may be an important consideration in the individual patient, knowledge regarding other toxins is still insufficient for general clinical purposes. The same point applies to environmental pollutants. Although, say, mobile telephony has recently been exonerated as a possible cause of neoplastic disease so subtle may be the changes induced by this as well as other common pollutants that all potential psychopathogenic elements cannot at any time be ruled out with confidence.

2.3 FAMILY INFLUENCES

The most important and obvious environmental factor in psychiatric practice is the family. It is ubiquitous and the centre of attraction for all kinds of professionals including the politician, but its role in the precipitation, propagation and prognosis in cases of mental disorder is as poorly understood as in the case of microorganisms or other environmental toxins. Some workers will continue to stress the biological basis of all mental disorders while others may consider psychological factors including the pathogenic family as a crucial environmental element in understanding mental disorder. Where the truth lies in between these two extremes is unknown and may even be unknowable for, to paraphrase Tolstoy, we could say pathogenic families may be toxic in their own way while all successfully nurturant families resemble one another.

One difficulty in studying family influences is that quite proper restrictions apply to safeguarding their privacy. One does not often see problematical families volunteering to be subjects of research. Then there is the problem of obtaining control samples for purposes of comparison from among the diverse kinds of families which exist in society with all their strengths and weaknesses. Few universal principles can be formulated from any such study, even if one were feasible to conduct, for every professional is aware of exceptions. There is the successful, well-adjusted individual arising out of horrific privation and there is his counterpart, perhaps a dangerously violent criminal psychopath, crafted out of a family which seemingly gave him every conceivable advantage in early life.

A problem family is often like an elephant – easy enough to spot but difficult to describe. The only conclusion to be safely drawn is to say it is necessary to study the individual family – the one containing the patient – and make any findings and arrive at conclusions with great care and caution. It is likely that one's results obtained from such a study of one family may not be transferable in all its particulars to any other family.

2.4 CULTURAL FACTORS

Cultural factors also require circumspection in their study and in their application to cases involving mental disorder. Many cultural practices are readily apparent, among which of relevance in family and child practice are the attitudes essayed in respect of women and children within any community. Aspects of these are dealt with under the relevant topics to be discussed in Part II of this book. In general terms it seems valid to say there are no general principles applicable. All cultures have evolved in circumstances and under conditions applicable to them. Those extant have obviously survived which, in social evolutionary terms, must be deemed a successful result. As far as mental disorder is concerned variations seen in symptoms and presentation may be due to both biological and social factors. In many developing countries the cause of the more common illnesses is still infection and deprivation. It is common in some circles to assert – at any rate privately, for these days one learns to guard one's tongue when making any public utterance – that individuals in these cultures have less well-developed psychological awareness and, for that reason perhaps, fewer psychological problems.

Two mental disorders, to be dealt with in greater detail in Part II, illustrate the complex interplay of biological and social factors and cultural influences. One is eating disorders. In most developing cultures the commonest eating disorder is due to the lack of food with the consequent physical and mental disorders. For persons in such cultures obesity is often a sign of success and prosperity, a state to which many aspire. To most inhabitants of such cultures the idea of eating disorders, in the sense in which we shall proceed to discuss them, is incomprehensible The idea of starving oneself in the midst of plenty – or taking other extreme measures to reduce weight in response to social pressures – appears to them to be a perverted one, perhaps even a sign of a specialised form of madness. There is little notion of such behaviour being otherwise pathological for there is no comprehension of such behaviour in those cultures. However, as we shall see, determined self-starvation may be undertaken in those cultures for religious and other social reasons. But, as the term developing implies, these cultures, communities and countries are expected to make economic and social progress, at a lesser or greater rate, and the intriguing question is at what stage of development there will be a general acceptance of eating disorders, as we understand them, as disease entities. Perhaps it will be a sign of arrival of countries such as China and India, now exciting much interest on account of their rapid rate of economic development, at the top table of economically most potent nations when they may also be able to boast of similar incidence of eating disorders as understood in the West.

The other illustrative mental disorder is psychopathy. Every culture and community contains its share of rogues, charlatans and scoundrels, but it is the impact these often disruptive individuals make on society that may be different. In most developing countries the family, in particular, and the community in general see it as their duty, a matter of honour and pride in fact, to contain these individuals so as not allow them to bring shame upon the wider community as a result of the actions of any individual members. It is thus virtually impossible to assess if there are a greater or fewer individuals showing psychopathic behaviour in these communities as opposed to individuals in Western societies satisfying the criteria for the disorder. The criminal justice system in such communities is often only comparatively rarely engaged in dealing with these anti-social individuals who are expected to be dealt with primarily by the family and community. A fascinating area of sociological study would be to try to learn what happens to these individuals when such communities are transplanted in the West. It is usual to assert that first generation immigrants from such communities will retain the mores and standards of their mother communities while the second and later generations will see their members absorbing the values of the host community and come to display the problems found there. How, and to what extent, this phenomenon extends to the incidence and type of mental disorder arising remains to be seen. Anecdotal evidence is conflicting. In London, a metropolis harbouring diverse communities, it is still uncommon to meet a member of the ethnic Chinese community who has become involved with the official criminal justice system. The suspicion is that miscreants are dealt with informally and unofficially within their own community.

2.5 SOCIAL CLASS

The term culture may evoke exotic vistas, but it is properly applied to any community – more or less precisely defined – which inhabits the wider society in any given nation, even in developed ones. One defining factor is social class, which may be associated with numerous subcultures. As is widely recognised, although classlessness is the accepted and desired outcome for the whole population today, membership of a particular social class may still determine many, perhaps most, outcomes. Illness is one area in which outcomes according to social class membership have been studied. It is common knowledge that while good health and an increased life expectancy can be generally expected in a country such as the UK, there are still pockets of deprivation where levels of morbidity and mortality exist on a scale which may not only be higher than in the country as a whole but may exceed even the rates to be found in many poorer countries (see the note above on the incidence of heart disease in the western regions of Scotland). Where mental disorder is concerned the picture is more complex, for the identification and classification of these disorders are altogether more complicated than in cases of physical illness.

In the past, there used to be a readier acceptance of the notion that illnesses, both physical and mental, were attributable to membership of particular social classes. Illness such as rheumatic heart disease and carcinoma of the stomach were believed to be preferentially found in the lower socioeconomic classes, while ischaemic heart disease was believed to afflict those higher up in the social scale. Psychiatric disorders were also believed to have a similar distribution. Schizophrenia was said to be found lower down the social scale, although social decline from previously higher levels of social class membership due to the illness itself was also to be observed. Suicide was believed to be a higher-class phenomenon while parasuicide (deliberate self-harm) was found lower down, as were psychopathic and anti-social behaviour. Nowadays, with the levelling down of all kinds of barriers, it is by no means certain that these neat distinctions can be convincingly made. In any event, it is not of any great value to the doctor assessing the individual patient before him who, while he can only properly be evaluated within the context of his personal, family and social circumstances, is primarily of interest because of the disorder, if any, he presents with. However, it is still necessary to take account of social beliefs – which may not always depend on social class membership – in any evaluation. Human beings live in a social context. They share values and beliefs. They are heavily influenced by what they see and hear, as is evidenced by the 'health scares' we see from time to time, whether it may involve the hospital-acquired MRSA infection or affliction by the mutant version of 'bird flu' which may cause, if the reports in the media are to be believed, a global epidemic on an unprecedented scale and even come to threaten the very survival of the species.

2.6 PERCEPTIONS OF DISORDER

Doctors have long been aware of a group of patients referred to as the 'worried well', individuals who have no known disorder affecting them but who persist in believing they may, in fact, have such a disorder or could imminently acquire it. As a rule such patients have an anxious and insecure demeanour and are particularly heavily influenced by what they happen to perceive around them. To call them hypochondriacs is merely to give them another name. How far a doctor should go in trying to establish disorder is always a problematical decision. There may be considerations of resources – both of time and money – in pursuing intensive investigation. With the form of informal rationing that one obtains in the NHS today, investigating such a patient extensively may deprive another, perhaps more deserving, patient of the necessary resources. But, in psychiatric practice in particular, there is another consideration. It is possible to reinforce the fears of such patients by too extensive investigation. Each time a negative result is obtained, the clamour may grow for more tests. Patients are well aware that tests such as CT and MRI scans are now available. They may arrive, say, with persistent headaches which the doctor believes is due to stress and tension but does not succeed in reassuring the patient. Every conceivable investigation may end up being undertaken. The doctor may be able to rule out a space-occupying lesion of the brain but in the nature of things he cannot be absolutely sure there is no pathology for it could have succeeded in concealing itself. But probabilities of pathology are of no interest to such patients. The honest doctor knows that pathology cannot always be ruled out on a negative test result; our knowledge of these matters is never complete and laboratory and radiological investigations have well-recognised limitations. The patient is also aware that the doctor cannot give him foolproof assurance and therein lies the dilemma. It needs a confident, self-possessed doctor who, while prepared to acknowledge there could be something that lies beyond available investigation, is nevertheless ready to call a halt to endless investigation.

We have spoken in terms of individual patients but these matters also have a public health dimension. The MRSA problem is a very good example of how inappropriate antibiotic treatment can lead in time to serious difficulties with resistant bacteria which affects the entire general public. While the emphasis is now on measures of hygiene in an attempt to restrict the spread of this infection, the problem arose in the first place, in part at least, through the promiscuous and unnecessary use of antibiotics. These have, of course, a recognised place in the treatment of bacterial infections but also used to be exhibited when the infection was viral – as the vast majority of respiratory infections are – when there is no therapeutic indication except in those few cases where, as a result of a pre-existing condition or some concurrent treatment such as with steroids and immuno-suppressive agents, prophylactic antibiotic treatment may be in order.

The benzodiazepine group of drugs (eg Valium) has posed a similar problem in psychiatric practice. We shall later discuss the properties of these drugs, but their use with anxiety states, probably the commonest form of mental disorder, appears to be continuing even when the dangers of dependence and other problems caused by these drugs have been known for some considerable time. A more recent example of misuse has involved fluoxetine (Prozac), which at one stage threatened to become a modern panacea and which came to be used on children (at a time when it was not licensed for such use) and even on domestic animals.

Class, culture and country have an influence on perception of disease. The French are said to have several times the rate of prescribed drug use as the British and lead Europe in the use of medicaments. The French health system – now under considerable strain despite its much-vaunted features – appears to have been planned on the basis of the patient's right to seek doctors who will prescribe him more drugs.

A different kind of cultural problem exists, as we shall see, in the perception and presentation of psychiatric illness in patients originating from the Asian and African continents. Here the patient tends to give primacy to the physical component of symptoms present in such common disorders as depressive illness or anxiety states. These conditions, as will be seen, do have physical symptoms present but these clearly are not the most significant part of the disorder. These patients focus on such physical symptoms because it is accepted in their cultures that it is proper to visit the doctor's for physical illness but not for mental disorder. The latter phenomena may still be attributed to moral weakness, not pathology, a matter of shame to admit to, let alone parade before a man of learning as the doctor is perceived to be. Much stigma may attach to psychiatric disorder and any hint of 'mental problems' may compromise many of the patient's social hopes including the prospects for marriage. Such patients will not accept any explanations for the symptoms based on psychological terms but the more sophisticated among them may be prepared to listen to explanations founded on, say, the functions of the autonomic nervous system. Technically they are lacking in full insight which is usually taken to mean the acceptance, first, that there is something medically wrong with oneself and which is the cause of symptoms and, secondly, that the explanation for this malfunction is psychological, not primarily physical. In a sense these patients may appear to be ahead of their time in that they do not accept the mind-body dichotomy and believe instead that there is a physical basis for their ills, but these philosophical approaches are of scant help to the doctor in his consulting room at present who has to furnish explanations in the here and now. Fortunately, modern drug treatment of psychiatric conditions is not dependent on the patient's insight or his lack of acceptance of psychological explanations. Provided he accepts and swallows the tablets and follows the advice for the taking of these drugs he is probably likely to benefit. Sometimes the doctor has to emphasise the effects of the drug on the physical symptoms – eg improved sleep, appetite, bowel functions and reduction in tremors and palpitations – to persuade the patient to accept the medication at all. It is an innocent ruse. Psychological treatments may be harder to sell.

2.7 STIGMA

A curious by-product of the fears of litigation, now apparently enveloping supposedly enlightened cultures, has been the revelation of behaviours which were more commonly associated with the cultures of the developing nations. In the West, as we are regularly reminded by mental health charities, there is stigma of a different kind attaching to mental disorders. Employment is one of the fields in which prejudice is widespread and, for all we know, discrimination is commonly practised. For all the anti-discriminatory sentiments they may espouse and express, it is hard to find, for example, parents who will employ a nanny who has a known and clear history of mental disorder. Many senior executives – and those aspiring to such positions – are often insistent on how their symptoms of depression, anxiety or alcohol misuse are written down in the clinical notes. GPs often use 'stress-related problems' on medical certificates as a euphemism for clearly demonstrated features of mental disorder. The reasons for this evasion and prevarication are perfectly understandable. It is only noteworthy as an example of stigma experienced by patients in developing countries finding conversion to a similar phenomenon of denial in practice of mental disorder in the West, even though the patient in the latter situation might have gained a full understanding of the psychological mechanisms at work in producing his symptoms and the nature of his disorder.

2.8 NORMAL, ABNORMAL AND PATHOLOGICAL

As will be seen throughout this book, a pervasive problem in all psychiatry is to determine the line between what is normal and what is abnormal, and also what demarcates abnormal from the pathological. What is normal is in these situations a contentious question. It could be reduced to manageable proportions for our purposes by taking a statistical approach to the issue. Biological features such as height or intelligence are amenable to such an approach. These have what is called a 'bell shaped' distribution in any given population, that is to say the ends are truncated while the middle is expanded. This means the vast majority of the population will be found congregated in the middle. This is obvious enough when one considers parameters such as height or intelligence. Very few persons are excessively short or tall; more are what is called of being of 'average' height. This kind of understanding is useful to have when considering a psychological phenomenon such as the mood. Most people are of a neutral temperament, some may be perpetually cheerful while others may be given to pessimism and are disposed to take a dark view of themselves and the world they live in. However, it is by no means clear that anything that may lie beyond the 'average' is necessarily pathological. In this respect mood is a particularly useful parameter to explore for an excess of mood in either direction may indicate pathology, being a feature of depressive illness or mania. Unhappiness, on the other hand, is merely a part of the human condition, which seems obvious enough to state. It is not so obvious when one considers the mood changes that are found in what are deemed to be normal forms of human behaviour such as found in ordinary grief, the premenstrual state or the 'baby blues' which commonly affect the mothers of the newborn. The challenge for the psychiatrist – in the present state of knowledge where no objective indices of measurement exist – is to see where normality ends and where abnormality/pathology begins.

At first sight it may be thought that psychotic phenomena involving hallucinations or delusions will provide clear-cut distinctions between what is normal and what is not, for, in the popular mind, these phenomena are associated with mental disorder. But this is not always a clear-cut matter. As we shall see, auditory hallucinations are common in schizophrenia. They are usually found to be distinctive and have particular characteristics such as the voices being clearly heard from outside one's head, voices referring to one in the third person and so on. But there are also phenomena called 'pseudohallucinations' which emerge from within one's head and are not at all uncommonly found in states of grief and other situations where the individual is in need of comfort and solace. The bereaved, those with learning disabilities or with personality disorders may be subject to them. Some individuals invent imaginary persons and conversations to stave off isolation and loneliness and may say they hear voices, often within, sometimes outside of, the head. Delusions are understood clearly enough in most cases involving pathology but some individuals do have odd ideas – the earth being flat, the literal truth of religious texts and so on – which while perhaps being perceived as odd are far from being pathological.

Apart from the personal element there are, as will be discussed in Part II, essential social and cultural considerations to be taken into account before one can establish a delusion. Many cultures have a persecutory tinge, no doubt an essential element in assuring survival of their communities. Thus, to be suspicious of one's fellows, even suspect them of potential malevolence and blame them for causing misfortune, may be perfectly normal behaviour in some cultural contexts and these beliefs cannot, by themselves, be taken to amount to delusions. Within any given culture these ideas are not even abnormal, using the crude statistical approach we have taken above. When these communities are transplanted in another society these beliefs may become, in the statistical sense, abnormal but they are not necessarily as yet pathological.

Psychiatry, in the present state of its development, is therefore hard put to determine when the abnormal has become pathological. Objective evidence of the kind feasible in the rest of medicine is still not forthcoming. Radiological and laboratory investigation are only undertaken to detect concurrent systemic conditions which may or may not have a causative bearing on the psychiatric condition or, sometimes, to find out if there are complications of the mental disorder, for example, liver function tests to detect liver damage due to heavy alcohol use, or to monitor treatment, for example, recording of serum lithium levels in the course of treatment with these drugs. What therefore psychiatry is left with is trying to give descriptions to symptoms and gather a cluster of symptoms which go to make up a disease entity. The procedure is almost entirely clinical and may be thought arbitrary but that is all that seems possible in the present state of knowledge.

2.9 DIAGNOSIS AND ITS RELIABILITY

The risks involving the making of diagnoses are ever present and not always fully appreciated by lay persons. The law appears to share these misconceptions. It is not at all uncommon for the law – including those branches dealing with family and child practice – to involve itself with the minutiae of diagnoses. Endless time may be spent in court – not to mention conferences – arguing as to what is or what is not the diagnosis in a particular case. Occasionally it is the law itself that is primarily responsible for these preoccupations. In personal injury law, a claimant cannot normally succeed in damages for tortious injury if he has not developed a clinically recognised psychiatric injury as a result of any trauma sustained. It is insufficient for the doctor to say the claimant had become depressed as a result of involvement in a road traffic accident; he must go on to say whether or not the claimant had developed a depressive illness. It is equally insufficient to say someone has suffered normal grief; to recover damages the claimant needs to have developed pathological grief. All this is well understood but it has to be said that in family and child practice it is most often the behaviour – on the part of spouse, partner or parent – that is the decisive consideration and not the bare diagnosis.

There are exceptions, of course, as in the case of a 31-year-old mother who suffered severe intractable bipolar affective disorder. Recovery from each bout of illness was painfully protracted. In the disposition of her children by the court it was legitimate to seek to know about her current mental state, her past history and the prognosis. These would all be guided by precise knowledge of the diagnosis of her condition. Another case involved a 40-year-old mother who was suffering from severe chronic schizophrenia with much deterioration in personality and of social functioning. The poor prognosis associated with such a diagnosis was a decisive factor in the care, and later adoption, proceedings that came to take place.

Diagnosis as communication

A diagnosis is also useful shorthand for communication. If a GP refers a patient to the specialist as having suffered paranoid disorder 5 years before it is useful information for the examining psychiatrist to have although the latter must still ensure in the course of the examination that such an illness was, in fact, experienced and it is not some observation in the clinical record which is being unreliably transmitted and thereby perpetuated. As already seen, a diagnosis is also useful for giving prognosis, although, in practice, the actual characteristics of the disorder suffered by the patient, his attitude to illness, his response to treatment and the support he is likely to have and accept are usually almost more relevant than the mere diagnosis.

However, a diagnosis does suffer from serious shortcomings when not employed in the proper context. The first reason for this, which is implied in the description given that it is shorthand mode of communication, is that it actually conveys, despite the impressive sound the term may make, very little information. It says, by itself, little or nothing about the origins of the disorder, its presentation in terms of the symptoms, its response to treatment and, hence, its prognosis. In the case of the 20-year-old girl previously mentioned who presented with recurrent schizophreniform illness, does one learn much from reading about the diagnosis given? In fact, one learns one useful detail from the fact that the condition she has suffered from has been called schizophreniform – meaning schizophrenia-like – rather than definitively schizophrenia. However, in the absence of knowing there had been very difficult family circumstances, childhood behavioural disorder affecting her, extensive abuse of illicit drugs and non-compliance with treatment previously offered, there is little that can be usefully conveyed to the court dealing with childcare proceedings she happened to be involved in. The prognosis for her condition will turn on whether she had a true schizophrenic illness or whether the illicit drugs she had consumed had been acting on a vulnerability on her part to precipitate her recurring bouts of psychosis. As for the former condition, future treatment will involve maintenance medication given over a relatively long period of time. If it is a drug-induced schizophreniform a settled lifestyle is a more important consideration than drug treatment which could be discontinued after a short period.

Secondly, it should be remembered that a diagnosis is applied to the collection of symptoms the patient has, not the patient himself. To gain a full understanding of the patient one needs to know far more than either the diagnosis given or the symptoms that led to the diagnosis being given. Information for this purpose must be derived from any available source. Even then understanding may be incomplete. Further, the symptoms presented do not always conveniently lead to precise diagnoses being made. Symptoms such as a depressed mood or anxiety are found very commonly and may be part of many disorders. Sometimes there are mixed states with features of schizophrenia such as hallucinations and delusions as well as significant mood change. Persecutory delusions may be found in paranoid disorders including schizophrenia as well as in states of depressive psychosis. Even the commonly cited distinctions between neuroses and psychoses may not avail in some hysterical (conversion/dissociative) states where gross behavioural disturbance may include features more usually seen in the psychoses as well as the patient lacking completely in insight.

Records

As we have already noted, psychiatric diagnoses still have a stigma attached to them in nearly all cultures and may considerably disadvantage an individual in diverse avenues of life. This may lead to a sympathetic doctor not revealing the true diagnosis in the clinical records. The opposite can also be true. There is a tendency also in medical records to repeat a diagnosis uncritically, even if it had been wrongly made in the first instance. One can readily imagine the effect of a diagnosis of schizophrenia or psychopathy on an individual who is seeking employment. A 34-year-old man, a father in childcare proceedings, had a long history of alcohol abuse. Many years before it had been suggested – he claimed by his mother (with whom he had long had strained relations) – that he might have schizophrenia. The GP had referred him in the past for psychiatric assessment at which it was concluded he did have some vague psychotic features – fleeting auditory hallucinations, short-lived ideas of persecution – but these were probably related to his alcohol abuse and the withdrawal state which followed forced detoxification whenever he found himself unable to afford the price of a drink. Yet, even 10 years later, the GP was still persisting in writing he had schizophrenia, a point naturally seized upon by the authorities investigating his fitness to care for his children. In another case, a 44-year-old woman had been called schizophrenic in childhood by her mother (a policewoman), an appellation which was propagated for over 30 years and which distracted attention from very serious personality problems which had caused her to become repeatedly involved in litigation.

A doctor may give a diagnosis but it is not just his fellow practitioners in medicine who will be considering the implications. Nowadays it is commonplace for medical records to be sought – in litigation as well as in other areas of life such as employment – and it seems it is mostly lay people who come to sit in judgment on the significance of a diagnosis.

Given the nebulous circumstances in which the subject operates, it is reasonable to ask if one doctor arrives at a diagnosis of a psychiatric condition whether another will agree with the first and what the rate of agreement might be. After all, in family and child practice, several doctors may be involved with a party, some treating him as a patient, others dealing with him as a client for the purposes of litigation. It used to be believed in the past that the degree of agreement between any two psychiatrists – in other words, a measure of the reliability – is relatively low. A doctor treating a patient might have arrived at one set of diagnostic formulations while the expert expressly commissioned to assist the court could have arrived at another, which could prove confusing to the parties, their representatives and to the court itself. The reasons for this poor reliability have been studied from time to time.

As we have seen already, there are few objective tests that can be applied in clinical psychiatric practice. If two doctors disagree as to whether the patient has anaemia or hypothyroidism, it is usually (but not always) possible to settle the argument with the aid of results of blood tests. Yet, those critical of disagreements between psychiatrists should know that even when apparently objective test results are available in general medicine or surgery there is still scope for disagreement as anyone sitting in with radiologists arguing over whether or not there is a fracture pictured on an x-ray finds out. In fact, it is now standard practice for two radiologists or pathologists to interpret mammograph or biopsy findings to avoid, as far as is possible, the kind of errors that from time to time make their way into newspaper headlines.

Symptom-finding

Psychiatric symptom-finding is undeniably more difficult because it depends on the questioning of patients when factors peculiar to both the patient and the examiner have a bearing on the result. The patient's intelligence, culture, grasp of language, the rapport established with the doctor, among many other factors, may determine the quality of the information the doctor succeeds in gathering. As for the doctor, his skills, experience, level of training and, also, grasp of language and idiom may determine the results obtained in what is, after all, the most verbal of medical specialities. Many years ago a study undertaken among trainee psychiatrists at the Maudsley Hospital purported to show that trainees at the beginning of their 3-year course as registrars were more inclined to diagnose psychopathology when compared with those ending their training. This is understandable, for lay persons – and those with relatively little experience of mental disorders – see pathology where those more experienced do not. It is part of the specialist's training to go through the process of learning how to evaluate the patient's experiences as being normal, abnormal and pathological. The distinction to be made between ordinary unhappiness (normal) and a depressed mood (pathological) is a case in point. The examiner must also learn about and come to understand matters which are not obviously technical but have an important bearing on psychiatric practice, namely about cultural (and subcultural and social class) influences when assessing whether pathology may exist. This is seen notably when assessing the presence of delusional ideas but extends also to the evaluation of habits and practices. For example, nowadays cannabis is commonly used as a recreational drug. A couple of generations ago it was still a minority activity, confined in the main to some cultures and subcultures. Today the challenge is to decide whether the use of lawful or illicit substances attains the levels when it becomes a mental disorder and earns a diagnosis. With alcohol use there is a kind of guide in which safe levels of consumption are set out. With illicit substances there is no such guide for safe use and one is left with an assessment of behavioural consequences of the use of these drugs.

Assessment

In psychiatric assessments, altogether a subjective process, the bias of the examiner must also be taken into account. There may be a tendency among those taking a special interest in a disorder to see it where others cannot. Anecdotal evidence, at least, is available to suggest that the condition of post-traumatic stress disorder (PTSD) is more likely to be diagnosed by those who do work substantially among victims of trauma. When, in the late 1960s, lithium salts became a recognised form of treatment for what used to be then called manic-depressive illness (bipolar affective disorder now) there was a conscious move to reclassify some patients from their previous diagnosis of schizophrenia (an untreatable condition although its symptoms can be contained through medication) to mania and/or depression which could now at least be effectively prevented and the prognosis improved thereby. When fluoxetine (Prozac) emerged on the scene, as we have already noted, depressive illness was seemingly to be found all over the place.

Previously we had had to be very cautious about using drugs after diagnosing depressive illness, for the older tricyclic antidepressant agents, while substantially effective, had numerous side effects, some of which were quite adverse, and they could also be lethal in overdose. Care had to be taken to balance possible risk with the prospect of a good result and decide if the scales were tipped in favour of the latter. If not, the patient received reassurance and counselling rather than medication. Prozac appeared, at any rate for a short while, to enable doctors to throw caution to the wind. Similar phenomena were observed when methylphenidate (Ritalin) became available for attention-deficit hyperactivity disorder (ADHD). There was an apparent explosion in the rates of diagnosis although many informed workers in this field believed the condition would previously have been diagnosed as a childhood behavioural disorder to be treated through psychological means, and also that some of the children now being treated with Ritalin might even then have been deemed to have been normal.

Bias

Another kind of bias, this time involving actual bias, may be altogether even more pernicious. Some persons, including a few psychiatrists, refuse to acknowledge the existence of the psychoses and some other mental disorders, rejecting the medical model altogether and believing that everything experienced or reported by the patient could be explained on the basis of the life experiences of the patient and his existence in a society which was more or less pathogenetic as far as he was concerned. Some others may have an axe to grind, most notoriously in the field of child protection where they proceeded to detect child abuse on the basis of tenuous or no evidence. The 'battered wife syndrome' and, perhaps, 'Munchausen Syndrome by proxy' are also examples of this kind reflecting more the examiner's personality and bias rather than a patient's disorder. Recourse to an agreed international classification of mental disorders is a useful corrective to such a view. The *Bolam* test (*Bolam v Friern Hospital Management Committee* [1957] 2 All ER 118) is useful when dealing with more extreme views concerning diagnosis for one can legitimately ask if a respectable, representative and reasonable body of doctors would hold such views.

It is implicit in the previous discussion that an examiner will need to decide what is normal, abnormal and what could be pathological. Could speaking to oneself, for example, be put in one of these categories? At one extreme, one can say it could be a perfectly innocent activity as when an individual rehearses a speech, learns a foreign language or practises his lines. At the other end, muttering to oneself was a feature seen fairly commonly in mental hospitals in cases involving chronic schizophrenia where the patient would either speak to himself without there being any obvious stimulus or appear to conduct a dialogue with a person or persons unseen where he seemed to be responding to voices he was hearing. Pathology could clearly be established on the basis of all the evidence that was available on such patients. In between these two extremes, there could be some difficulty in establishing if pathology did exist. Patients with learning disabilities, individuals experiencing grief or in need of solace when lonely or isolated may also comfort themselves by muttering or speaking to themselves and these individuals could even invent imaginary persons for this purpose. In this category of individuals in some cases (eg involving learning disabilities, pathological grief, perhaps depressive illness) some underlying pathology may clearly exist but the behaviour of speaking to oneself is not necessarily a part of that condition. Hallucinations may also show a similar distribution among both normal and disordered individuals. Different examiners may ascribe varying significance to such behaviour which may also prove to be a source of unreliability in diagnosis.

In the past what features a particular condition needed to have before a diagnosis could be given to it sometimes caused an impairment in reliability as between doctors. Some insisted that there needed to be certain 'pathognomonic' features such as specific types of auditory hallucinations before diagnosing schizophrenia. Others demanded there be present a particular pattern of life history in which social decline and deterioration in functioning were noted before making the diagnosis.

US, British and Soviet Union approaches

Even when there is broad agreement present on what criteria are required before diagnosis, there could still be disagreement on how the clusters of symptoms are to be classified. The most notorious of these disagreements, at any rate the one best publicised, involved the USA, Britain and the Soviet Union in the 1960s when the latter, of course, existed as a nation and was much feared on account of its perceived ambitions to take over the world. As between US and British psychiatrists there were significant differences in the diagnoses they gave to comparable patients, the Americans being twice as likely to diagnose schizophrenia as the British who were content to diagnose affective illness (depression and mania), the neuroses and personality disorder in these patients. There was evidence that this discrepancy could be attributed largely to practice in New York rather than finding application in all the states. Now, of course, there is no reason to believe such differences continue to exist as between national practice, at least in the countries of the West, now that international systems of diagnosis and classification are widely applied. The explanations given for this difference in practice were never very convincing. One suggestion – admittedly made from a British point of view – was that the ragbag of disorders which ended up by being called schizophrenia was due to the psychotherapeutic and psychoanalytical traditions that influenced US psychiatric practice at that time, the diagnosis being on the basis of the amenability to treatment of the patient rather than, say, on any objective medical approach to the evaluation of symptoms and their significance. In the British tradition, schizophrenia, as conventionally diagnosed, precludes any psychotherapeutic approach, at any rate in the early stages of the illness. Also, Britain has followed the rigorous German and continental tradition of giving primacy to phenomenology in eliciting symptoms and the medical model has been the approach unashamedly used in British psychiatric practice. This entails the weighing up of symptoms and seeking the proper place for any cluster of symptoms in a classification. Nevertheless, even in advance of international consensus, US practice changed and many came to believe this was due to a point we have discussed before, the emerging promise of lithium salts which had been recognised in the management of manic-depressive illness and which gave hope for successful treatment of these conditions so that it was now felt appropriate to reclassify schizophrenia as manic-depressive illness.

The Soviet experiences were altogether more sinister. Ostensibly, the approach appeared to be the perfectly respectable one in which the course of the illness in a suspected case of schizophrenia was given primacy over the symptoms, thereby leading to a somewhat broader conception of the illness. However, what happened in practice was that it was the behaviour of the patient that came to be taken into account. This in turn led to dissent, usually on political, sometimes for religious, reasons, leading to a label of misbehaviour which, after a short step or two, led further to the evaluation of this alleged misbehaviour as being a feature of illness. The upshot was that many dissidents were incarcerated, not in prison after a proper trial in a court on any evidence available, but in mental institutions since a psychiatric diagnosis had been given. (In the interests of fairness and balance one must say the authorities in the West were themselves not immune to the occasional practice of political psychiatry. It was alleged in the 1970s that a militant trade union leader had been seized and propelled into a police cell. It was further alleged that he had been taunted and provoked so successfully that his response bore all the hallmarks of an acutely disturbed psychotic patient so much so he was assessed and compulsorily detained under the Mental Health Act 1959, the forerunner of the current Act, to the delight of his numerous political enemies.)

Occam's razor

Finally, in considering the problems of reliability of diagnoses in psychiatry one must look also at how multiple features in any mental state are to be dealt with. Does one proceed to make an all-encompassing diagnosis or does one consider the components of the symptoms and give as many separate diagnoses as are merited? There is a long tradition in medicine of following the cut of Occam's razor where, in accordance with the thought of the fourteenth-century philosopher William of Occam, one seeks to make the fewest possible assumptions in trying to explain disorder. Medicine has long followed this reductive principle which is not always convenient for psychiatric practice. A case will illustrate the dilemmas arising. We have come across the 34-year-old man, the father in childcare proceedings, who had a long and serious history of alcohol consumption. He showed many of the neurological and psychiatric complications associated with alcohol abuse and forced withdrawal from it when he lacked the means to support his habit. The symptoms on occasion included auditory hallucinations and persecutory ideas. These symptoms all responded to anti-psychotic drugs even when he was continuing to drink heavily. Some doctors who examined him believed he was entitled to a dual diagnosis – paranoid psychosis as well as harmful use of alcohol. Others saw all these features as being part and parcel of his alcohol misuse. The problem was compounded by his inability to remain sober long enough to allow any other pathology to emerge. Patients with personality disorder often become depressed, largely on account of the situations they get themselves into. The depression may require treatment in its own right. These patients may also abuse alcohol and illicit substances. Personal preference among doctors appears to dictate the way such patients are investigated and presented, although we shall later take up the concept of co-morbidity which has come to find acceptance in clinical psychiatric practice.

2.10 INTERNATIONAL CLASSIFICATION OF MENTAL DISORDERS

Illness and disorder, whether physical or mental, are universal phenomena and it was bound to be the case that there would be international collaboration in studies to compare, contrast and co-operate when dealing with disorders. The differences in US and British psychiatric diagnostic practice noted above came from the US/UK Diagnostic Project in the 1960s. In the 1970s the International Pilot Study of Schizophrenia carried out pioneering work on the disorder over nine disparate cultures. As far back as 1948 the sixth revision of the International Classification of Disease (ICD-6) was available for use in Britain though mainly for the classification of non-psychiatric conditions. Further revisions were made under the auspices of the World Health Organization (WHO) and, in time, the ICD-8 came into being. It demonstrated the confusion present as a result of the medical roots of psychiatry by sometimes classifying disorders by symptomatology and sometimes by aetiology. Some said the solution to this could be achieved by having two axes for disorders, one for symptomatology and the other for aetiology.

The case for international agreement on classification is a strong and obvious one. National jealousies being what they are, a national classification is not likely to find widespread international acceptance. Further, the role of the WHO is widely respected as not many international bodies are and, ironically, a world body is more likely to bring about acceptance even in, say, British practice to an extent that may not be possible if one knew the Department of Health or the Royal College of Psychiatrists were alone instrumental in the venture. However, there are also drawbacks. International co-operation involves many committees and international classification of disorders often have an uncomfortable and unfamiliar feel to them, much like the proverbial elephant which had been put together by a committee. These classifications are at once conservative – for progress must be at the pace of the slowest vehicle in the convoy – and unfamiliar as international committees tend to demand that national sensitivities must be taken account of. Thus, depressive illness started off by including manic-depressive illness, reactive depression of the neurotic kind and involutional melancholia (agitated depression which used to be believed possessed special characteristics). At the instance of the Scandinavian psychiatrists the category of reactive depressive psychosis – a disorder recognised in those countries – was added. In time the category of mood (affective) disorders in the ICD-10 came to have over 50 entries. The clinical utility of this enterprise is not always clear but one persists in deferring to the spirit the law refers to as the comity of nations.

2.11 ICD-10

Several innovations feature in this the tenth and latest edition of international classification of mental disorders. Some of the relevance of this work will be taken up here. For example, there were changes made to the way that alcohol and other substances are classified as being misused. It used to be the case that substance abuse was classified by the clinical syndrome which was present at the time of examination of the patient. Now, the substance of abuse is first classified such as F 10 for alcohol, through opioids, cannabinoids, cocaine, other stimulants and so on up to F 19 which is for other/multiple substances. There is then a coding for features which may follow misuse which go through intoxication, harmful use, dependency syndrome, withdrawal state, withdrawal with delirium, psychotic disorder, amnesic syndrome, residual and late onset psychotic states, other and unspecified problems (0.0 to 0.9). Thus, the 34-year-old man abusing alcohol and suffering complications discussed previously could have been accommodated within F 10.0 (intoxication), F 10.1 (harmful use), F 10.2 (dependency syndrome), F 10.3 (withdrawal state), F 10.4 (withdrawal state with delirium), F 10.5 (psychotic disorder) and F 10.6 (amnesic state).

Another innovation has been in respect of schizophrenia which has been separated from other acute psychotic syndromes. The reasoning behind this change appears to be a sound one. In many developing countries there are numerous patients who present with acute short-lived psychotic conditions (which appear to be close to the Scandinavian conception of reactive depression). Whether these disorders are due to stresses experienced or infections harboured is not always clear. These patients respond very well to treatment and long-term drug management is not usually necessary. To lump these conditions with schizophrenia is to do a disservice to patients, doctors and researchers, for classical schizophrenia, even in its recent mutation in the direction of a relatively benign condition, remains a beast of very different stripe. However, in deference to the apparently changing face of schizophrenia the time-limit of one month for the symptoms to be present has also been adopted. This approach rejects the notion, long held, that schizophrenia is invariably a chronic and unrelenting disorder. Recent research has shown that in all cultures there are patients who make a good recovery within 6 months of treatment. In an exemplary formulation, which could serve right across the board in the study of all mental disorders, the ICD-10 describes schizophrenia as 'a syndrome with a variety of causes and a variety of outcomes depending on a mixture of genetic, physical, social and cultural influences'.

There is a recognition also of mixed anxiety and depressive disorder. While it is traditional to separate these two disordered mood states, it is a commonplace clinical observation that distinction can rarely be made between the two with any great confidence. These symptoms go together, although one kind of mood disturbance may be prominent in one patient, the other in a second patient. In fact, their drug treatment nowadays follows similar lines of management. There are many psychiatrists who would question whether depression and anxiety should be separated, while a minority will allocate separate categories to depression and anxiety and, in addition, place irritability in a third category.

Culture-specific disorders have also been given their place in the sun. As we shall see repeatedly stressed in this book, cultural influences – the term to be used in its broadest sense – must always be considered in any psychiatric assessment. There is also an exotic collection of disorders which are seemingly peculiar to individual cultures. We shall make the briefest reference to them in Part II.

The problematical area of personality disorder also finds consideration. Borderline personality disorder, generally believed to be the most severe kind among these disorders, finds a place under emotionally unstable personality disorders. These are conditions which, above all, require considerably more research in order to elucidate their properties.

2.12 TERMINOLOGY

As might be expected in a system of classification formulated for use around the world, there are problems of terminology for terms are used in very different senses in different cultures. But terms such as 'psychotic' and 'neurotic' continue to be used; the former referring in a descriptive way to the presence of hallucinations, delusions, severe abnormalities of behaviour such as gross excitement and overactivity, marked psychomotor retardation and catatonic behaviour such as excitement and stupor

It is not surprising there is much misunderstanding of terms such as 'mental illness' and 'mental disorder'. The usual practice – also followed in this book – is to confine the term illness to formal mental illness such as schizophrenia, depressive illness or anxiety states. As the ICD itself remarks, 'disorder' is not an exact term but is used to describe the existence of a clinically recognisable set of symptoms or behaviour associated in most cases with distress. It is a useful shorthand term for a motley collection of categories which include personality disorders and learning disabilities. The ICD points out that disorder is not to be inferred from disturbances of social functioning alone and gives express warning that social deviance or conflict alone is not a mental disorder. This finds an echo in s 1(3) of the Mental Health Act 1983 (MHA 1983) which provides that a person cannot be dealt with under that Act as suffering from a mental disorder, or any specific form of it, 'by reason only of promiscuity or other immoral conduct, sexual deviancy or dependence on alcohol or drugs'. MHA 1983 does not define mental illness. The Butler Committee (*Report of the Committee on Mentally Abnormal Offenders*, Cmnd 6244 (HMSO, 1975)), defined mental illness as a 'disorder which has not always existed in the patient but has developed as a condition overlying the sufferer's usual personality'.

In *W v L* [1974] QB 711, a case which involved the gross maltreatment of animals and also the expectant wife of the appellant, Lawton LJ considered the meaning of mental illness:

> 'The words are ordinary words of the English language. They have no particular medical significance. They have no particular legal significance ... ordinary words of the English language should be construed in the way that ordinary sensible persons would construe them ... I ask myself what would the ordinary sensible person have said about the patient's condition in this case if he had been informed of his behaviour to the dogs, the cat and his wife? In my judgment such a person would have said, "well, the fellow is obviously mentally ill".'

Such a variant of the Clapham omnibus test, with all due respect to judicial authority, will not do justice to the complexities that exist in the clinical situation. A useful 'rule of thumb' in such situations is to consider mental illness to be those conditions which are susceptible to standard forms of treatment and which have recognised symptoms and signs apart from showing the distinctive break with habitual personality the Butler Committee noted. Some observers have suggested that mental illness is what remains after the term mental disorder has been applied to the various forms of personality disorders and disabilities. In fact, s 1(2) of MHA 1983 defines mental disorder as 'mental illness, arrested or incomplete development of mind, psychopathic disorder and any other disorder or disability of mind'.

Interestingly the ICD-10 now does not use the term 'psychosomatic' on the ground that the term should be avoided because its use might be taken to imply that psychological factors play no role in the occurrence, course or outcome of diseases that are not so labelled. We are back to the 'mind-body' problem where this medieval distinction appears to still stand in the way of our achieving a complete understanding of the mechanisms by which 'physical' symptoms of disorder come to be displayed. As we shall persist in noting in this book, there is no mental disorder – for all we know, there may be no disorders at all – where 'psychological' factors play no part.

The terms 'impairment', 'disability' and 'handicap' may also give rise to confusion, not to say offence. Any psychiatrist with a generation's experience of the speciality has seen the phenomenon now described as learning disabilities move from being called mental retardation thorough mental subnormality and mental handicap. MHA 1983 uses the term mental impairment while the ICD-10 persists with mental retardation. The ICD-10 refers to 'impairment' as being the loss or abnormality of a structure or function (eg memory loss or loss of a limb), while 'disability' is the restriction or the impossibility to perform social and professional roles and 'handicap' refers to the disadvantage which society imposes on an individual with a disability.

As must be clear by now, a diagnosis, by itself, is of limited value in achieving an understanding of the functioning within society of any individual who may be afflicted by a disorder. The ICD-10 sets out a possible approach to resolving this problem by suggesting a multiaxial presentation of mental disorders. Axis I refers to the clinical diagnosis which we shall see summarised shortly. Axis II refers to disability resulting from mental and/or physical disorder. These disabilities are rated in respect of personal care and survival, occupational functioning, functioning with family and household members and broader social behaviour (eg leisure activities). Axis III refers to the factors contributing to the presentation or course of the disorder. The group of factors covered on this axis include problems related to negative life events in childhood, education and literacy, family circumstances, social environment, housing or economic circumstances, family history of diseases or disabilities and lifestyle.

2.13 CLASSIFICATION

The list of categories of disorder in the ICD-10 is vast and we can only give a bare summary here. As will be seen, there is no necessary logic in this classification – or, for that matter, in any other system – when it comes to setting out mental disorders in a systematic way.

1. F 00–09 refers to organic, including symptomatic, mental disorders. The term organic, as opposed to functional, can, as we have seen already, be subjected to criticism but it is the best we can do in the current state of knowledge. This category includes the various dementias (including Alzheimer's disease), organic memory problems, other mental disorder due to brain disorder or dysfunction and also personality and behavioural disorders due to brain disease, damage and dysfunction such as the frontal lobe syndrome following brain damage.

2. F 10–19 includes the mental and behavioural disorders due to psycho-active substance use. Apart from the abuse of alcohol and the better-known illicit substances, this category also takes account of the problems due to misuse of otherwise lawful substances such as prescribed drugs, caffeine and tobacco.

3. F 20–29 accommodates a variety of disorders including schizophrenia and related conditions. Apart from schizophrenia, persistent delusional disorders, the acute and transient psychotic disorders and the schizo-affective disorders find their place here.

4. F 30–39 is for the mood (affective) disorders which, given their multi-faceted forms, require a feat of imagination to be corralled into any category. This category does not exhaust the possibilities of mood disorders, for the next, too, includes them.

5. F 40–48 is employed to include such disorders as the anxiety states, obsessive-compulsive disorder, stress-related disorders, dissociative (conversion) disorders (hysteria) and somatoform disorders which include the hypochondriacal disorders.

6. F 50–59 involves the behavioural syndromes associated with physiological disturbances and physical factors. While physical symptoms are
   commonly found associated with psychiatric conditions, notably with
   depressive illness and anxiety states, this category places within it eating
   disorders, non-organic sleep disorders, sexual dysfunction, puerperal
   (post-partum) disorders not classified elsewhere and also abuse of non-
   dependence producing substances such as laxatives, steroids and
   hormones.

7. F 60–69 deals in disorders of adult personality and behaviour which
   include not merely the personality disorders as commonly understood
   but also habit and impulsive disorders such as pathological gambling,
   pyromania and kleptomania, gender identity disorders, disorders of
   sexual preference such as paedophilia and sadomasochism.

8. F 70–79 deals with mental retardation in all its forms.

9. F 80–89 categorises disorders of psychological development including
   specific disorders of speech and language development as well as the
   pervasive developmental disorders including childhood autism and
   Asperger's syndrome

10. F 90–98 deals with behavioural and emotional distress occurring in
    childhood and adolescence.

Any mental disorder which cannot be shoe-horned into this capacious
receptacle can always be accommodated under F 99 – unspecified mental
disorder.

Chapter 3

THE PSYCHIATRIC EXAMINATION

As a medical specialist, the psychiatrist, when conducting an examination, sets out to elicit symptoms and signs which are then evaluated in order to produce a diagnosis (if applicable) following which, he hopes, treatment will be feasible. The state of development of psychiatry is such that clear-cut approaches to this task are not always possible. Symptoms in the rest of medicine are what the patient complains of and signs are what the doctor elicits, usually through some means of physical examination. In psychiatric practice it is not always possible to separate symptoms and signs and some professionals refer to all clinical features as symptoms. These symptoms may be described by the patient or by another party who could be a friend or relation of the patient. It used to be said that a history given by the patient, especially one suffering from a psychotic disorder, should be deemed to be part of that patient's mental state.

3.1 THE HISTORY

Nevertheless, it is possible to divide with some logic, even in psychiatry, as between history taking and the mental state examination. Many patients are referred by the GP and in most instances in this rushed age what the GP's referral contains is a summary, often brief, of what the patient has said to the doctor. Some patients are reluctantly present at a psychiatric examination, attending there under greater or lesser duress, often, in family and childcare cases, only to comply with orders and directions of the court and allowance must be made for the lack of reliability which may follow protest in those circumstances. The history taken follows the pattern established in all medicine – the onset of symptoms, their nature and the duration of symptoms (by asking the patient when he last felt well). The information elicited is recorded with the patient's view of how the symptoms might have originated, that is, any stressful situation or other precipitating factor that he feels could have been causative.

Family history

It is logical to inquire at this stage into the presence of any family history of similar or other psychiatric problems or, indeed, a history of physical illness. These matters are not always reliably investigated by speaking to a patient or even by looking into his medical records (where what is entered might only have been information supplied by him on a previous occasion). In cases where a clear genetic basis to some disorder is suspected there may be no alternative to interviewing family members and, with their consent, examining the relevant medical records.

Personal history

The next logical step is to consider the personal history of the patient. For what it is worth he should be asked about his childhood. It has been said by experts in the field of childhood memory development that no valid or systematic memory is available to a child until it reaches the age of about 7. This must put in some doubt any claims to a reliably recounted history of early childhood abuse or unhappy experiences before that age; often what is believed to be early childhood memory is a result of later hearsay. Questions routinely asked about family life, the atmosphere therein, relationships between family members and the stability of the family also suffer from this potential source of unreliability. Educational and employment history are more reliably established, or at any rate capable of being independently verified. The school history is not only valuable for information to be gained about academic accomplishment (which has a bearing on the evaluation of intelligence possessed by the patient which is a feature in every psychiatric examination) but also for evidence of behavioural and conduct disorders which have their onset in childhood and adolescence. As we shall see later, the diagnosis of personality disorder – to be undertaken at deemed psychological maturity of an individual – also requires investigation of the presence of childhood misconduct in that individual. In those individuals who are thus afflicted not all childhood naughtiness is seemingly outgrown.

The employment record is equally valuable for any lack of correspondence between academic attainment and intellectual promise and the employment that has actually come to be secured may indicate some mental problems as well, usually in terms of personality, sometimes due to formal illness, which is deserving of further inquiry. Furthermore, the employment record itself, if procurable, often gives an independent and objective account of the individual's capacity for work and also his personality.

In family and child practice the sexual and marital history of the patient is of obvious relevance. Sadly, reliability is not always achieved when it comes to evaluating the quality of the relationships formed but the bare enumeration of the number and duration of relationships is capable of independent verification. Any current relationship is noted as are mundane matters such as the nature of accommodation and the receipt of social benefits.

Alcohol and illicit substances

An important subcategory of the personal history involves inquiry into the consumption of alcohol and illicit substances. These are usually recorded from personal report, objective or independent verification from any available witnesses and a limited range of laboratory investigations. It cannot be emphasised too often that a proper evaluation of alcohol and illicit drug use requires a comprehensive assessment of all areas of personal and psychological functioning, for, especially in family and child practice, what one is looking for is some disturbance in behaviour which is likely adversely to affect the patient's responsibilities as spouse, partner or parent. Absolute levels of consumption of these substances may have general forensic relevance (eg convictions for driving with an excess of alcohol, possession or distribution of illicit substances) but in itself it is not necessarily of direct significance to the issues arising in family and child proceedings.

Forensic history

A forensic history is of similar importance. A recent history of convictions and cautions gives objective support to what could otherwise, in many domestic instances, be emotionally charged accusations of violent and aggressive behaviour. Ideally, one should also have available the facts of any incident leading to conviction although much useful information may be found in previous forensic psychiatric and pre-sentence reports.

Medical history

Following an evaluation of personal history the next step is to consider the past medical history of the patient. This would appear to be an obvious step, for many disorders tend to recur. The most useful source of this information is the full medical record of the patient. Often the GP records are retrieved more easily than the hospital records. The former are less complete when hospital intervention has taken place but copies of all correspondence routinely sent from hospitals – letters, discharge summaries including results of investigations – should be available as part of the GP record. Sometimes they are not and it remains a matter for scandal that in an age which purports to be one dedicated to the proper transmission of vital information so many patients do not have readily available access to a comprehensive and reliable record of their medical history to present to any examining doctor. The time has probably come – and the necessary technology is available – for information concerning patients to be given to them, to be held responsibly and to be produced to authorised professionals. It strikes one as being a more useful investment of public funds than attempts to confirm mere identity.

Be that as it may, the past medical history is divided conventionally into physical illness and mental disorder, which is not strictly logical but convenient. The details of physical illness suffered in the past must also include details of therapeutic drugs used previously and those which may continue to be taken by the patient, for many drugs do have adverse side effects which may themselves precipitate or aggravate psychiatric disorder. The importance of past history of mental disorder is self-evident. The patient may not have reliable information to give in respect of past psychiatric disorders or interventions – it is striking how many patients lack such essential information as the diagnosis or treatment previously given, length of hospital stay or whether admission had been voluntary or under the compulsory provisions of MHA 1983. A study of the past medical record is essential although its availability is not always assured.

From what has been said already – and will be repeated through the course of this book – the personality of the patient, that is, the element on which any illness comes to be grafted, is important to evaluate. The study of ante- or pre-morbid personality is a well-recognised feature of the psychiatric examination. However, as with his reputation, what is the true personality of an individual is a matter to be determined by other persons. Individuals are notoriously unreliable in the self-assessment of personality. Sadly, in family and child practice, the significant other person in an individual's life – spouse or partner, especially when estranged – can himself or herself come to provide information which materially distorts the picture that more independent or objective witnesses may draw of an individual. Despite the protestations of psychologists, there are few reliable tests of personality assessment for use in ordinary clinical practice. The doctor is left with evaluating the evidence as a whole and it is in this respect that independently made records such as employment history or the documentation of the criminal record may give a more reliable picture. One must also always bear in mind the huge variations that are possible in the attributes of a personality, and what is the normal range for any attribute is scarcely to be ascertained with any convenience. The distinctions invariably to be made with any behaviour of psychiatric relevance – what is abnormal, what is pathological – is to be borne in mind also when assessing personality. It should also always be remembered that one could be grossly abnormal in one's behaviour in terms of the norms of any society but that fact alone does not preclude acceptable participation as spouse, partner or parent. And the world would be a duller and more primitive place if not for the abnormal personalities who have existed in every age.

3.2 THE MENTAL STATE EXAMINATION

This is the equivalent of the physical examination in general medicine and surgery. It is, of course, a vital part of any examination of a patient but it is possible to overstate its importance. By that one means both a history and examination must be undertaken and many experienced psychiatrists will argue that the history – with its scope for eliciting objective, independent information – is the more important component. In fact, in family and child practice, with the possibility of a study of the papers which are routinely disclosed to the psychiatric expert along with the available medical record, it should be possible in the average case to predict about 90 per cent of the contents of the report that waits to be written on a study of these documents alone. If sufficient knowledge has not been obtained in this way, one of two situations exist. First, the papers are incomplete, in particular the medical records might not have been included within them. Secondly, sufficiently careful reading of the papers has not been undertaken. While psychotic conditions and other obviously revealing disorders such as a depressive illness may be detected by an examination of the mental state alone, other conditions of particular relevance to family and child practice, especially the personality disorders, may be difficult to identify without access to the kind of information which makes up the history, whether such information is to be found in the papers in cases where litigation is afoot or is derived from persons independent of the patient such as friends and relations, although care must be taken to see that those acquainted with the patient do not exaggerate – by maximising or minimising pathology – so as to make their own case.

Notwithstanding this, a current mental state examination is essential if a fully informed diagnostic formulation is to be arrived at. It sometimes happens that a spouse, partner or parent refuses to undergo a psychiatric examination as directed and the expert may be left to work on the available papers alone, sometimes by a further direction of the court, more usually on the instructions of the solicitor. Although, in view of what has been said above, it is perfectly feasible to produce a report in those circumstances to assist the court, the expert must ensure that he conveys to the court the information that the peculiar insights that may be possible on examination – the 'feel' of a patient, so to speak – is only possible on personal contact with a patient.

For our present purposes we shall merely summarise the heads of the mental state examination and briefly note the significance of any findings.

Appearance and behaviour

It used to be said to medical students that a skilled and experienced doctor could make a diagnosis even while a patient was walking through the door of the consulting room. This art was carried to its peak in the works of Sir Arthur Conan Doyle who based his fictional creature, Sherlock Holmes, on a real individual, his teacher at Edinburgh Medical School, Dr Joseph Bell. Conan Doyle said of his mentor that he would sit in his room 'with a face like a Red Indian, and diagnose the people as they came in, before they even opened their mouths. He would tell them their symptoms and even give them details of their past life, and hardly ever would he make a mistake'. The maestro Bell himself explained the basis to his apparently wondrous facility:

> 'The precise and intelligent recognition and appreciation of minor differences is the real essential factor in all successful diagnosis.'

Things are a little more complex in psychiatric practice. Eccentricity of manner and exotic dress may indicate psychiatric disorder and is especially common to see with exuberant manic patients. Self-neglect, on the other hand, may not necessarily indicate pathology; lack of means could be the reason. However, alcohol and illicit drug misuse may also lead to self-neglect on the part of the patient as can schizophrenia or some forms of personality disorder. Overactivity is characteristic of mania although some depressed patients appear agitated. The paranoid patient may be suspicious and the occasional sufferer from paranoid psychosis or paranoid personality disorder may insist on tape recording his encounter with the doctor and may also be given to misinterpreting even the most trivial of occurrences (eg the doctor speaking on the telephone or into a Dictaphone). Yawning is not merely a sign of boredom but could indicate oversedation and may be one of the withdrawal symptoms seen in opiate dependence.

Physiological symptoms

These are usually the most straightforward features to elicit in the examination of the mental state. Sleep in mental disorder may be disturbed in a variety of ways, and dreams and nightmares may indicate an underlying anxiety state. No intricate exploration of dream phenomena is undertaken in mainstream psychiatry; that is the historical task of psychoanalysis and even there the analysis of the content of dreams is now deemed of doubtful value. Appetite, as will later be discussed, may be altered in many psychiatric conditions as may bowel habits, menstrual regularity and libido.

Mood

Under this head depression, anxiety and irritability are investigated. These mood states are commonly found within the affective disorders. Schizophrenia may be associated with subtler changes involving incongruity or flattening of affect. Indifference – *la belle indifference* – was once believed to be a classical feature of hysterical or dissociative states (although see later pages for current belief). The examination of suicidal thoughts also comes within an investigation of mood. As will be discussed later, there are gradations in suicidal ideation passing from fleeting ideas that life may not be worth living through to active suicidal ideas to elaborately crafted plans to take one's life. Anxiety states may include features of generalised anxiety with or without the presence of phobic states and a particular feature of anxiety states is the presence also of the symptoms of depersonalisation and derealisation where the patient feels he has changed or the world has changed.

Speech

This is studied from the point of view of both form and content. Form refers not only to the rate of speech – considerably slowed as with all other functions in depressive illness and speeded up in mania – but also the quantity and quality. Poverty of speech is noted in those with compromised intellectual functions. The pattern of speech is also considered when logic may be lacking in speech, a state of affairs which is believed to reflect thought disorder, characteristically seen in schizophrenia. The terms 'speech' and 'thought' are often used interchangeably although speech should be reserved for actual talk while thought is to be inferred from the content of talk which gives a window into the mind.

Thought content

These may include the variety of delusions to be discussed later in the book. There are rarer phenomena such as thought insertion, thought withdrawal and thought broadcasting which refer to abnormal processes involving thinking that reach delusional proportions. An extreme variant of this is passivity where the patient feels his body has been taken over and is controlled by some extraneous or alien force. These are, characteristically, features of an acute schizophrenic illness. Obsessional thoughts and compulsive behaviour, although normally features of a non-psychotic illness, may also be dealt with under the investigation of the processes of thinking.

Abnormal perceptions

These include illusions and hallucinations. The former are common and usually harmless. One is not uncommonly startled by the shadow of an object, say a tree in moonlight, and come to believe it could be a person, usually one carrying a malevolent design. Hearing a chiming church bell calling out, 'Turn again, Whittington', is an example from legend. The significance of auditory hallucinations can only be evaluated within the context of the entire clinical picture. It is a common symptom of acute schizophrenia although normal individuals experiencing stress or grief or unwanted solitude can also have these perceptions. Visual hallucinations are invariably significant and suggest organic brain disorder. They are notoriously experienced in states of withdrawal from alcohol and also with illicit drug use. This and other hallucinations may also be a presenting feature of space occupying lesions of the brain such as tumours.

Cognitive functions

It is traditional to make a clinical examination of the higher brain functions although full psychological testing is recommended for all formal purposes such as litigation. The latter are labour-intensive and time-consuming although resources are normally available for psychological testing in family and child cases. Consciousness is not usually a problem in the parties involved in these proceedings although it is the first cognitive state to be examined usually. There is much confusion regarding the state of confusion itself and disorientation. Confusion, although colloquially applied to any state where an individual does not know what is going on, technically means a state of disturbed consciousness. Disorientation, on the other hand, concerns a lack of knowledge which leads to impaired appreciation of such details as time (not knowing day, date, month, etc), place (where one is) or person (who people are). As a rule demented patients are disorientated, not confused, though these patients, like anyone else, may also become confused when afflicted, say, by an infection. Attention and concentration are impaired most commonly in states of depression and anxiety, although almost any condition, not to mention its treatment, can lead to this phenomenon. Their importance lies in the fact that they may give rise as a consequence to poor short-term memory which is not to be attributed to 'organic' factors but is related to the poor registration of memories which follows poor attention and concentration. There are more specialised tests for higher function such as those for dysphasia (difficulties in receiving or expressing spoken speech) or dysgraphia (difficulties in receiving or expressing the written word) but these are matters for specialist neuropsychological testing. Short-term and long-term memory may also be clinically tested. The focus is usually on the former which, as is well known, is preferentially affected in most disorders. Remote memory is preserved for a long time even in fairly severely demented patients who can, for instance, converse knowledgeably about Mr Churchill as prime minister but who may have no idea who the current incumbent might be. The formal detailed testing of memory function is also a matter for expert psychological testing. As was said earlier, it is usual also to make some assessment of intelligence possessed by the patient. In fact, the purpose of seeking information about schooling and educational attainment is at least, in part, directed to the aim of seeing whether later occupational achievement has matched intellectual promise or whether there has been a shortfall possibly related to mental disorder. Questions on general knowledge of current affairs, intellectual interests admitted to by the patient and the content of the patient's talk in interchanges with the examiner may also indicate the level of intellectual functioning of the patient. Needless to say, formal detailed assessment of intelligence also resides in the province of the specialist psychologist.

Insight

It is usual to end any examination of the mental state with an assessment of the insight possessed by the patient. This term refers to the understanding, in general terms, the patient has achieved in regard to the nature of the disorder he has suffered and its cause. At its most basic, the patient is able to recognise he is ill although he does not acknowledge mental disorder. One level up, he accepts he is ill and also that the disorder is of nervous or mental origins. When insight is completely lacking, disorder is denied *in toto*. Psychotic conditions are usually associated with some impairment of insight while those patients with non-psychotic disorders usually retain insight. However, there are exceptions. Hysterical patients are notoriously lacking in insight, sometimes totally, even while hysterical (dissociative/conversion) states are classified usually as non-psychotic conditions. As has already been indicated, and will also be discussed in detail later, cultural beliefs may decisively influence whether mental or nervous disorder is acknowledged by the patient.

Chapter 4

CONSENT, CONFIDENTIALITY, CAPACITY AND THE MENTAL HEALTH ACT 1983

4.1 CONSENT AND CONFIDENTIALITY

These issues are common to all forms of medical examination. Consent is not usually an issue in cases involving family and child practice. A party may, of course, withdraw from the proceedings or refuse to participate in such procedures as undergoing a psychiatric assessment. What steps are then to be taken is a matter for the court. It may direct the psychiatric expert to produce a report on the available papers which may include the medical record. From what has been said previously, a substantial amount of relevant information is available in these proceedings for the papers are usually full and likely to give accounts of the individual's behaviour in a variety of settings. The medical records, when available, will give relevant information about past medical and psychiatric history and any ongoing treatment. Writing a report under these conditions is not ideal but in the circumstances, especially when the child's welfare is the paramount consideration, one must do what one can.

Confidentiality becomes an issue, apart from the usual considerations, by reason of the special status accorded by the law to family and child proceedings. Experts who, as professionals, are, of course, familiar with the concept of the confidentiality attaching to patient-client relationships do not always appreciate that the information in and derived from the papers in a case involving family and child proceedings is to be treated in the strictest confidence. In ordinary clinical practice, as we have noted, it is common for doctors to communicate informally with their colleagues and satisfactory clinical practice cannot be achieved unless a patient's medical record is also consulted. In family and child proceedings even a seemingly innocent act such as disclosing a medical report one has written to a treating doctor to commence treatment without delay is a breach of confidentiality if the consent of the court has not first been obtained. In fact, no document may be disclosed to any person unconnected with the proceedings without the prior authority of the court. Doubtless any such breach will constitute a contempt of court and may also be the subject of a reference by the court to the regulatory and disciplinary body of the professional involved.

4.2 CAPACITY

While consent and confidentiality are reasonably well understood, the issue of capacity – despite it being a consideration in virtually every branch of the law – often appears to raise problems as both lawyers and doctors appear easily led into confusion. One reason for befuddlement appears to be the tendency to equate illness and disorder – especially when mental illness or disorder is involved – with possible loss of capacity. Conversely, it is not always appreciated that sound physical and mental health does not preclude a loss of capacity. Capacity is a function of the exercise of autonomy on the part of an individual. Many of the cases in which the concept of capacity has been investigated have involved consent to medical treatment although the principles derived are generally applicable to any situation where capacity becomes an issue. The classic formulation of the policy lying behind capacity are the words of Cardozo J in *Schloendorff v Society of New York Hospital* (1914) 105 NE 92:

> 'Every person of adult years and sound mind has a right to determine what shall be done with his own body.'

The implications of this view go well beyond issues of consent to medical treatment and affect every aspect of a person's existence in a free modern society. There is an acknowledged right to be wrong, absurd, bizarre, eccentric or capricious as long as one has capacity. The state can impose its paternalistic view only if one is incapable. English law has jealously guarded this right, as evidenced by the wide discretion given to testators to dispose of their property after their death and has even now extended the principle to mature children on matters involving contraceptive advice, abortion and sexual health.

A useful summary of what the law requires comes from this passage of a judgment by Boreham J in *White v Fell* ((unreported) 12 November 1987):

> 'To have capacity [the party] requires first insight and understanding of the fact that she has a problem in respect of which she needs advice. Secondly, having identified the problem, it will be necessary for her to seek an appropriate adviser and to instruct him with sufficient clarity to enable him to understand the problem and to advise her appropriately. Finally, she needs sufficient mental capacity to understand and to make decisions based upon, or otherwise give effect to, such advice as she may receive.'

A leading case on capacity is *Masterman-Lister v Brutton* [2003] 1 WLR 1516 which involved personal injury litigation. Some passages from the judgment will help to set out the essence of the issue of capacity.

> '1.   The mental abilities required include the ability to recognise a problem, obtain and receive, understand and retain relevant information including advice, the ability to weigh the information (including that derived from advice) in the balance in reaching a decision.
>
> 2.   Capacity is an important issue because it determines whether an

individual will in law have autonomy over decision-making in relation to himself and his affairs. If he does not have capacity, the law proceeds on the basis that he needs to be protected from harm. Accordingly, in determining an issue as to an individual's capacity, the court must bear in mind that a decision that an individual is incapable of managing his affairs has the effect of removing decision-making from him.

3. Capacity must be approached in a common sense way, not by reference to each step in the process of litigation but bearing in mind the basic right of any person to manage his property and affairs for himself, a right with which no lawyer and no court should rush to interfere.

4. What, however, does seem ... of some importance is the issue-specific nature of the test, that is to say the requirement to consider the question of capacity in relation to the particular transaction (its nature and complexity) in respect of which the decisions as to capacity fall to be made. It is not difficult to envisage claimants in personal injury actions with capacity to deal with all matters and take all "lay client" decisions related to their actions up to and including a decision whether or not to settle but lacking capacity to decide (even with advice) how to administer a large award.

5. It is not the task of the courts to prevent those who have the mental capacity to make rational decisions from making decisions which others may regard as rash or irresponsible.

6. The court is concerned with the quality of the decision-making and not the wisdom of a decision.'

The other leading case on capacity is *Re: MB (an adult: medical treatment)* [1997] 2 FLR 426 in which Butler-Sloss LJ set out the requirements for capacity. The facts of that case involved a caesarean section operation but the decision in the case has had a profound influence on other areas of the law concerning capacity. It was stressed that a decision in any individual case had to be based on the particular facts of that case.

'1. Every person is presumed to have capacity unless and until that presumption is rebutted.

2. A competent woman, who has the capacity to decide may, for religious reasons, other reasons, for rational or irrational reasons or for no reason at all, choose not to have medical intervention even though the consequence may be the death or serious handicap of the child she bears, or her own death. In that event the courts do not have the jurisdiction to declare medical intervention to be lawful and the question of her best interests does not arise.

3. Irrationality is here used to connote a decision which is so outrageous in its defiance of logic or of accepted moral standards that no sane person who has applied his mind to the question to be decided could have arrived at it. It might be otherwise if the decision is based on a misperception of reality (eg the blood is poisoned because it is red). Such a misperception will be more readily accepted to be a disorder of the mind. Although it might be thought that irrationality sits uneasily with competence to decide, panic, indecisiveness and irrationality in themselves do not as such amount to incompetence but they may be symptoms or evidence of incompetence. The graver the consequences of the decision the

commensurately greater the level of competence is required to take the decision.

4. A person lacks capacity if some impairment or disturbance of mental functioning renders the person unable to make a decision whether to consent or refuse treatment. That inability to make a decision will occur when:

   (a) the patient is unable to comprehend and retain the information which is material to the decision, especially as to the likely consequences of having or not having the treatment in question;

   (b) the patient is unable to use the information and weigh it in the balance as part of the process of arriving at the decision. If a compulsive disorder or phobia from which the patient suffers stifles belief in the information presented to her, then the decision may not be a true one. As was said in *Banks v Goodfellow* (1870) LR 5 QB 549, "... one object may be so forced upon the attention of the invalid as to shut out all others that might require consideration".

5. Temporary factors (confusion, shock, fatigue, pain or drugs) may completely erode capacity but those concerned must be satisfied that such factors are operating to such a degree that the ability to decide is absent.

6. Another such influence may be panic induced by fear. Again, careful scrutiny of the evidence is necessary because fear of an operation may be a rational reason for refusing to undergo it. Fear may also, however, paralyse the will and thus destroy the capacity to make a decision.'

A simpler form of test used by the courts in assessing a patient's capacity is the three-stage test outlined by Thorpe J in *Re C* [1994] 1 All ER 891. The patient must be able to:

1. comprehend and retain the relevant information;

2. believe it; and

3. weigh it in the balance so as to arrive at a choice.

The patient must be able to understand the 'nature, purpose and effect' of any step that has been proposed. The Law Commission in its report *Mental Incapacity* (Law Com No 231 (1995)) gave as its view that to have capacity the patient should be able to understand or retain 'the information relevant to the decision, including information about the reasonably foreseeable consequences of deciding one way or another of failing to make the decision'.

As far as medical treatment is concerned, no one, including a court, is able to give consent to treatment on behalf of an incompetent adult. According to *Re F* [1990] 2 AC 1, in these circumstances doctors are under a legal duty to treat incompetent patients in accordance with the 'best interests' principle.

Capacity is not a question of the degree of intelligence or education of the person concerned. Some persons may permanently lack capacity, for example, due to severe mental handicap; others may lose capacity from time to time, for example, due to periodic severe mental illness; yet others may be temporarily deprived of competence owing to transient factors such as unconsciousness, pain, confusion or drug treatment.

The Mental Capacity Act 2005 formalises the common law presumption that an individual is presumed to possess capacity (s 1(1)) and the other presumption that a decision, provided it is made by a competent individual, may be unwise, imprudent or eccentric (s 1(4)).

4.3 MATRIMONIAL CAPACITY

One cause of confusion in a consideration of capacity to marry is the different meanings that can be ascribed to the phrase 'capacity to marry'. Here we shall consider only the psychiatric aspects involved in impairing marital capacity. The starting point for any analysis must be s 12(c) of the Matrimonial Causes Act 1973 ('the 1973 Act') which provides that any marriage shall be voidable if 'either party to the marriage did not validly consent to it, whether in consequence of duress, mistake, unsoundness of mind or otherwise'.

Section 12(d) of the 1973 Act provides that a marriage is voidable if 'at the time of the marriage either party, though capable of giving a valid consent, was suffering (whether continuously or intermittently) from a mental disorder within the meaning of the Mental Health Act 1983 of such a kind or such an extent as to be unfitted for marriage'.

As far as the first ground is concerned, as *Re Park* [1954] P 112 showed, mental illness or disorder will only affect the validity of consent if either spouse was, at the time of the ceremony, by reason of illness or disorder, incapable of understanding the nature of marriage and the duties it creates. This is a true test of capacity.

The ground in s 12(d) of the 1973 Act is, strictly speaking, not concerned with capacity but with the fact of mental illness or mental disorder which unfitted a spouse for marriage. Here, the spouse suffering from such an illness or disorder may be capable of giving a valid consent – in other words, has capacity – but on account of the mental disorder is incapable of carrying on a normal married life (*Bennett v Bennett* [1969] 1 WLR 430). A spouse may petition on the basis of his own mental disorder.

The facts may involve – as they did in *R: Davey* [1981)] 1 WLR 164 – the marriage of an elderly resident in a nursing home suffering from severe dementia with an unscrupulous attendant in that home. The fact that such a marriage may be voidable is no comfort to the relations of the elderly woman if she, having died, is deemed to have died intestate, the marriage, being only voidable, having revoked any previous will she might have made in their favour.

The more fundamental meaning to be attached to the term marital capacity – an ability to understand the nature and quality of the transaction – was explored recently in the case of *Sheffield City Council v E and Another* (2005) *The Times*, January 20. A local authority had responsibility for E, a woman aged 21 with hydrocephalus and spina bifida who functioned at the level of a 13-year-old. She had formed a relationship with an older man who had a substantial history of sexually violent crimes. It was feared this association had become abusive. The local authority wished to test E's capacity to contract a marriage. E's representatives proposed that the questions should address whether E had the capacity to understand the nature of the contract of marriage, the responsibilities generated by that contract and the capacity to give valid consent to marriage in general. The local authority, which sought to prevent E marrying the man she had become involved with, wished to give the questions a wider ambit. The matter reached the Family Division as a preliminary issue.

The court reiterated the general points arising on any question of capacity such as it being issue-specific. Further, it was said that it was not enough that someone appreciated he was taking part in a marriage ceremony or understood its words, he had also to understand the nature of the marriage contract which meant he had to be mentally capable of understanding the duties and responsibilities that normally attached to marriage. The court rejected the local authority's contention – based on consent to medical treatment – that the particular marriage proposal had to be taken account of. If a woman aged 21 had the capacity to marry, she had the capacity to marry anyone and it was not the business of the local authority or the court to adjudicate on the wisdom of her choice; that was her business and nobody else's. The court had no role in the vetting of E's suitors to select an appropriate partner. The analogy of consent to medical treatment was wrong, not least because medical procedures varied in scope while the contract of marriage was the same for everyone; nor was marriage something the average person needed to obtain expert advice or assistance on, in contrast to both medical treatment and litigation. Furthermore, the Family Division, when exercising its inherent jurisdiction in relation to an adult incompetent, had no power to give consent on behalf of the adult (see also above). The lawfulness of a marriage depended exclusively upon consent, and a test of best interests was neither here nor there; nor, if there was capacity, was it necessary to show that someone also had the capacity to take care of his own property and person. Therefore, the proper questions to put to the experts assessing capacity were those formulated by E's representatives.

At the other end of the spectrum of marriage – divorce proceedings – litigation capacity is to be determined as with any other proceedings bearing in mind the injunction that capacity is issue-specific. The essential questions are, however, similar to those arising in the assessment concerning litigation capacity in childcare proceedings.

4.4 CAPACITY IN CHILDCARE PROCEEDINGS

It necessary now to consider the capacity necessary to engage in childcare proceedings. The psychiatric expert is usually instructed to examine a party, usually a parent, with a view to seeing if the latter can give proper instructions and take sensible part in the proceedings. This examination invariably takes place in the course of a general psychiatric examination. The papers in the proceedings and the medical records may be available. The first pitfall to avoid is to desist from coming to any provisional view that the individual under examination could have compromised capacity on the basis of what one has read in the papers. These may include medical records giving evidence of current or past mental disorder. There could be psychological test results indicating low levels of intelligence. There may even be a certificate of mental capacity in which a previous medical examiner has opined that the patient had no capacity to manage his property and affairs in respect of financial matters. Despite this evidence the first rule to observe is that capacity is presumed to be intact. That is a common law principle which will be given statutory force when the Mental Capacity Act 2005 comes into operation. This presumption is to be displaced where appropriate on the evidence the examiner finds upon examination. Capacity, as has been made clear in the paragraphs above, is also both issue-specific and subject-specific. Capacity in childcare proceedings is to be evaluated in terms of the issues arising in these proceedings. As will be seen shortly, although childcare and adoption proceedings usually proceed about the same time, the issues arising in adoption proceedings in respect of capacity are quite different and must be separately assessed. The fact that an individual has been deemed to be lacking in capacity in respect of one matter – say, to handle his financial affairs in a proper and prudent way – is a fact to be taken into account when evaluating his capacity in regard to another matter but is by no means determinative on the issue of capacity in respect of the instant matter.

The fact that the individual has made contact with solicitors – from whom the instructions to the expert emanate – is an indication that he acknowledges the need for legal advice, one of the requirements for the possession of capacity in this situation. Also, by this time, the allegations in regard to any deficient parenting would normally have been made and perhaps even have been tested in court at a preliminary hearing. The examiner must ensure that the patient has fully grasped the nature of the allegations made. Many parents in this situation will protest vigorously and challenge the local authority's views in trenchant terms but that is not quite evidence of having achieved a preliminary understanding in general terms of what the accusations might have been about. The examiner must next place himself in the position of the patient's legal adviser and invite the patient to say how he proposes to counter the accusations in specific terms, in other words to give instructions. Occasionally the instructions to the expert might have indicated that the patient has changed his instructions from time to time apparently on a whim. It is useful to learn why instructions might have been changed by the patient. A 25-year-old woman, with a significant degree of learning disabilities, kept changing her instructions in childcare and, later, adoption proceedings. It transpired that what impelled these changes was the state of her relationship with her husband. They had a volatile relationship in which much violence involving both parties featured. They would break up once in a while and then be reconciled. It appeared the instructions the woman gave reflected her state of mind as to whether or not she was currently living with her husband or was estranged from him. In other cases it may be the ungovernable impulses arising from his mind – notably a feature of personality disorders but not unknown in other forms of mental disorder – that may dominate the mind of a patient at any given time to such an extent as to give the impression of capriciously changing instructions being given by him. The patient in this situation may even be of normal or high intelligence, be free of formal mental illness and appear to have no difficulty in understanding the issues. He may be disabled only in coming to a decision on the issues he has come to understand on account of his emotional state.

Capacity is a reflection and expression of an individual's autonomy. As such, it should be the individual who should be the focus of attention at an examination for the purpose of determining capacity. Occasionally, the individual under examination could be in a relationship with a stronger, perhaps intellectually and emotionally better endowed spouse or partner and be subjected to his influence. It is necessary to ensure the individual being examined is not having his will overborne by a mentally stronger person, in other words being subject to undue influence, to the extent that the examiner (and by extension the legal adviser of the individual) cannot be certain the instructions he is being given are the patient's or the spouse or partner's. Separate legal representation of the spouses or partners will not avoid this problem altogether if the couple are still living under one roof. It is essential to insist on examining the individual alone for a strong-willed spouse or partner may also insist on being present at the examination.

Being present in court is a double-edged weapon as far as any patient with impaired capacity is concerned. On the one hand, a court is a public setting – at any rate within the meaning as understood in family and child proceedings – and allowance can be made to ensure the patient can sensibly follow proceedings. On the other hand, many even quite normal persons possessing full capacity are often quite overawed by the nature of the proceedings and the atmosphere of the courtroom, even given the informality prevailing in these proceedings. The examiner must satisfy himself that, even with the support that will be forthcoming in court from the solicitor and the court itself, the patient will still be able to follow the proceedings, in particular when those situations arise where he will be called upon to further instruct or amend previous instructions in a less restful atmosphere than a solicitor's offices.

Ultimately, in evaluating capacity in these circumstances, the examiner's task is to ensure the tests applicable on the issue of capacity are, in fact, applied to the special circumstances of childcare proceedings. The patient is required to understand what is being alleged, should be able to grasp and retain the information, weigh it up and come to an informed decision so as to be able to instruct his legal advisers properly and, then, be able to sensibly follow proceedings in court.

4.5 CAPACITY IN ADOPTION PROCEEDINGS

Given that capacity is issue-specific it is implicit in that statement that adoption proceedings will be a special case. Under s 16 of the Adoption Act 1976 ('the 1976 Act') an adoption order cannot be made unless the child is first free for adoption by virtue of a freeing order made under s 18 of that Act or that each parent freely, and with full understanding of what is involved, agrees unconditionally to the making of an adoption order. This agreement can be dispensed with, *inter alia*, if the parent is incapable of giving agreement or is withholding the agreement unreasonably (s 16(2)(a) and (b) of the 1976 Act).

Section 18(1)(a) of the 1976 Act allows a court to make an order declaring the child free for adoption if each parent freely, and with full understanding of what is involved, agrees generally and unconditionally to the making of an adoption order.

What is 'freely and with full understanding of what is involved' is not statutorily defined but the parent must understand that in agreeing to an adoption he recognises that an adoption order:

1. takes away a birth parent's parental responsibility for a child; and

2. means that the child will be treated in law as the child of the adopters, and not as a child of the birth parents.

The test of capacity laid down in *Re: MB* [1997] 2 FLR 426 is applicable for this purpose. The Official Solicitor has said that until recently successful applications to dispense with a parent's agreement on grounds of incapacity were rare. Perhaps because of increased awareness about the question of decision-making capacity generally, the ground now appears to be pleaded more often. It will usually be necessary for medical evidence specifically addressing capacity to be obtained. In some rare cases (eg where a patient has sustained severe brain damage and is unable or virtually unable to communicate) the evidence of incapacity to give agreement may be so strong that specific medical evidence on the point need not be sought.

The test is applicable for both adoption and freeing cases. If a patient:

1. refuses agreement to the adoption; and

2. is capable (following the above test) of understanding the meaning of
    adoption,

the likeliest ground will be that the patient is withholding his agreement
unreasonably.

Adoption proceedings naturally involve a different set of circumstances to
childcare proceedings and, capacity being understood to be issue-specific
and subject-specific, the general principles associated with an assessment of
capacity must be specifically applied to this situation. Confusion appears to
arise in some patients' minds as to the rights they are bound to lose when
adoption takes place. Often this misunderstanding arises on account of the
parental rights they might have previously exercised, especially in terms of
the contact they were allowed during the course of childcare proceedings. A
40-year-old woman, suffering a significant degree of learning disabilities,
became involved in adoption proceedings concerning one of her children.
She also had an older child who resided with its father under a care order and
the mother enjoyed informal and flexible contact with this older child. She
also believed this older child could at some future time come to reside with
her. When examined with a view to seeing if she could understand the
implications of the adoption of the younger child she could not grasp that the
two situations involving her were different. In fact, she had formulated a
scheme in her own mind by which her family could be reunited with her at
some point in the future and she could not understand therefore any loss of
parental rights that would follow adoption of the second child.

4.6 MENTAL HEALTH ACT 1983 (MHA 1983) – CIVIL PROVISIONS

Parties to proceedings in family and child law cases may occasionally be
subject to the compulsory provisions of MHA 1983, or might have been so
subject in the past. Occasionally parties may well be confined in secure or
special hospitals following conviction and disposal under provisions
applicable in criminal matters. The subject of MHA 1983 is therefore briefly
dealt with here and reference will only be made to the compulsory
provisions that are in common use and which are necessary for the
practitioner in these fields to understand.

MHA 1983 emerged after a long evolution in the course of which Parliament
and the public had struggled to develop measures to contain and, later, to
treat those suffering from the effects of mental disorder without unnecessary
impairment of personal liberty. This evolution – which some may stigmatise
as regression, in view of recent experience – is still not ended as can be seen
in the debates and disputes the Government has been engaged in when
attempting to amend MHA 1983.

It seems logical to begin with s 4 of MHA 1983, which is used in emergencies. Under this provision, assessment may be made in an emergency with only one medical recommendation being required. The doctor involved need not have s 12 (MHA 1983) approval (granted when a doctor can demonstrate expertise in relation to mental disorders) and is most usually a GP with or without experience of the patient. Detention for up to 72 hours is permitted but it is usual (and good practice) to subject the patient, who will inevitably be in hospital soon after the single doctor makes his application, to a formal MHA 1983 assessment as soon as it is possible. Only emergency treatment under the common law principle of necessity is permissible under this provision if there is no consent given by the patient to any treatment.

The far commoner provision in use is s 2 of MHA 1983 which allows assessment for up to 28 days. Assessment may also include the giving of any provisional treatment. There must be two medical recommendations, one by a doctor with s 12 approval, and an approved social worker is normally involved. There is a right of appeal to a Mental Health Review Tribunal (MHRT).

Detention and treatment under s 3 of MHA 1983 is similarly made on the recommendation of two doctors (at least one approved under s 12) and an approved social worker. The patient may be detained in the first instance for up to 6 months. Detention may then be renewed for a further 6 months and thereafter for a year at a time. Treatment may be given against a patient's consent; indeed this admission under compulsory powers is made with a view to treatment being given.

From the point of view of the family and child practitioner, the significance of any particular application of these provisions must be noted. A s 4 (MHA 1983) admission without further assessment and extension of compulsory powers is probably of little significance (see also s 136 of MHA 1983 intervention below). It may imply that there had been some short-lived disturbance of behaviour on the part of the individual concerned which might or might not have been related to a mental disorder. The lack of further compulsory intervention usually means that s 4 of MHA 1983 could have been disapplied with the patient going on to accept help on a voluntary basis. Thus, a s 4 order may be of little significance in itself and the medical records need to be studied for the actual presence and significance of any mental illness or disorder.

Sections 2 and 3, given the time periods of detention involved, are of potentially greater significance although s 2 of MHA 1983 is expressly used for assessment and it may involve a case of compulsory hospital admission being sought for a clearer view to be obtained of what could be ailing the patient. While the need for compulsion in these circumstances may generally point to a loss of insight and unco-operativeness on the part of the patient, matters may need to be evaluated with some measure of caution. Family attitudes, hostility to one hospital or generally to all institutions after some unhappy experiences in hospital, even for an unrelated condition, or simply the desire to avoid getting a 'record' given the prejudices against mental disorder generally present in the community, may all be capable of explaining the resistance to accepting medical help shown by some patients. It is therefore wrong to use the fact of compulsory detention involving especially a s 2 order to draw, on that fact alone, some conclusion about the patient's mental health, though it is not uncommon for this to be done in family and child practice to the prejudice of a party. Section 3 of MHA 1983, on the other hand, generally indicates a significant degree of mental disorder having been previously present. In either case the outcome of an appeal to an MHRT may be informative as in these tribunals three independent persons, including a medical professional and a legally qualified chairman, come to cast their eye on the appeal made by the patient.

One of the odder but most useful uses of MHA 1983 resides in s 136. If a constable (the term applies to the office, not necessarily the rank) finds in a public place a person causing a disturbance which he believes to be due to mental disorder, and the individual in question is deemed to be in need of care or control, he may, if he thinks it necessary in the interests of that individual or for the protection of others, remove the individual to a place of safety. A place of safety usually means a police station or a hospital. There are regional differences influencing where a patient is taken but an increasing number of hospitals now have suites of rooms dedicated to the reception and assessment of such patients. Good practice dictates that any person brought in under s 136 powers must without delay be assessed under MHA 1983 to see if detention should be converted to a s 2 or the s 136 powers disapplied. Although often a temptation – as the least damaging option in cases where the clinical picture may be unclear and should be given a short time to show itself – a s 136 order is not expected to run till expiry in 72 hours after an MHA 1983 assessment has taken place; it must be disapplied or converted after an MHA 1983 assessment. Many of these cases involve the use of alcohol and/or illicit drugs, family disputes or some emotional crisis through which the person is living although it is not altogether unknown for mental disorder to declare itself to the authorities in this dramatic fashion. Despite the powers granted to constables – and officers on the beat likely to come across these disturbed persons are usually of low rank with no great training in mental health care – few will deny that the police, using simple good judgment with a lashing of common sense, usually achieve creditable results in this endeavour.

4.7 MENTAL HEALTH ACT 1983 (MHA 1983) – CRIMINAL PROVISIONS

Here we shall deal only with those powers used upon conviction, usually for fairly significant offences. The basic provision is s 37 of MHA 1983 which enables any court to make these 'hospital orders'. The effect is very similar to a s 3 civil order. The patient's ultimate disposal is left in the hands of his responsible medical officer (RMO) and the receiving hospital. The Home Secretary has no role to play in these cases. As could be imagined, the offences for which these orders are given following conviction are relatively minor.

Section 41 of MHA 1983 deals with altogether more serious offences. Only the Crown Court can make these 'restriction orders' which are tagged on to a MHA 1983, s 37 'hospital order' to restrict the movements of and administrative arrangements to be made in respect of such patients with a MHA 1983, s 37/41 order (hospital order with restriction). In such cases the court takes regard of the nature of the offence, the antecedents of the offender and the risk of his committing further offences if set at large, and decides whether it is necessary to make this restriction for the protection of the public from serious harm. Medical evidence from two doctors, one approved under s 12 of MHA 1983, is required. Most administrative matters involving these patients come within the purview of the Home Secretary and discharge of such a patient is only possible after a decision of the Home Secretary or an MHRT usually chaired in these appeals by a circuit judge. When the decision is taken to discharge the patient, absolute or conditional discharge is possible, the latter being conditional on good behaviour, compliance with medication, keeping of appointments, etc. In the event of breach of these conditions the patient may be recalled to hospital at the behest of the Home Secretary. The most seriously mentally disordered offenders involved in the graver crimes are usually brought to secure hospitals and units under this provision.

There are also 'remand orders' available under ss 35 and 36 of MHA 1983 (the latter power confined to the Crown Court) by which the courts are able to send an unconvicted defendant to hospital, normally for observation and for medical evidence for use at the trial to be gathered. The Home Secretary has similar powers to transfer to hospital remanded prisoners under s 48 of MHA 1983. Under s 47 of MHA 1983 the Home Secretary may also direct the transfer of convicted prisoners serving a custodial sentence from prison to hospital. This is a very useful power as it is by no means always certain that the full extent of a defendant's mental state is clear at the time of the trial and it is only later, upon definitive incarceration, that the scope of his mental disorder becomes known. It is obviously the case that if these patients need to be examined for purposes of family and child proceedings the procedures will have to be undertaken while they are held in conditions of considerable security.

PART II

THE PSYCHIATRIC DISORDERS

Chapter 5

ORGANIC MENTAL DISORDERS

In considering details of the individual mental disorders, we start with what are by convention called the organic mental disorders. Thereby we immediately confront, as we have already noted, an anomaly, an odd situation, in fact. It is this: modern research has revealed that most, perhaps all, psychiatric disorders appear to have their roots in brain dysfunction. Whether the means exist at present to pinpoint their precise location of dysfunction in some part of the brain is, however, a more problematical issue. One therefore, for the time being at any rate, presumes their source of dysfunction being in the brain. In some conditions of mental disorder, such as with the neuroses or the addictive disorders, the evidence at present for any brain involvement is very small and is presumed to be at a microbiochemical level. It is anticipated that in time, as technology advances and becomes available for practical use, more and more disorders will become susceptible to confident delineation as definitely arising in the brain but in the meantime we reserve the use of the term organic mental disorder to those conditions where there is little or no dispute that brain dysfunction, as currently understood, is the primary cause of the mental disorder.

It is customary to classify organic mental disorders as between acute disorders such as delirium and chronic conditions such as the dementias. Further, consideration in this category is also given to the consequences of head injury and to the psychiatric effects of systemic illness such as endocrine disorders. As might be imagined, it is a huge area of study and it is not our intention in a book such as this even to attempt to undertake an outline sketch of the entire field of study of organic mental disorders. Where appropriate in the relevant subsequent chapters we shall consider such effects as, say, the results on behaviour of particular aspects of brain damage or dysfunction, for example, with alcohol-related psychiatric problems, but in this chapter we shall only consider the dementias and the psychiatric effects of head injury, conditions which may affect behaviour involving cases in family and child law proceedings.

5.1 THE DEMENTIAS

Dementia refers to a condition in which there is an acquired global impairment of brain functions which usually leads to a progressive loss of intellectual and memory powers and a deterioration of personality and social functioning. These are conditions that have come upon the public consciousness fairly rapidly in recent years on account of an ageing population, although there still tends to be a degree of confusion, as we have already seen, concerning these conditions. The first element causing confusion is the term 'confusion' itself. It is common to hear even health care professionals referring to a demented patient being 'confused'. This is an inaccurate use of the term. Confusion is a result of a disturbance in consciousness. A demented patient is not confused, his consciousness is normally clear. What he usually displays is disorientation, that is to say, he does not know where he is, what day or place it is, what date or year it is, or who his intimates might be. A demented patient may, like anyone else, become confused as well, say, as a result of an infection but the primary underlying problem in dementia is a brain disorder which has global effects on the intellect, memory and personality which, at some stage in the course of the disorder, also comes to display disorientation.

Dementia is also an acquired condition. Childhood brain dysfunctions which lead to impairment in intelligence, memory and character (as personality can be called before maturity has been reached, at least in chronological terms) is more properly referred to as mental handicap or learning disabilities, which we shall take up in a later chapter. As already suggested, the impairment in dementia is also global, that is, it refers to a considerable range of the brain's functions being affected, a state of affairs to be distinguished from focal deficits where one part of the brain, for example, the parietal or frontal lobe, is a specific area to be affected. Finally, dementia refers to a clinical description of the phenomena observed. It does not suggest the cause of the brain dysfunction leading to the features of dementia, which requires further investigation and analysis for its elucidation.

The term senile dementia is to be found in popular usage. In its strict sense the term is doubly descriptive as it refers to a dementia found in the senium. The senium is conventionally defined as being the period after the age of 65 has been reached. The origins of this figure – which, of course, now has enormous social, financial and political significance the world over – are usually attributed to the age at which in 1884 Otto Von Bismarck, then Chancellor of Germany, decreed that citizens became entitled to their state old age pensions. There is no discernible medical significance in this age. Therefore any dementia arising after the age of 65 is a senile dementia, if before that age it is called a pre-senile dementia.

The causes of the dementias are various. The commonest cause is believed to be a degenerative brain disorder called Alzheimer's disease. There are rarer degenerative conditions of the brain such as Huntington's disease, Pick's disease, Creutzfeldt-Jakob disease (in its classical form as well as the more recently emerged variant CJD) and the dementias associated with Parkinson's disease. Cerebrovascular disease can lead to several forms of vascular dementia. Other causes of dementia include endocrine disorder (eg thyroid deficiency), head injury, poisoning (eg by heavy metals), excessive alcohol consumption, brain tumours and a variety of infections affecting the brain.

The prevalence of the condition varies with age. At the age of 65 some 5 per cent of the population are believed to be affected, the figure rising to 20 per cent when the population reaches the age of 80, hence the association with the growing elderly population. There is believed to be a genetic basis to the dementias related to the degenerative brain disorders although its precise nature in conditions such as Alzheimer's disease is still unclear. Certainly, a family connection is sometimes seen in the dementias which commence at a relatively young age and progress in a notably aggressive way.

The symptoms of dementia are attributable to the global nature of the brain dysfunction involved. Their course is insidious and it is usual for the short-term memory to be first affected, invariably unnoticed at first when it may be put down to the forgetfulness long associated with ageing. The growing impairment of intellectual functioning may also be similarly dismissed at first. These are not matters that usually concern the practitioner in family and child law although these features may in the course of time come to cause inconvenience and distress to the sufferer and his intimates. Litigation may involve the feature of a change in personality. There may be what is called a 'coarsening' of personality. Any individual is usually made up of many elements forming an amalgam of his personality, there being good, bad or indifferent parts to any personality. The whole is usually held together with the glue usually attributable to good manners and the appreciation of the need to conform and behave according to the expectations of a civilised society. Dementia has a tendency to cause this glue to dissolve or, perhaps as it may be more aptly described, this coat of civilising varnish to be removed. The result could be the emergence of an exaggerated or parodic picture of the characteristics in the individual's habitual personality. Thus, a person known to be careful with money now begins to acquire a reputation as a miser and a hoarder of objects, mostly valueless except in his eyes. A domineering person who managed nevertheless to keep his need to dominate others within acceptable bounds now turns into an aggressive, even violent, bully. Behaviour on the part of an individual may become unreasonable with implications for family lawyers. The couple which to all the world had appeared to be ageing gracefully together may now end up behaving disgracefully to one another. This kind of behaviour is not in all cases, of course, to be attributed to the effects of illness but the possibility of pathology affecting one partner must always be borne in mind especially when there has been a quite marked change from his previous conduct.

Another effect of dementia is disinhibition. Persons with an intact and reasonably well-adjusted personality are usually able to keep rogue impulses in check and thereby conform to the expectations of social and legal norms. A dementing illness may result in these inhibitions and restraints coming undone with aberrant behaviour the result. Anti-social behaviour especially leading to sexual misconduct, in particular involving young children, is a not unknown phenomenon and may be a cause for great alarm and distress to patient and families and of concern to the authorities. Any behaviour of this kind, especially when novel and out of keeping with the previous character of the individual, is an indication to explore further the possibility of some form of supervening brain pathology including those associated with the dementias.

The treatment of dementia depends on the cause. If the cause is correctable, for example, a deficiency in thyroid function, early treatment usually provides a good result. As for the commoner dementias due to degenerative disorders there is little by way of reliable treatment in any accepted sense available today. Claims for slowing the progress of the cognitive disturbance seen in the early stages of Alzheimer's dementia through drug treatment remain to be sustained.

5.2 HEAD INJURY

This is a vast subject primarily of neurological and neurosurgical interest. However, head injury being a common phenomenon, its victims not uncommonly interest the psychiatrist on account of the behavioural changes that may follow any insult given to the brain. These very same behavioural effects may also become of interest to practitioners involved in family and child proceedings as the roles and responsibilities of a spouse, partner or parent could be adversely affected as a consequence of a head injury.

One area of interest is the post-traumatic state following concussion where no specific lesion may be traceable to the brain. In this state are to be found numerous symptoms which include headache, giddiness, irritability, poor attention and concentration, with impaired short-term memory and an intolerance of alcohol. Post-traumatic epilepsy may also be found although that is commoner with penetrating wounds of the head where up to 50 per cent of patients may develop this condition. Mild organic dysfunction is not uncommon in the early days following minor head injury and during the subsequent few months. During this time psychological features can develop and/or pre-existing psychological vulnerabilities may be activated. When post-concussion syndrome persists, psychological factors may entirely account for the symptoms in some individuals, and organic or quasi-organic features will entirely account for the symptoms in others. Most patients will be found in between these extreme situations. A complicating feature in symptoms persisting over 6 months may be the expectations from a claim for compensation. Treatment of the post-traumatic state is often difficult partly because the patient is convinced that there is organic pathology underlying his symptoms, partly as the symptoms are often so vague and also in part because the personality of the patient may be the most important factor behind the symptoms and, accordingly, so much harder to deal with.

Personality change following concussion or more serious injury to the brain is occasionally to be found. Sometimes the change in personality can take a dramatic turn as a previously peaceable and respectable citizen commences a career of psychopathic excess. A couple of examples of this phenomenon are given in Chapter 10 when we take up the personality disorders. Those are personality changes of a fairly gross kind but many patients following head injury leaving little or nothing by way of obvious physical sequelae complain they are not 'the same person' following an episode of trauma involving their heads.

Head injury actually affecting the gross structure of the brain may leave behind specific deficits. One such state is the frontal lobe syndrome following injury to that part of the brain. There is often dramatic change in personality and behaviour of patients so affected. Patients may become euphoric or apathetic. Their character can turn gross and they have little regard for social norms and conventions or for the concern of others. They can be irresponsible and cruel and prone to excesses involving all their appetites. Their aggression and violence may lead to involvement with the criminal law. The interest in such individuals for practitioners in family and child law is obvious.

Chapter 6

THE PSYCHOTIC DISORDERS

These are the major psychiatric disorders and involve the patient losing touch with reality, also with loss of insight, and displaying symptoms such as delusions, hallucinations, disorders of thinking and of speech. As such, these features demonstrate a quite fundamental disruption of the higher functions of an individual and it is easy to see how family and child law practitioners may become involved with a spouse, partner or parent who suffers from such a condition. In this chapter we shall concern ourselves with schizophrenia and related conditions but not with those affective disorders of a psychotic kind, which we shall leave for consideration until the next chapter.

6.1 SCHIZOPHRENIA

Schizophrenia refers to a group of disorders whose features we shall take up shortly. It is best considered a form of brain dysfunction whose neurological lineaments are still far from well understood thereby causing us to study the illness (or, more accurately, the group of illnesses) at a descriptive rather than at any deep pathological level. There is one matter we shall summarily dispose of at the outset. Lay persons – encouraged by the journalistic use – appear to hold onto a notion that schizophrenia refers to some entity called a 'split personality'. It is nothing of the kind. The 'split' in schizophrenia refers to the dissociation between the various functions of the mind such as thinking, feeling, behaviour and perception so that contact with reality comes to be lost. This illness is a far cry from any personality disorder.

6.2 AETIOLOGY – GENETICS

The schizophrenic disorders are found the world over in virtually all communities and in fairly uniform distribution apart from a few pockets of increased incidence. They affect young men and women in late adolescence or early adult life and, although nowadays there is not believed to be a social class difference in the affliction, the tendency of patients with these conditions to drift socially downwards may suggest a poorer class distribution in surveys. There is sufficient evidence now of a genetic predisposition although the precise mechanisms still elude us. The closer the relationship to a schizophrenic patient a person has, the higher the risk that individual runs of developing the illness. However, the genetic risk is not 100 per cent which allows scope for environmental influences, both good and bad, to affect both onset and outcome. In fact, it appears it is a predisposition or vulnerability that is inherited rather than the illness itself. It has long intrigued observers – as we have already noted – that some of those who could have inherited this predisposition often tend to be gifted and highly creative individuals who, moreover, do not go on to develop the illness. There is a suggestion therefore of evolutionary advantage to be had in possessing some of this genetic material which is thereby propagated and kept in circulation.

6.3 THE ENVIRONMENT

The environmental influences remain unclear. A viral theory has been mooted. Over the past generation or two the condition appears to have become milder in presentation, at least in some cultures, and less chronic in outcome. The kind of inhabitant seen in the old lunatic asylums – still to be recalled by an older generation of psychiatrists – is now rare and the change is exemplified also by the 'care in the community' approach, much traduced on account of its shortcomings, but an infinitely better and more humane way of dealing with the appropriate patient than incarcerating him, perhaps for ever, in primitive institutions offering little by way of comfort or treatment. The diminished severity of the condition has suggested to some observers there could be a possible infective aetiology for viruses, in common with other microorganisms, have a well-recognised tendency to mutate to greater or lesser virulence. That apart, there have been some neurological changes noted on brain studies of patients with schizophrenia, although these findings, as yet, do not provide any reliable basis for diagnostic purposes. The role of environmental pollutants also remains unclear. Closer to home, pathological and dysfunctional family relationships have been suggested both as being aetiological as well as relapse-inducing elements.

Drug-taking

Finally, some presentations of schizophrenia-like conditions are virtually indistinguishable from the traditional presentations of the illness and may arise in the presence of systemic illness or following some illicit drug-taking. The strong association between self-reported cannabis use and the earlier onset of psychosis provides further evidence that schizophrenia may be precipitated by cannabis use and/or that early onset of symptoms is a risk factor for cannabis use. One study showed that half of all patients treated for cannabis-induced psychosis will develop a schizophrenia-like disorder and that almost a third will be diagnosed with paranoid schizophrenia. The first episode of schizophrenia occurs several years earlier in these patients compared with those with no history of cannabis-induced psychosis. Another study has suggested that compliance with antipsychotic medication by someone with schizophrenia may not prevent a relapse or worsening of psychotic symptoms if stimulant drugs (such as the amphetamines and cocaine) are used. Another study has reported that cannabis use in adolescence leads to a two to threefold increase in relative risk for schizophrenia or schizophreniform disorder in adulthood. The earlier the onset of cannabis use, the greater appears to be the risk for psychotic outcomes. Cannabis does not appear to represent a sufficient or necessary cause for the development of psychosis but seems to form a part of a causal constellation. A minority of individuals therefore experience a harmful outcome consequent on their use of cannabis. However, this minority is significant from a clinical point of view as well as at a population level. It is estimated that about 8 per cent of cases of schizophrenia could be prevented by elimination of cannabis use in the population. Given all this evidence, it is tempting to believe that the picture of schizophrenia one sees in a clinical setting is but the result of some 'final common pathway' of brain dysfunction which may be instigated by diverse means.

6.4 CLINICAL FEATURES

The onset of the illness may be variable. Some patients may harbour the illness for months or years and come only casually to medical attention. Others may suffer an explosive presentation which is drawn to the attention first of the police force or the criminal courts. Symptoms used to be described as being positive (such as hallucinations) or negative (such as apathy and social withdrawal) and extensive classificatory systems used to be drawn up with many subcategories but these are of little practical help nowadays. The symptoms may nevertheless still be varied in presentation. Self-neglect or a bizarre appearance and behaviour may be in evidence. Speech disorders indicating disordered thought used to be believed to be virtually pathognomonic of schizophrenia. Concrete thinking, neologistic constructions, irrelevant sentence structures and illogical speech patterns may be seen. Disorders of thinking may be further manifested by the possession of delusions, usually persecutory in kind.

Delusions

A delusion may be defined as a false unshakeable belief held despite the evidence to the contrary and out of keeping with the social norms and the cultural practices of the individual in question. Discussion of the features of a delusion arising in terms of such a definition has kept phenomenologists and philosophers happily occupied for years. It is plain that no false belief by itself necessarily amounts to a delusion. A belief in God may not appear rational by the usual standards but, quite apart from there being lack of definite proof to the contrary, it is also a belief sanctioned by social norms and cultural practices. Patients from parts of Asia and Africa may hold varying beliefs in 'evil spirits' or witchcraft but these may also be appropriate according to the norms of their cultures. More problematical diagnostic considerations may arise when an individual complains, say, of being hounded by the security services which, on investigation, turns out to be true. He may still be mentally ill if the means by which he arrived at his belief are shown to be pathological. This matter does not feature in the definition of a delusion given above but one needs also to inquire in practice as to how the belief was come by. Thus, the story is told of the man who, having paused at a red traffic light, came to the overwhelming conclusion that his wife was being unfaithful to him on account of the colours changing from red to amber. That state of affairs was true, as it happened, but the way the belief arose suggested it being pathological. So, one may say that just because they are really after you does not necessarily rule you out as also being paranoid.

Auditory hallucination

The other dramatic symptom is auditory hallucination which in schizophrenia takes a distinctive form with voices talking about the individual in the third person, the tone often being derogatory, and there may also be voices commenting on the individual's actions and thoughts.

Mood changes

Mood changes may not be remarkable in this condition but depression not uncommonly co-exists with other phenomena. Whether the behaviour is related or not to this mood change, there is an increased risk of suicide in schizophrenia, especially in the early phase of the illness where the changes in the mental processes may be bewilderingly incomprehensible and therefore distressing to the still insightful patient. There has been considerable recent interest in suicidal behaviour among schizophrenic patients. Previously, a depressive component in schizophrenia was believed responsible for this behaviour. Then it became known that the disorder, without any obvious depressive element, could also give rise to this phenomenon. The incidence of suicide in schizophrenia was put at about 10 per cent. Recent studies have shown this figure to have been exaggerated and, at any rate in the pre-community care age, does not seem to have exceeded one per cent. What the post-community care era will bring forth remains to be seen for it is believed that the single most important factor determining suicide rates in patients with schizophrenia is deinstitutionalisation – that is, the protective asylum function of institutions having now been lost – although drug treatment seems also to make a contribution to increasing risk. Insight, by which one means in this situation an appreciation by the patient that he is ill and that it is a mental disorder that is involved in his problems, may be lost when the illness progresses but it is often preserved in the early stages, a feature which, as we said, compounds the distress experienced. Cultural factors, as we have already noted, may inform the issue of insight. In many cultures, especially of Asia and Africa, there is a notable lack of enthusiasm for acknowledging mental disorder, whether on the part of the patient or his family and the wider community. It is customary among these persons to try to understand the phenomena of disease in physical terms. In such cases it would be wrong to suggest that insight has been lost when all the patient is trying to do is to explain his symptoms in terms of the acceptable cultural norms he subscribes to.

6.5 TREATMENT

The cornerstone of modern treatment of schizophrenia is drug treatment. In broad terms, the drugs used may be classified as the 'old' type and the 'new' type of drugs. The older drugs – the stalwarts among them were chlorpromazine, haloperidol and trifluoperazine – tended to be effective but were also sedative and in addition caused movement difficulties, some of which became permanent, causing a considerable degree of secondary disability. Versions of injectable depot preparations of these types of drugs, by which a patient may be given periodic injections thereby reducing the risk of non-compliance (a notoriously intractable problem in all medical practice), were also available.

The newer type of anti-psychotic drugs includes agents such as amisulpride, clozapine, olanzapine, quetiapine, risperidone, sertindole and zotepine. These drugs, it is claimed, have fewer of the adverse effects, especially the atypical movement disorders, associated with the older drugs. By and large the efficacy of both sets of drugs is comparable. Special mention may be made of clozapine which is said to have properties against the 'negative' symptoms of schizophrenia – apathy, lack of motivation, etc – which appear to be largely beyond the reach of the other agents more commonly used. However, clozapine is a notably toxic drug capable of producing lethal adverse effects by causing bone marrow suppression of white cell formation. It is therefore never to be considered as a first-line treatment in the average case of schizophrenia, its utility being rather in its availability when the conventional drugs have failed to produce improvement especially with the negative symptoms which may also be present. It has to be used under strict medical supervision with periodic blood testing being a mandatory requirement. It goes without saying its use is limited to those who are specialists in this field who are able to weigh up the balance of benefits and risks. The patients being considered for this treatment must show motivation – however apathetic they may be – to take the drug as well as being able to submit themselves to regular blood testing.

If a firm diagnosis is made of schizophrenia, drug treatment, following a first episode of illness, is normally required for a period of at least 2 years. If there have been recurrent episodes of illness this period of treatment may have to be extended. If stresses are present – including such stress as ongoing litigation – longer periods of treatment may need to be advised to avail of the protective functions of drug treatment. Therapeutic drugs have been shown to have a prophylactic function in the face of most stressful situations. Recourse should be had, wherever possible, to depot anti-psychotic injections which will also ensure a reliable record being kept of compliance with medication. Contact with doctors, community nurses and other health care professionals is advantageous as is the prompt reinstatement of vigorous treatment early in the course of any relapse. Modern drugs, including clozapine, offer alternative choices which were not available in the past.

The drugs commonly used today are usually successful in controlling the acute symptoms of the illness and, unlike in the past, in-patient treatment is not always necessary. This form of treatment in the community also has the supplementary benefit that rehabilitation can be started straightaway. This is essential as one can be successful in treating the disease and yet end up with a patient that becomes a chronic invalid who tends to make the most of his illness for conscious and unconscious motives. The rule should always be to aim for as rapid a return as is safely possible to the patient's pre-morbid state of physical and psychological functioning and minimise, as far as possible, the dangers of secondary disability and chronic invalidism.

6.6 PROGNOSIS

The prognosis of schizophrenia has notably improved in the past generation or two. The shuffling, muttering disengaged patients seen in such vast numbers inhabiting the Victorian lunatic asylums – and their more recent successors – is a thing now of the increasingly distant past, although if the theory of viral infection as a possible cause of schizophrenia holds any water it is not wholly inconceivable that the condition could once again in the future regain its previous severity – viruses, after all, are known to mutate in all directions. It used to be believed that a schizophrenic illness of early onset and of insidious progression associated with prominent negative symptoms heralded a poorer prognosis than an illness which came on at a later stage of life, announcing itself with an acute onset and the spectacular presence of positive symptoms such as delusions and hallucinations. A clearly identifiable stress factor acting as a precipitant, good compliance with medication, satisfactory social support and a sympathetic family environment are all known to improve prognosis. It also used to be believed that few sufferers from a schizophrenic illness could successfully resume professional, academic or social life. This is no longer true – a function of the reduced severity of the illness and the generally good prognosis it carries now – and most individuals, with treatment and support, could reasonably expect to reclaim the life they used to lead before they were struck down by the illness. Abuse of alcohol and illicit drugs – and non-compliance with prescribed drugs – remain a potent cause of a future relapse and consequently of a poorer prognosis

6.7 IMPLICATIONS FOR FAMILY AND CHILD LAW

As for the legal practitioner, the symptoms of schizophrenia may be seen to have an impact on many areas of family and child law. The acute phase of the illness – marked as it usually is by disordered thinking, perception and loss of insight – may significantly impair functioning as a spouse, partner or parent. If response to treatment has been good, and the compliance and co-operation with the authorities maintained, there is no reason to believe that a recovered patient cannot resume his activities in relation to family and childcare responsibilities as he previously did. A greater cause for concern may be expressed when there is a situation of non-compliance with medication (usually accompanied by unco-operativeness generally), when the response to treatment has not been good (when negative symptoms may also prevail) and when symptoms such as apathy and lack of motivation are at the fore. These features are especially disabling to family and childcare responsibilities. Any co-existing abuse of alcohol and/or illicit substances may also adversely affect functioning in such cases. There are few hard and fast rules permissible in these circumstances but it remains a truism that schizophrenia (and, for that matter, any mental disorder) does not, by itself, necessarily lead to any significant impairment of the activities that are required in respect of being a spouse, partner or parent. Every case must be studied on its own particular facts and, where childcare responsibilities are concerned, medical opinion on the nature of the illness, its treatment and prognosis can offer only general guidance. Whether the parent can, in fact, become, or resume being, a satisfactory and safe parent is a matter for parenting assessments undertaken by those who are expert in that field, not usually the province of an adult psychiatrist.

6.8 OTHER PARANOID DISORDERS

There are paranoid disorders – usually involving persecutory delusions with little or nothing else by way of other psychotic symptoms – which for a long time have been observed not to fit into the diagnostic categories reserved for the schizophrenic illnesses. The primacy of delusions was always evident in these cases. Sometimes these delusions became well systematised – meaning they existed as a near-complete system within the patient's mind and usually involved conspiracies against him – and there was little other impairment, intelligence and the personality in other respects being well preserved. A famous case – and a patient of Freud's – involved a German judge who apparently carried out his judicial tasks satisfactorily even while harbouring such a delusional system in his mind. The term paranoia was given to this class of paranoid disorders. Another kind of paranoid disorder afflicted the elderly in whom it showed virtually all the features of a paranoid schizophrenic illness, apart from the obviously late onset, and this condition usually carried a good prognosis. This condition was referred to as paraphrenia or, where appropriate, as senile paraphrenia. All these conditions have now been brought under the heading of persistent delusional disorders which are to be diagnosed in the absence of brain damage or schizophrenia. Their treatment is essentially on the lines taken in cases of schizophrenia. Good results are usually to be expected in those cases previously called paraphrenia but there is usually little impact on well-established cases of paranoia, as they were called, and these patients carry on with their life with their delusions well encapsulated in their minds.

Chapter 7

DISORDERS OF MOOD

In the traditional classification of psychotic disorders, mood disorders tend to be included with schizophrenia. As will become apparent on a consideration of the contents of the next chapter, depression can also, when it is milder in presentation, find itself classed among the neuroses or the minor psychiatric illnesses. As far as the psychoses are concerned, the modern understanding of mood disorders is that it involves mania, depression or a combination of the two conditions which are called bipolar affective disorders or manic-depressive illness. These conditions are characterised by pathological mood changes, usually in the form of depression or elation. In fact, it is a useful rule of thumb to remind oneself that the symptoms found in mood disorders should generally be capable of being explained by the central change in mood, whether downward or upward.

7.1 DEPRESSIVE ILLNESS

The term depression is not wholly satisfactory for it is capable of bearing many meanings. It could refer to a mood state, a personality type or the constellation of symptoms that makes up a depressive disorder. These symptoms can involve bodily or physiological changes such as those involving sleep, appetite, sexual desire, gastro-intestinal function or the menstrual rhythm. Symptoms may also involve psychomotor function.

Mood change

The mood change in depressive illness must involve a pathological lowering of mood. This refers to a significant and sustained diminution of mood which transcends the regular variations of mood that all human beings (indeed, probably all animals) are subject to. Where normal variation ends and pathological change begins remains a problematical area of definition for there are no objective measures available to discern this shift (cf the measurement of body temperature or blood pressure). There is no alternative to a detailed inquiry being undertaken into the individual's perceptions of changes in mood for different persons may also differ in their habitual setting of mood. Any change must be sustained and persistent, normally lasting at least 4 weeks. The mood change may lead to a variety of ancillary subjective changes such as the inability to enjoy the things the individual habitually used to. There may also be present a pervasive feeling of gloom, pessimism and dark foreboding which is not in keeping with the previous character of the individual. The sufferer may echo the Bard by saying, 'How weary, stale, flat and unprofitable/Seem to me all the uses of this world'.

These feelings may intensify to accommodate ideas of guilt and worthlessness which may extend even, in severe cases, to expressing delusions of guilt and worthlessness such as being convinced that one is responsible for all the ills, sins and wickedness found in the world. A related delusion is one involving a sense of nihilism in which the patient believes he does not exist, that his mind and body do not exist and that the world itself does not exist. As these delusions are to be derived from a pathological lowering of the mood, these ideas far transcend any philosophical notion one can hold that the world and the individuals within it are but an illusion. As might be imagined, these pathological ideas may co-exist with a sense of bleak hopelessness which leads on, with perverted logic, to suicide, an ever-present risk in any patient with a depressed mood.

Sleep

The changes in physiology or bodily function are common in depressive illness and have long indicated to some observers the ultimate biological provenance of any significant depressive disorder. The sleep rhythm may be upset early in the course of the illness. Although the classical feature is noted to be early wakening, that is waking 2 or more hours before the usual time of awakening for the patient, in practice sleep may be disturbed in diverse ways. There could be difficulty in getting to sleep, repeated wakening during the course of sleep, waking early or a combination of all these disruptions over several nights. Sleep may also be disturbed by intrusive dreaming. The upshot is disrupted sleep of poor quality which leaves the patient unrefreshed even after he has apparently been sleeping for several hours. This ensures the next day is started off on a shaky footing and, thereby, a vicious circle is also set in motion, making the consequences of a depressed mood worse through a lack of any 'balm of sleep'. Many patients complain it is their poor sleep, above all other symptoms, that contribute most to their feelings of black despair and demoralisation. However, a small minority of patients tend to oversleep, giving the impression to observers that they could be attempting to escape their torments in a loss of consciousness. These patients do not, however, appear to enjoy much refreshment as a result of their prolonged somnolence.

Appetite

Parallel biological change may be seen in respect of appetite. Loss of appetite is common and may be severe with consequent weight loss which, in graver cases, could come to cause a medical emergency through loss of nutrition and hydration. Changes in bowel function may reflect poor appetite with ensuing constipation the common feature although diarrhoea may also be present when it is usual to attribute it to features of anxiety which are commonly found in depressed states. There could in some cases be a paradoxical feature of overeating when with the overconsumption of what is called 'comfort food' there could be excessive, even gross, weight gain. Reduction in sexual interests – as with other appetites and sources of pleasure – is a common feature in depressive illness as are changes in menstrual rhythm.

Psychomotor

Psychomotor retardation refers to slowness of both mental and physical activity. It is a common observation that patients with depressive illness often appear to be functioning like an under-powered engine, being laboured in thought, word and movement. In extreme cases – rarely seen these days – stupor can overcome patients when, mute and immobile, they enter into a catatonic state. On the one hand, minds can, in equally severe depressive illness, become seemingly overactive when agitation may be an accompanying feature. In severe psychotic forms of depressive illness, delusions of a kind already mentioned could be seen along with auditory hallucinations – the voices characteristically saying things in keeping with the patient's mood, abusing him, invoking feelings of guilt and, sometimes urging him to suicide to put an end to a worthless existence. In these cases the differential diagnosis must also consider other psychotic conditions such as schizophrenia.

Attention span

An invariable feature in a depressive illness of any significant severity is loss of attention and concentration. Patients may report having difficulty keeping track of events when following popular pastimes such as watching the television. Serious intellectual activity may become impossible. Commonly complaint is also made of a poor short-term memory, of being forgetful and mislaying objects. There is usually no evidence of anything unduly serious underlying these memory difficulties which are attributable to poor attention and concentration, and full recovery can be confidently predicted with successful treatment of the depressive illness.

7.2 MANIA

What is popularly regarded as the mirror image of depressive illness is mania, which appears to sit on the other pole of bipolar illness, although this stark distinction between 'polar opposites' is not by any means entirely accurate either in description or in terms of an analysis of underlying pathology. As with depressive illness, it should be possible, at a superficial level at any rate, to derive all the features of a manic illness from the central pathological elevation of mood. In mania, this elevation of mood is elation, a sustained elevation of mood. It must be stated, however, that in many cases what strikes (possibly in more senses than one) the observer is not elation or pathological happiness but a mood of aggression mixed with irritability and hostility. Nevertheless, many of these patients do appear unduly cheerful, for a time at least, with a limitless supply of energy which – in stark contrast to the more severe cases of depression – causes them to act like an overpowered engine, being in constant overdrive, humming with activity and exhausting those around them. These patients may talk without end, make endless plans and are pathologically optimistic. The future is scanned by them with lofty regard, money may be scattered on all and sundry, extravagant purchases (including the fabled elephant ordered through Harrod's, other exotic creatures, jewellery) made, largesse bestowed. Relations usually have to pick up the pieces at the end of the episode of illness.

Their excessive talk is characterised by what is referred to as a pressure of speech and the overpowered mind may give rise to a 'flight of ideas' which means a form of speech disorder is present.

So active are some of these patients that they have little time for food, drink or sleep and very occasionally they may collapse into utter exhaustion. Elation of mood is also mirrored in the patient having a grandiose or even fantastic conception of himself, occasionally believing he is of noble or royal birth, possessing special talents or powers and given also to possessing limitless wealth. There is also disinhibition in sexual matters and unwanted pregnancies in women patients is not uncommon. With the lack of any insight being present, all these excesses may appear to give the impression of behaviour by a celebrity albeit one who actually possesses little or no talent, which may, of course, be not unusual these days.

Depressive and manic illness may be, indeed are commonly, found as separate illnesses. However, when serially combined, for instance, when depression and mania tend to occur in the same patient, the appellation bipolar affective disorder, replacing the former manic-depressive disorder, is given.

7.3 AETIOLOGY

As with schizophrenia, all the evidence suggests that pathological disturbances of mood originate in brain dysfunction although the precise mechanisms are far from clear in the present state of knowledge. There is a discernible genetic influence (greater in bipolar than in unipolar disorders) and close family relations may show an increased tendency to these disorders. But the environmental effect, as might be imagined, is also strong and in any given case of these disorders it is not uncommon to find an interaction between genetic susceptibility and environmental effects bearing responsibility for the illness. The role of life events may be particularly decisive. It appears to be the case that it is not so much the effect of the adverse life events themselves – which, after all, everyone is heir to – but the impact they could have on a person who might have been rendered vulnerable as a result of genetic and prior psychological influences. Among the psychological factors deemed significant in making an individual vulnerable to disorders of mood, especially depressive illness, are unemployment, having several young children living at home and having no confiding or intimate relationship to sustain the person.

Neither depressive illness nor mania needs to be of primarily psychiatric origin. These disorders can follow a host of medical or surgical conditions or the treatment given for those. The primary cause in such cases could be systemic illness of infective, metabolic, endocrine, haematological or neoplastic origins. Treatment of the underlying condition may be sufficient in some cases to improve the mood disorder although not uncommonly both the secondary depressive illness or mania requires treatment in its own right whatever other condition might have been primarily causative of the mood disturbance.

7.4 TREATMENT

The treatment of depressive illness usually involves some combination of drug and psychological therapy. The mainstay of drug treatment for many decades used to be the tricyclic group of antidepressant drugs. This group includes such drugs as amitryptiline and dothiepin. Their efficacy was, on the whole, acceptable but their adverse effects occasionally proved tiresome. They could be unduly sedating and, more crucially, they could be dangerous, even lethally so, in overdose, a situation that is potentially capable of arising in every case of a depressive illness. These drawbacks led to a search for drugs with different modes of action and in time was born the group of drugs called the selective serotonin reuptake inhibiting agents (SSRIs). As the name suggests, their biochemical action is to block the reuptake of an important brain chemical called serotonin, thereby, in effect, flooding the nerve endings where this chemical is believed to modulate mood function. These drugs do not have the same sedating properties as the older tricyclic agents and, more pertinently, are believed to be far less dangerous in overdose. Among their number are fluoxetine, citalopram, paroxetine and sertraline. In time other atypical drugs such as mirtazepine, nefazodone, reboxetine and venlafaxine also made their way to the marketplace. There is no doubt that we now possess a considerably improved armoury of drugs for use in depressive illness but in all drug treatment there is a cautionary tale to be told and remembered when it comes to the use of any pharmaceutical agent.

These newer atypical drugs were taken up with an almost messianic zeal, the drug fluoxetine (Prozac) in particular achieving notoriety by being promiscuously exhibited in subjects for whom it was never intended – very young children, domestic pets, not to mention individuals who were disaffected with life rather than suffering from a depressive illness – and the term Prozac nearly came to signify a synonym for panacea. Over a period of time adverse reports gathered and there is some evidence now that these newer agents may not be as risk-free, never mind of universal benefit, as they were once believed to be. In particular this group of drugs has been implicated as a possible cause in some cases of suicide and homicide where it is believed they might have enhanced aggressive tendencies already present in some depressed patients – might even have precipitated these tendencies in other patients – causing them to turn on themselves or towards others with violence. Litigation was mooted. The caution that was enjoined following these reports was wholly beneficial for in all medicine a balance has to be struck in every patient between the reward and risks possible with any treatment that is being contemplated. The result now is that a more balanced view appears to be once again taken of all antidepressant drug treatment.

Psychological treatment

Psychological treatment for depressive illness is often suggested but is more sparingly offered or taken up. Resources are limited, it is a vastly time-consuming business and considerable intellectual and emotional demands may be made on often vulnerable patients while they are experiencing a sensitive mental state. Nevertheless, in carefully selected patients, considerable benefit may be reaped through the deployment of psychological methods of treatment used as an adjunct to drug treatment. The role of cognitive behavioural treatment in particular has been studied with interest and there is no doubt that in suitable groups of patients better results may be obtained by the use of this technique with medication than by drug treatment alone. An associated form of treatment is what may be called social therapy. There is often little doubt that in a significant number of depressed patients underlying the disorder are adverse social factors such as uncongenial or non-existent employment, unmanageable debt, poor marital relationships, adverse housing and a host of similar influences. If anything can be done to ameliorate these adverse influences there is greater scope for successful treatment and rehabilitation involving these patients.

Electroconvulsive treatment

A brief word needs to be said about electroconvulsive treatment (ECT) given the notoriety the procedure has attracted over many years. It is a procedure that is not without its risks but there is no gainsaying its potent efficacy in the most severe forms of depressive illness involving a seemingly intractable disorder that could be leading the patient into a serious state of ill health. Its use lies in specialist hands and with carefully selected cases. Despite its even greater notoriety, nothing will be said here about psychosurgery. Its use is not likely to feature largely in the kind of individual routinely encountered in the practice of family and child law.

Antipsychotic agents

The treatment of mania involves the use of the kind of antipsychotic agents that were discussed in the management of the schizophrenic disorders. The essence of treatment is to bring symptomatic relief and curb the various excesses involving the case of a manic patient. But in the case of depressive illness or mania or both (bipolar states) there is also scope for prophylactic treatment, that is, attempting to prevent the recurrence of these conditions. The primary agent available for use for such purposes is the salts of the metal lithium which has now been employed for this purpose for four decades. The benefit from lithium use can be considerable but, once again, it is not without risk, especially in terms of kidney and thyroid functions. There are also other adverse effects associated with this drug. Further, it is safely and satisfactorily used only with regular blood level monitoring available to the patient and accepted by him. The demands on the patient may be considerable and some selection as to who might be suitable is necessary. Carbamazepine is an alternative drug for use in this form of prophylaxis.

7.5 PROGNOSIS

The prognosis for individual episodes of illness, whether of depression or mania, is generally good these days. Fairly rapid response to modern drug treatment may be expected. If recovery from a depressive illness appears to be slow, apart from non-response to medication (which may necessitate a change of drug), other factors may need to be considered or reviewed, in particular personality and social elements in the patient's life. Recurrence of illness is always possible. It is usual to advise that drug treatment be continued for 6 months following full recovery from symptoms so as to minimise the risks of relapse. The role of lithium in prophylaxis has been mentioned above. Recurrence following specific risk factors, for example, the post-partum state, is always possible (see later).

7.6 IMPLICATIONS FOR FAMILY AND CHILD LAW

As far as involvement with family and child law are concerned, the symptoms of acute depressive or manic illness given above may indicate how sufferers from such conditions could be affected in their roles as spouses, partners or parents. The generally good response to modern drug treatment and the non-response that could be caused by adverse personality and social factors are worthy of note in these proceedings. It is generally the case that elements within the habitual personality or factors such as employment (or lack of it), marital or relationship difficulties, the impact of drink and illicit drugs, poor housing and criminal involvement with all its complications are usually more potent agents of impairment of function as spouse, partner or parent than pathology involving affective illness alone. The other factor to be taken into account in the course of litigation is the possibility of recurrence of affective illness, serial bouts of illness being more disruptive than any single bout of illness, however severe. As we shall see later, a post-partum state of depression may tend to recur in a subsequent pregnancy and this may have obvious implications for childcare.

Chapter 8

THE NEUROSES

This ragbag of conditions makes up the minor psychiatric disorders. The qualifying term 'minor' refers to the presentation of symptoms as seen from the perspective of a detached professional observer who finds them less severe than the features of a psychotic disorder. To a patient with a neurotic condition it may be anything but minor as he carries around pressing symptoms of greater or lesser chronicity which respond poorly to conventional treatment and causes him to become the despair of doctors. The old joke with a US flavour – that 'the neurotic builds castles in the air, the psychotic lives in them and the psychiatrist collects the rent' – conveys much truth as jokes often do. A neurotic patient, whatever his symptoms may be and however inexplicable they are, usually has some grasp on reality and, generally, some measure of insight; the psychotic patient may invariably fall down on both scores. There is also a strong contribution made to neurotic conditions by the personality of the patient whereas psychotic conditions are usually studied as 'true' disease conditions with distinct biological origins and with the disease condition usually overwhelming any observable feature in the habitual personality and forming a distinguishable break from it. Perhaps to the public the best-known neurotic in the world is Mr Woody Allen whose anguished confessions bear all the hallmarks of a neurotic personality with neurotic symptoms. By his own account he has been in 'therapy' for decades with little discernible change being made in his life or behaviour. Mr Allen's understanding of the gap between his feelings and the realities of the world – the source, in fact, of his humour and wit – reveals why, despite the sufferings of many of these patients, we persist in calling these conditions minor psychiatric disorders.

8.1 MINOR DEPRESSIVE ILLNESS

The first of the conditions to be considered under this heading are the depressive illnesses. We have already considered depressive illnesses under the psychotic conditions and, at one level, the differences between the conditions appearing under the two rubrics is merely quantitative – depressive neurosis may appear to be a less severe illness and is not usually associated with a bipolar affective disorder. If the term is to be taken literally, depressive neurosis also will be expected to lack psychotic features such as delusions and hallucinations which may be a feature in some very severe depressive illnesses. These patients also retain a good hold on reality and their insight could be considerable and, in fact, contribute to their perception of their disorder. However, it is usual also to observe other differences between the two forms of depressive disorder. One of these is the contribution made by the patient's personality to his disorder which may be of greater significance than with cases of 'psychotic' depressive illness where the illness element is usually the more prominent observable feature. That apart, the symptoms may appear to be similar, with, as stated, the obvious absence of any psychotic features. Onset of illness may be less marked and there is a 'grumbling' (in all senses) feel to the condition as reported by the patient. In other words, the distinction between the patient's habitual mood state and the way he usually feels and the state of disorder seen at examination may be far from clearly drawn. It is a feature of the neuroses that there is considerable interaction between personality and response to stress or life events in the causation of the conditions and this is usually seen in cases of the depressive neuroses. The management of the condition is on similar lines to any other depressive illness with the difference that more obvious attention should be paid to psychological approaches to deal with elements in the personality once the symptoms have been dispersed with the help of medication.

8.2 ANXIETY STATES

One of the commoner neurotic states involves the presence in the patient of pathological levels of anxiety. Anxiety in this context refers to unnatural and inappropriate feelings of fear. It is normal – and an important part of survival, both personal and collective, in the evolutionary sense – to feel fear. Most animals keep a watchful eye open for predators. The human animal is naturally concerned for its personal security when living in its modern habitation and is understandably concerned for the future. In anxiety states this natural and appropriate fearfulness appears translated into an overwhelming sense of fear in regard to ordinary and seemingly normal situations. A patient may feel a sense of impending disaster when seated indoors, behind locked doors and in the absence of any obvious threatening stimulus. Another patient may become fearful about walking outdoors among people going about their routine and unremarkable business. A third may become exceedingly fearful in the presence of common and generally harmless creatures such as domestic pets where, in no obvious way, is such feeling serving any protective purpose.

Anxiety states may be classified as being generalised anxiety states, panic states or as phobic disorders.

Generalised anxiety states

In generalised anxiety states the patient is subject to 'free floating' anxiety which may arise without any provocation or warning and in the absence of obvious stimuli. There is a feeling of great unease and of foreboding, a sense of some disaster waiting to strike imminently. This feeling is accompanied by physical symptoms such as palpitations, a dry mouth, a tightening in the chest, excessive sweating, a tremor of the extremities, sleep disturbance (characteristically an inability to get to sleep), diarrhoea and an increased feeling of the urge to urinate and in the frequency of this sensation. There are also symptoms of physical tension such as a particular type of headache (usually described as feeling like a band around the head) and stiffness in the region of the back and neck. There is loss also of attention and concentration which, in turn, may lead to poor short-term memory. Insight is normally preserved, meaning the patient can recognise all these effects (will, indeed, complain about them and ask for help), attribute them to a nervous or mental phenomenon and confirm that something has definitely gone wrong.

Panic states

Panic attacks were previously considered to be part of any state of generalised anxiety but are now believed to exist in a subcategory of the disorder. The symptoms of a panic state are well known and combine the physical symptoms seen in generalised anxiety states with an overpowering mental reaction which may give rise to feelings in which the patient's life may seem unreal or the world itself may appear unreal (depersonalisation and derealisation). Attacks tend to recur and are unpredictable, a state of affairs leading to much distress and also tending to feed the anxiety.

Phobic disorders

Phobic anxiety states refer to pathological and irrational fearfulness experienced in specific situations. There is both quantitative and qualitative elements distinguishing these phobic states from normal responses. Children may fear the dark as a normal response and anxious adults become apprehensive in unlit locations. These fears do not usually handicap them in their daily existence and is a response shared by several persons and may, in fact, both be seen to be normal and sensible responses to reality. Phobic anxiety states are of a different order for the fear may be out of proportion to any threat inherent in the situation, it cannot be reasoned away, is beyond the control of the individual and leads to the avoidance of these situations. These fears are not shared by any large number of other citizens and, on occasion, may be socially disabling. Common phobias involve outside locations (agoraphobia), confined spaces (claustrophobia), social settings (social phobia) and such situations as heights, flying, spiders, domestic animals, needles and of contracting illnesses.

Causation

Anxiety states are common and their prevalence comfortably outstrips the distribution of the psychotic conditions. The symptoms of anxiety are strongly suggestive of involvement of a part of a brain called the limbic system. There is a significant genetic component and features of anxiety may be seen to run in families where sometimes psychological contagion may also be implicated as a cause, unnaturally fearful parents infecting children under their influence. The environment undeniably plays a part. Anecdotal observation suggests that the modern overprotective parent can induce unnatural fearfulness in children so much so that a child today appears to be more apprehensive of situations, especially concerning outdoor activities, than its predecessor of a few generations ago (similar explanations are given for the apparent increase in allergies to all manner of stimuli among children and young adults believed to have been reared in excessively sanitary conditions). The other psychological explanation of note regarding causation involves faults in attachment in childhood, where early feelings of insecurity may be reactivated later in the form of anxiety in relation to the world.

Treatment

Drugs

Treatment of the anxiety states partakes of both pharmacological and psychological approaches. The best-known drugs for use in anxiety states are the benzodiazepine group including such agents as diazepam (Valium) and lorazepam. There is no doubt that these drugs are effective in treatment in virtually all forms of anxiety but for some considerable time now their primary adverse effect has become all too well known – that they are also remarkably addictive. In fact, the anxiety in the patient having been successfully dealt with, the problem then arises that the patient needs to be weaned off these drugs, a process which sometimes causes far greater trauma to the patient than the symptoms of anxiety did in the first place. There is still a place for these drugs in the treatment of anxiety but that lies in the hands of specialist practitioners who may use it under strictly observed conditions – for short periods of time and as an adjunct to other treatments. These drugs may also have a place in the treatment of some phobic anxiety states where the anxiety-provoking situation is only met with occasionally, for example, when the prospect of air travel looms to a patient suffering from the relevant phobia.

Other drugs have useful anxiety-relieving properties as side effects of their primary therapeutic use. The tricyclic antidepressant drugs discussed in the previous chapter have such effects which can be usefully mobilised in the treatment of anxiety. However, the more serious adverse effects of these drugs such as a fatal result in overdose constrain their widespread use. The modern SSRI group of drugs such as paroxetine and citalopram also have well-recognised effects in reducing anxiety although the paradoxical effect of making anxiety worse in some susceptible cases must be borne in mind. For all these reasons drug treatment of anxiety should be approached with care and left in specialist hands. Another group of drugs with useful anxiety-reducing features is the beta-blocking group of drugs such as propranolol. Their effects are on the physical manifestations of anxiety such as palpitations, which they may be successful in reducing. The mind-body relationship may well be in evidence in these situations for it is believed a reduction in physical symptoms may lead in turn to an amelioration of the psychological effects and a virtuous circle is thereby caused to come into being.

Psychological treatment

Psychological treatment is well established in the management of anxiety states. At its simplest the procedures involve techniques of relaxation and anxiety-management being taught to the patient. Phobic anxiety states, in particular, submit well to psychological approaches. Perhaps the best known of the techniques employed with cases of phobic anxiety is called graded exposure by which the patient very gradually becomes attuned to approaching the object or situation that has caused dread previously and either comes to deal with the situation with greater equanimity or has his previous feelings replaced by not too disabling nervousness. If the irrational fear, say, has involved dogs the approach is to start by talking about dogs and then looking at pictures of them. As anxiety is coped with, and confidence gained, a step-by-step scheme of approaching dogs may be put in place – starting with smaller, friendlier, known animals, then moving on to a larger creatures of unknown temperament, ending perhaps with an amble in the showground at Cruft's. The treatment is individually tailored and the subject of agreement is between patient and therapist. Cognitive behavioural treatment, which essentially involves shifting the cognitive bias of the patient in a more positive direction, may also be useful.

Prognosis

The prognosis of anxiety states is variable but is generally satisfactory. If an anxiety state has followed discrete trauma, say, a road traffic accident leading to a phobic state about driving or travelling in a motor car, the results are generally good if treatment is undertaken swiftly and the patient previously had had a sound personality. As a general rule, the longer the symptom persists the less good is the outcome with any treatment, for symptoms can become entrenched. With generalised anxiety states the previous personality of the patient may intrude upon treatment and may be a bar to successful recovery. Such patients may continue to be predisposed to relapse even while temporary improvement can be produced. As might be imagined, the exigencies of the modern world inform the anxieties of many patients. Relationship insecurities, financial difficulties, employment uncertainties, poor housing or a run of misfortune, for example, being a victim of street crime when one is recovering from a previous assault (something not unknown to happen in certain neighbourhoods) may defeat the best efforts of the therapist.

Given its pervasive prevalence, anxiety states do tend to have an influence on the practice of family and child law. A spouse, partner or parent afflicted with anxiety may find his functions impaired. The difficulties that arise in consequence, largely in the context of relationships of the patient, may be harder to deal with than when symptoms of an anxiety state alone have primarily affected the individual. There is little one can add to this observation except to say that where stable relationships involving the patient continue to exist – or once did exist – a better medical result is likely to be obtained than when relationships – whether involving spouses, partners or children – have ceased or are in danger of breaking down irretrievably.

8.3 OBSESSIVE-COMPULSIVE DISORDER

A relatively uncommon neurosis, but one which has been given some prominence in recent years, is obsessive-compulsive disorder. This condition is characterised by obsessional thinking and/or compulsive actions. The former involves persistent and intrusive thoughts which are unwelcome to the patient who attempts to resist them and yet fails. This is not to be confused with being preoccupied with some thought, a common enough and perfectly normal experience. Compulsions or rituals are their motor equivalents leading to repetitive, usually non-productive or inefficient, behaviour. The patient may spend many hours engaged in rituals of diverse kinds which are meaningless to the observer. Thoughts and actions of this kind involving a patient can cause immense distress to the patient and eventually lead to destruction of family, social and occupational life.

As some forms of brain damage can cause the features of obsessions and compulsions to emerge, it is believed the locus for pathology in this condition exists somewhere in the brain (very severe forms of the disorder are one of the rare indications for modern psychosurgery which may achieve good results where all other treatment has failed). However, as with all neuroses, the personality of the patient cannot be ignored when evaluating this disorder, for a substantial majority of patients do have a pre-morbid obsessional personality which is characterised by a tendency to unusual orderliness and conscientious attention to detail, admirable characteristics in those in clerical or administrative occupation but not always tolerable when it forms the basis for pathology of this kind. Treatment involving both drugs and psychological approaches can achieve reasonably good results in the average case, although recurrence is not uncommon.

8.4 STRESS REACTIONS

While all neurotic conditions may generally be understood as being the reactions of vulnerable personalities to stress of some kind, as perceived by them, stress reactions involve situations where the stress has been overwhelming or threatening in some way to the patient. It can be an acute reaction, arising immediately after the stressful event, or it could be delayed. The probably much overused diagnosis, post-traumatic stress disorder (PTSD) may partake of both forms, although usually seen and assessed after a period following the trauma. This condition may be defined as 'a delayed and/or protracted response to a stressful event or situation of an exceptionally threatening or catastrophic nature'. As is well known, this condition has been associated with serious disasters such as train crashes or where explosions have occurred. There is little doubt in many observers' minds that this condition might have been overdiagnosed and some feel the features reported were previously quite satisfactorily accommodated within the categories of anxiety states and depressive reaction, usually in a mixed type of condition. If it is to be diagnosed at all strict diagnostic guidelines should be followed. Treatment of the condition, as previously mentioned, has raised surprising controversy given its widespread diagnosis in recent years. There is a place for drug treatment but it is still not clear what form psychological intervention should take. The extensive 'debriefing' that was routinely practised soon after the victim had emerged in the immediate aftermath of the tragedy has been questioned in some quarters with some holding that this activity may tend to make things worse or even retard recovery. Others have even gone as far as saying these victims should be left alone to recover with the help of their 'stiff upper lips'. The truth, no doubt, will appear in the course of time as to what, if any, approach should be taken, although clinical experience already suggests that, as with any clinical procedure, there should be careful sifting of victims to see who is most likely to benefit from counselling. Statutory agencies, charities and commercial organisations often automatically offer their services to victims following traumatic events. Fearing litigation, some companies require their employees to undergo 'debriefing' following certain incidents. More promising are studies which show good results when the intervention was not offered to everyone indiscriminately but only to a minority with acute stress disorders who are at higher risk of developing subsequent psychiatric disorder. The interventions in this successful situation involved multiple sessions and was based on a cognitive-behavioural model. Another study involved work with the Marines. All ranks had been offered simple training so that when disasters happened the 'therapist' and 'patient' shared a common culture and outlook which gets over the problem of using strangers unknown to the patient and invariably coming from another 'culture'. From the point of view of family and child law what is important to recognise is that traumatic situations faced by a party could have taken the form of acute trauma (eg a grave accident) or a chronic form (eg following prolonged domestic violence). Both kinds of situations are capable of having an adverse impact on the mental state of one who is a spouse, partner or parent. What form any ensuing mental disorder has taken is a matter for detailed clinical analysis rather than shorthand diagnostic descriptions such as PTSD. What treatment, if any, should be given to the patient in these cases will depend on the precise delineation of symptoms present, the past history and an evaluation of the patient's previous personality, and not on any diagnosis alone. A study undertaken among service personnel found that PTSD and post-traumatic stress symptoms were not associated with consequent disability. Rather, it was the co-morbid symptoms of depression that were significantly associated with disability. The clinical importance of PTSD and post-traumatic stress symptoms may therefore become questionable if they are not a cause of disability.

8.5 HYSTERIA

The only justification for the inclusion of hysteria in a book of this nature is that it has historical sanction and the condition, in its way, helped to define both neurology and psychiatry. The disorder involves unconscious mechanisms which, perhaps as a result of their subterranean presence, are far from clearly understood despite several years of study. There is undeniably a strong cultural and social background to the condition for gross examples of hysteria are now rare in the West although still observable in many parts of the developing world. The short explanation to be proffered in seeking an understanding of this condition is to say that when a patient is confronted by unbearable and unresolvable anxiety as a result of some inner conflict, the unconscious mechanisms at work translate this conflict into physical symptoms thereby giving the patient what is called primary gain through relief from anxiety. Secondary gain may then arise from any practical advantage to be accrued by sporting the symptom to the world. The symptoms in question are manifold and may include amnesia, wandering (the fugue state), stupor, trance and possession states, motor paralysis and sensory loss and, in extreme cases, multiple personality disorder. The other symptom of note is *la belle indifference* which refers to an apparent lack of concern shown by some patients towards their symptoms and is often regarded as being characteristic of conversion/dissociative states. Recent studies, in fact, have shown that true 'organic' illness may underlie conversion symptoms and that this finding of indifference actually discriminates poorly between 'organic' and 'functional' symptoms. In fact, serious physical illness such as multiple sclerosis may initially present with symptoms which, as they often nonplus the clinician in the early stages of the disorder, are not uncommonly damned as being hysterical. Treatment is by way of intensive psychological investigation for which relatively few of these patients are suitable. Notwithstanding this, the results in the acute state, for instance, where symptoms are short-lived, may be surprisingly good although recurrence is not uncommon.

Related to hysteria are the somatisation disorders where recurrent complaints of physical symptoms yield little or nothing by way of physical investigation, which, in some of these cases, can be extensive and prolonged. The strong cultural influence should always be borne in mind, for in cultures where it is more socially acceptable to present with and accept physical rather than psychological symptoms of illness these disorders are still not uncommon. Hypochondriacal disorder is closely related. There is no alternative to full investigation of these symptoms for the elusive 'real' cause of the symptoms; the skill comes in knowing when to put a stop to investigation and to resist the entreaties and importunities of the patient.

Hysterical personality disorder is taken up in Chapter 10, which deals with the personality disorders.

Chapter 9

DISORDERS OF DEPENDENCE AND APPETITE

Perhaps the most common psychiatric problems met within the course of work involving family and child proceedings are those associated with the abuse of alcohol and illicit substances, with and without the presence of some form of personality disorder, the subject matter of the next chapter.

9.1 ALCOHOL

Substance abuse, the term used collectively to designate misuse of alcohol and illicit substances, is much misunderstood, which is paradoxical given the prominence the subject attracts in the media. One reason for this is that, despite the vast resources given to the study of the problem, objective scientific evidence in respect of many aspects of the difficulties concerning these substances is still sparse. Take the terms commonly used in connection with the misuse of substances – reliance, addiction, dependence and abuse. They all appear to have a similar meaning to the lay eye. These are useful terms as they go, but far from precise when it comes to understanding the problem despite their everyday use. For our present purposes we could define abuse of alcohol and illicit substances very simply as where their consumption has led to behaviours which impact on cases involving family and child law. This implies that an individual may have problems or difficulties, say, with alcohol even when he may not be addicted to, reliant upon or dependent upon alcohol. Let us take an example to illustrate this point. Imagine a man who is habitually abstemious, is a teetotaller, in fact. One day, at a function, much against his better judgment he is induced to consume a few alcoholic drinks. Being a novice in these matters, he feels the drink going to his head. Nevertheless, despite not feeling his usual self, he drives home, is stopped, breathalysed, charged with driving with excess alcohol in his system, and convicted. He is fined, he pays the costs and he is disqualified from driving. Already he could face serious financial and social difficulties and his livelihood could be put at risk. Worse, if he is a professional – certainly if he is a doctor – he could attract the interest of his professional regulatory body. It will require abuse of the language to say he has problems with alcohol but, undeniably, he has an alcohol-related problem, for he has got into difficulties after consuming alcohol, albeit after only a few drinks on one occasion. This example also illustrates the importance of looking at the facts in any individual case. It is not always the quantity of alcohol or drug abused or the prolonged history of misuse that may be in point but the behaviours engaged in by the individual and that are recorded in the facts of the case. A practical definition, based upon one given by the WHO itself, is that abuse of alcohol occurs in those who drink excessively to such an extent that alcohol use has attained a degree which shows noticeable disturbance or an interference with their bodily and mental health, their personal relationships and smooth economic functioning or who show prodromal signs of such a development and, therefore, require treatment.

9.2 ALCOHOL – THE EFFECTS

Alcohol can cause physical dependence. By this it is meant that tolerance has developed, in other words, more and more needs to be drunk to obtain the same behavioural effect. This also means a hardened drinker can consume considerable quantities before showing signs of intoxication, whereas someone like the novice described above needs only a few drinks before showing obvious changes in behaviour. Next, there may be withdrawal effects in the absence of sufficient alcohol in the system, which include tremors, agitation, sweating, nausea, irritability and feelings of anxiety and panic along with a craving for more drink. These withdrawal symptoms can be quelled by drinking a sufficient quantity of alcohol, which leads to a vicious circle being brought into operation. Regular drinking to avoid the symptoms of withdrawal sets in, the individual becomes preoccupied with drinking and drink-related behaviour. Soon, if measures are not taken to curb the consumption of alcohol, drinking becomes the primary activity in the individual's life at the expense of all others.

Physical and mental effects follow persistent drinking. Bodily effects include damage to the liver. At first, fat infiltrates the liver cells. Later, the liver shrinks with the onset of cirrhosis. Alcoholic hepatitis may present itself. If drinking continues in these circumstances the liver may fail altogether in its functions, and coma and death supervene. If abstinence can be brought about, and sustained, repair of the liver can take place for the organ has remarkable powers of recovery and regeneration. Effects may also be seen in the gastro-intestinal system with oesophageal and peptic ulceration. Bleeding from oesophageal varices leads to the well-known symptom of vomiting of blood in these patients. Heart and circulatory problems may also follow with an enlarged heart and elevated blood pressure in consequence. Considerable disturbance may also be seen in both the central and peripheral nervous systems. Effects on the brain may lead to blackouts, amnesia and fits. Peripheral neuropathy may give rise to motor and sensory deficits along with paralysis later on. It is no exaggeration to say that every bodily function may be adversely affected through persistent alcohol abuse.

Running in parallel are the mental complications due to persistent alcohol abuse. The symptoms due to states of withdrawal have been noted above. Fits may follow as well as the dangerous and potentially lethal condition called delirium tremens in which consciousness fluctuates and, classically, visual hallucinations involving usually small animals (rats or insects) but occasionally larger creatures ('pink elephants') are seen. Fleeting persecutory ideas may be present. Alcoholic psychosis of a more sustained kind may also be seen later. There is a notorious connection between alcohol and depression. Alcohol is a depressant, a fact not always recognised by those who see mainly its disinhibiting properties. The depression it induces leads usually to more drinking in an attempt to dull the senses and, thereby, more depression ensues which means there is another vicious circle also in operation. Sexual dysfunction ('it provokes the desire but takes away the performance') and deterioration in personality and social functioning are common consequences. The impact on social life can prove considerable. Apart from involvement with the criminal law, there are also consequences for employment, and accidents are commoner in these individuals. The impact on family life may be substantial and, of obvious relevance to this work, will be taken up later.

9.3 ALCOHOL – THE RISK FACTORS

Despite many years of intensive study, those at risk of developing alcohol-related problems cannot be pinpointed with any accuracy. There is a clear genetic factor but this generally shows a predisposition not only to alcohol abuse but also to depressive illness, in other words there may be 'alcohol equivalents', a predisposed individual going onto suffer depressive illness rather than having problems with alcohol. Environmental factors are dominant influences. Cultural influences may also play a part. One report suggested that in Taiwan in the 1960s drinking was largely an act of celebration after the harvest but nowadays it is considered a more widespread problem. Prevalence rates for adolescents in that country are high. Alcohol use among adolescents there was initially more likely to be affected by social and cultural factors, and the behaviour of parents and peers, but less by genetic factors. However, as these adolescents started to misuse alcohol, genetic factors came to play a major role in influencing the frequency and amount of drinking. There seems no doubt that the ready availability of alcoholic beverages in the community can contribute significantly to an increased prevalence of problems concerning alcohol misuse. Economic factors are also important. It has been shown that alcohol has become cheaper in 'real terms' over time, making its routine use within the reach of most pockets. Thus, there seems to be a close relationship between *per capita* alcohol consumption and alcohol-related problems and an inverse correlation between the 'real' price of drink (as a percentage of average disposable income) and national *per capita* consumption of alcohol. Finland is among several countries where relaxation of previously restrictive licensing laws had been shown to cause significant increases in alcohol consumption. As the recent debate on the relaxation of the licensing laws showed, there are also quite considerable cultural and subcultural influences at work. It seems possible, it is said, for responsible and convivial social drinking to be inculcated according to the pattern prevailing in many parts of Continental Europe in distinction to the 'macho' excesses which habitually disfigure British urban life.

The short answer to the question as to who might be at risk of developing alcohol-related problems is 'almost anyone'. Social change had rendered out of date the assertions that certain occupations – bar staff, journalists, manual workers, mariners – were preferentially at higher risk. Clinical practice reveals virtually all trades and professions are now represented, not to mention those who have no occupation. The professional bodies concerned with both doctors and lawyers have expressed their alarm at the prevalence of alcohol-related problems among their members and have established dedicated 'help lines' to render advice and assistance. One striking social change is the presence now among problem drinkers of women and, increasingly, younger children. The advice, which is somewhat conservative in its import it has to be admitted, as to what might constitute 'safe' drinking allows 21 units of alcohol per week for adult males and 14 units of alcohol for adult females. What constitutes a unit of alcohol is not without controversy. A half pint of standard bitter beer, a measure of spirits or a glass of wine were conventionally deemed to make up a unit of alcohol. But this assumption has been undermined by the growing alcoholic strength of beverages. Bitter beer may range from 3 per cent alcohol strength to 7 per cent. Lager beer comes in varying strengths and some continental beers, especially of Belgian origin, can be of substantial alcoholic strength. Wines from the Old World were traditionally about 12 per cent alcohol in strength but they have grown in potency. Some wines of the New World may approach 15 per cent in alcohol strength. It is wise to consider a glass of these wines to hold 1.6 or 1.7 units of alcohol, which is now increasing practice to note on the label at the back of the bottle. *Ad hoc* adjustments therefore need to be made in these calculations, and it also must be admitted that many individuals comfortably exceed these 'safe' thresholds without suffering any obviously discernible problem.

9.4 ALCOHOL – TREATMENT

The treatment of alcohol-related problems is often a concern of the law, especially family and child law. There appears also to be considerable interest in objective indices of alcohol abuse. Liver function tests are commonly utilised for this purpose. As a snapshot of current heavy drinking they may have some use but their limitations must be understood. Increased liver enzymes, in the absence of liver disease or concurrent medication, may be indicative of heavy persistent drinking. But the liver, as we have seen, has substantial powers of recuperation and regeneration and absence of disordered liver function may denote little more than a temporary period of abstinence. There is little alternative to taking a holistic view in relation to any patient suspected of heavy drinking, clinical observation being supplemented by the reports of witnesses. Heavy drinking, in itself, can be concealed but its effects – on domestic life, childcare, social activity, occupation – can rarely be kept hidden over any period of time. Any deficiency in behaviour will usually be apparent if observation continues long enough.

The actual treatment is more problematical than allowed for by many lay persons. The truth is that there is little by way of any specific treatment for alcohol-related problems. What there is is advice and support to assist such a person to bring his problems under control. It is *par excellence* a problem which requires self-help. It follows that the single most important determinant of success in treatment is the motivation and attitude shown by the individual. Without this, all help will be futile and fail. The patient must accept with true insight – mere lip service is insufficient – that he has a problem with alcohol and has to take steps to counter this problem and bring it under control. This means the patient must also feel he has the necessary incentive to turn over a new leaf.

Too much emphasis is often laid on the 'treatment' aspect of management of alcohol-related problems. In truth, specific help by means of pharmacological treatment is very limited, being reserved for some select and exceptional cases and has no application in the vast majority of cases seen in practice. Treatment therefore ordinarily means counsel, advice and support deployed through community-based agencies. Hospital in-patient detoxification may be required in only a small minority of cases where dependence is heavy, previous attempts at community-based detoxification have failed or raised complications, or where there are significant concurrent medical conditions which may cause concern. Counselling provided by public agencies may be complemented with attendance at Alcoholics Anonymous, an organisation that is sometimes mocked but which has a useful ancillary part to play in assisting the motivated patient with his rehabilitation.

9.5 ALCOHOL – THE PROGNOSIS

A common problem often arising in family and child practice is to advise on how long rehabilitation following treatment will take and what the prognosis might be. Since the disease concept of alcoholism is largely a matter of form and convenience, and the specific medical element in any treatment is so small, it is a somewhat artificial exercise to talk of prognosis in any accepted medical sense. However, over a period of years, clinicians have utilised their experience of these cases and the accumulated knowledge to arrive at a 'rule of thumb'. It is believed 2 years usually have to elapse before one can sign off a patient as being 'cured' of the disease of alcoholism, albeit perhaps only for the time being. There are those who argue that a tendency to alcohol misuse is a life-long affliction and that as a result one can only speak of remissions and exacerbations. Be that as it may, the patient has to show evidence that he has attained mastery over drink, however temporarily.

Whether he can aim for controlled drinking in the future rather than total abstinence is usually determined entirely on an individual basis, by trial and error in most cases, and there can be no hard and fast rule as to who could aim for moderate social drinking and who should aim for abstinence for life. Some individuals will not be able to touch another drop, others may be able to develop a much more socially appropriate *modus vivendi* with alcohol. It is one of those decisions that patient and counsellor need to work out following a course of treatment.

Once alcohol has been defeated, on however short-term a basis, the patient needs to be reassessed in terms of his mental state. Alcohol can mask many problems and once it is out of the picture one may be able to see if there remain difficulties such as depressive illness, anxiety states, chronic pain, etc, which might have induced, or contributed to, the original bout of heavy drinking. It is obviously more rational to treat any underlying condition which might have been a significant causative factor in the previous drinking in its own right rather than leave the patient at risk of relapse into further drinking. More ordinary social repair work can also be contemplated for such matters as marital or relationship difficulties, financial problems, poor housing or occupational concerns.

In the ultimate analysis, any prognosis to be given, as might be expected, is very variable. The only valid point to make is that if there is any underlying problem, and if this remains or recurs, the danger of relapse could be high. In the end, one is reduced to saying that if the patient derives greater satisfaction from alcohol – or, at any rate, greater relief from emotional pain through drinking – than from more normal social pursuits and satisfactions then he may have greater incentive to take or return to drinking. On the other hand, if the physical and mental well-being associated with a freedom from excessive drinking enables him to pursue worthwhile and rewarding social goals, it is likely the balance will shift in the opposite direction. The practitioner in family and child law confronted with a client with alcohol-related problems will do well to see how the balance sheet in respect of these matters reads.

9.6 ILLICIT DRUGS

There are many drugs that are in common use. Some of these drugs include those which are legitimately prescribed and have genuine medical properties for use in those for which there is a need for them to be prescribed but which, occasionally, find their way in large quantities into the hands of patients (whether those for whom they were originally prescribed or others). We are not here concerned with these prescribed drugs. Rather, we shall concentrate our attentions here on cannabis, the opiate drugs, the amphetamines and cocaine, which, in the public eye, are the illicit drugs, so to speak, of substance. The problem involving illicit substances is not uncommon. It has been estimated that at least 3 per cent of the population, that is about two million people in Britain, will take illicit drugs at any given time. Their involvement with mental disorder (co-morbidity, as it is called) is significant. More than 40 per cent of patients managed by community mental health teams reported problem drug use and/or harmful alcohol use among the patients in the previous year. The general perception is that co-morbidity has a much greater impact on services than its single components with increased psychiatric admission, violence and poor treatment outcomes.

9.7 CANNABIS

This is probably the most commonly used of the illicit drugs. It is used as marijuana, hashish and ganja and consumed on virtually every continent on the globe. It is imported from what used to be called the tropics although *Cannabis sativa*, the hemp plant from which these substances are derived, can be grown with success in Britain and aficionados of the drug relish the superior quality of the homegrown product. Cannabis is usually smoked neat or combined with tobacco, but can also be eaten on its own or after being baked into cakes and biscuits. Its fumes have a distinctive odour when smoked, nowadays considered to be part of the smells of the street. It has been a drug which has been used in some cultures for centuries and has the status of a staple recreational agent much as tobacco used to have elsewhere. Its effects are very variable and dependent on the purity of the source, the amount taken, the route through which it is absorbed, the personality of the consumer and the social and cultural expectations in play. In cultures where its use is traditional it is accepted as a relaxant and as an aid to social intercourse and conviviality. However, it has long also been associated with apathy and lack of motivation, and debate has raged as to whether it is the laid-back individual who is drawn to its use or if the drug itself induces feelings of relaxed indifference and insouciance. These effects are deemed to be psychological and it is not clear whether physical dependence can also arise as with alcohol or the opiate drugs.

There have been reports of pulmonary complications following prolonged use though confirmation of this is awaited. However, what is of renewed psychiatric interest is the implication of cannabis in cases of psychotic breakdown where it has been alleged that the drug can precipitate or induce psychotic symptoms in a predisposed individual. Similar claims have also been made for the precipitation of violence following its use. Neither the inducement of psychosis nor the production of violence is a universal feature and it appears to be the case that a susceptibility, probably of the genetic kind, is required as a pre-condition for psychosis and/or violence to arise. In the meantime, it is probably true to say the drug is by no means as benign as claimed by those who campaigned for its decriminalisation, a revised point of view now seemingly accepted by the authorities who fear another problem drug may have fallen into their hands.

9.8 THE OPIATE DRUGS

Like many drugs that are now abused socially, the opiates have had a parallel history of having been very valuable weapons in the medical armamentarium for decades. Morphine, heroin (diamorphine) and codeine along with synthetic derivatives such as pethidine and dextropropoxyphene continue to have legitimate medical use. Opium has, of course, been used and abused for centuries and a subculture of abusers, some intellectuals, others mere addicts, has existed probably in every age and in every society. The most important illicit use nowadays concerns heroin, which finds its way into the streets of Britain from origins in Afghanistan and Pakistan. As with cocaine, commerce is difficult to control largely because of the importance of the substance to the local economies; intricate networks of supply supplemented by the financial infrastructure needed to support the trade are in place. The effects of the drug are virtually indistinguishable from those seen when it is used in some form in legitimate medical practice save for the complications due to contaminants. Purity is variable and when a pure supply of the drug occasionally hits the streets many deaths not uncommonly occur as users do not allow for the strength of the uncontaminated product when they unwittingly consume it. Dependence of the physical type can supervene – sometimes following single use – and withdrawal effects are similar to those seen in alcohol deprivation with an added element of more intense craving, a state in which the individual is prepared to sacrifice everything, including his liberty and even his life, in the pursuit of the drug. In general the severity and length of withdrawal depends on the nature of the drug being abused, shorter-acting drugs tending to have more severe withdrawal symptoms over shorter periods as compared with longer-acting drugs. It is as socially destructive as any substance that can be imagined and life expectancy used to be drastically reduced in untreated cases, quite apart from the complications arising from infections due to contaminated needles, intercurrent infection and concurrent medical disorders. Two thirds of heroin users have had drug overdoses and a third of them have done so in the previous year. Part of the reason attributed to this is that, as we have seen, the purity of heroin can vary so that, especially when injecting, the exact dose being taken is unpredictable. It has also been suggested as an alternative explanation that near-death experience may form part of the desired euphoric effect due to heroin. Methadone overdose has also been reported to be on the increase. The drug may be smoked, inhaled or injected. Respiratory depression, with possible death, and constipation are common features. The euphoric feeling which follows its immediate use is difficult to replicate with the same repeated dose, so the amount taken needs to be increased, resulting in the phenomenon of tolerance.

9.9 AMPHETAMINES

These drugs also had legitimate medical use in the days before standard antidepressant drugs came into being to elevate the mood in depressive illness. It is freely available on the streets nowadays – methyl amphetamine use is now said to be the biggest public health hazard in terms of illicit drug use – and its commonplace nature sometimes leads to these drugs being treated with disdain by the authorities. Its effects are initially to produce euphoria along with the appearance of increased physical and mental energy. However, persecutory ideas along with paranoid states and convulsions are not unknown. The actions of the drug are short-lived – no more than a few hours – and, if the effect is not sustained by repeat use, there is the 'downer' element in which depression and lethargy supervene. Sleep and appetite, both suppressed with use, may remain permanently impaired.

9.10 COCAINE

This drug has effects similar to the amphetamines. It is derived from the coca plant in South America and the substance is a mainstay of the economy of countries such as Colombia. A more powerful part-synthetic derivative is called 'crack cocaine', which is notoriously even more addictive than native cocaine. The substance is conventionally inhaled, or snorted. Its effects last an even shorter time than the amphetamines and repeat use has to be resorted to. There is an increase in physical and mental energy and feeling of euphoria following use. As with the amphetamines, a complication of recurrent use can be paranoid psychosis and there may be present a combination of psychological and physical dependence. A stimulant dependence syndrome – usually involving the amphetamines but increasingly also cocaine and 'crack' cocaine – has been reported.

9.11 ILLICIT DRUGS – TREATMENT

The assessment and treatment of illicit drug abuse follows the principles set out in regard to the treatment of alcohol misuse. In general terms there is little by way of an underlying medical reason – save those cases where opiate dependence has followed therapeutic use of these drugs – for becoming dependent on or abusing these substances. Social conditions are now such that problematical abuse of these drugs mostly follows the casual or recreational use of these substances. Medical complications may, of course, follow their use. Dependence in the physical sense is common with the opiates and is occasionally probable with amphetamine and cocaine use but only psychological dependence is normally seen with cannabis use. Psychological dependence means, broadly speaking, the patient feels he can take or leave the substance, but its effects being such – the sense of relaxation, increased sociability, confidence and well-being – that the patient is drawn into continuing use of the drug. It may be thought that a distinction between physical and psychological dependence in these circumstances is little more than academic.

An important aspect of alcohol and drug use is the social scene in which these substances are indulged, in other words the social relationships and networks fostered among users, along with the sense of camaraderie which follows any involvement in what could be seen to be daring and unlawful activity. This may mean breaking away from the illicit drug scene is difficult – conveying also perhaps a sense of betrayal or treachery in respect of one's comrades – even when the patient is otherwise motivated and has the incentive to desist from further use. Motivation is the key to stopping the use of these drugs. Counselling, support and advice are available if the patient wishes to avail himself of these services. Progress in treatment may be monitored with the aid of objective measurements such as by testing hair strands for the presence of illicit substances. These measures are most useful when a patient is under treatment and regular hair strand testing for drugs can be undertaken to see if progress is being made in respect of controlling the use of the drug and, later, to ensure abstinence is maintained. Random drug tests are occasionally undertaken in family and child proceedings and are of limited value, whether positive or negative values are obtained. It cannot be overemphasised that, as in the case of alcohol misuse, what is really in point in these proceedings is the actual behaviour of an individual whether he be spouse, partner or parent. With opiates, withdrawal effects are such that medical assistance is usually required. Methadone – another opiate agent – may be substituted in oral form to reduce withdrawal effects and as this drug, although itself addictive, is dispensed under medical supervision some control may be achieved over the patient's opiate use by substituting a legitimate product as part of his treatment. The majority of patients with opiate dependency tend to be managed, at least at some point, in a maintenance programme. It is said that maintenance treatment of this kind retains patients in treatment, reduces illicit drug use, diminishes criminal activity and may also lower the incidence of HIV, hepatitis B and hepatitis C infection. It may also improve the chances of resocialisation. The dosage of methadone given is on the basis of the minimum dose necessary to avoid symptoms of withdrawal but a higher dose may be needed if the aim is to reduce illicit drug use. Other specialised drug treatment regimes are now also available for a suitable patient. However, the cornerstone of any treatment remains the psychological approaches undertaken in the form of individual or group help. The prognosis must always be guarded as there are so many imponderables and as so much remains dependent on the patient's own motivation, his attitudes and his social and personal circumstances.

Untreated, the picture can be dire. Apart from accidents and suicide, intercurrent infections and those complications directly attributable usually to intravenous drug use, there is the ever-present risk of entanglement with the criminal law as these substances remain unlawful to possess or distribute and the cost of their consumption is not negligible. Apart from medical and legal complications there is always also the risk of social and personal degradation involving the patient. Family and child law are naturally concerned as so much of illicit drug use impacts directly on family life. A person who seriously abuses alcohol or illicit drugs invariably puts himself in the position where he becomes of primary concern to himself, a state of affairs not usually compatible with satisfactory family life, in particular those aspects concerning childcare, where spouses, partners and parents are expected to show responsibility and care towards others including those who may be more vulnerable than themselves. However, recent studies have shown that some hope is permissible in cases of opiate dependence. On a 30-year follow up of patients who had suffered injected heroin abuse, 42 per cent of patients had been abstinent for at least 10 years following treatment. Ten per cent of patients were continuing to take methadone and 22 per cent were dead.

9.12 PATHOLOGICAL GAMBLING

A few words need to be said about this condition in view of the social and legislative changes that have led to the easing of previous restrictions on gambling. Pathological gambling is a hidden menace for indulgence in gambling, at any rate in Britain, is not unlawful, is seemingly encouraged by the State and its effects are not as obvious as may be, say, with problematical alcohol use. There are believed to be about 300,000 persons who could be described as problem gamblers in Britain and their number is believed to be growing. Problem gambling, in the clinical sense, does not usually involve such glamorous activities as playing the roulette wheel or engaging in the activities of well-appointed clubs in Mayfair. It normally involves an impecunious individual who has become pathologically dependent on such humble activities as playing the lottery and scratch cards besides engaging in the more traditional pastime of backing horses and dogs in insane hope. The poor are selectively more afflicted because they are the least likely to afford the inevitable losses associated with gambling. The point made earlier about the self-absorption and the relentless pursuit of personal gratification at the cost of all else, in respect of alcohol and illicit drug use applies equally well here, helping to bring the subject within the purview of the family and child lawyer. Treatment is entirely by psychological means – unless there is some underlying medical condition predisposing the individual to pathological gambling – and success of any therapeutic endeavour depends, once more, on the motivation and the desire for change exhibited by the affected individual.

9.13 DISORDERS OF APPETITE

These disorders are included in this chapter for completeness and as they appear to have at least a superficial resemblance to the kinds of perverted appetites found in the cases involving alcohol and illicit drug misuse. We leave obesity from any consideration here. This is no doubt a subject of considerable and expanding medical importance but it is one that does not commonly touch the professional working lives of practitioners in family and child law. We shall concentrate instead on anorexia and bulimia nervosa.

Anorexia nervosa

Anorexia nervosa is a condition that has been known for some centuries although it has come into greater prominence in more recent generations. There is a 'fear of fatness' in the individuals who suffer from these disorders – the vast majority adolescent girls and young women – which leads to their imposing a low weight threshold upon themselves. The disorders are characterised by the refusal of the individual to maintain a minimum normal body weight, often to the point of starvation. The core feature is an intense fear of gaining weight. This lower body weight is maintained at least 15 per cent below the standard norm applicable to such an individual. The behaviour aimed at achieving this self-imposed target includes the avoidance of high calorific foodstuffs, self-induced vomiting, self-induced purging, excessive exercise, and the use of appetite suppressants (the attraction of these properties of amphetamine drugs is obvious) and diuretic agents.

The onset of the condition is in early adolescence and a feature is the preoccupation with food in all its aspects apart from eating it. The condition may go unnoticed for many years for a preoccupation with figure and weight is otherwise considered normal in young girls. The female predominance is notable and there is no doubt that, at present, this is a condition found primarily in the developed world. The eating disorders, as conventionally understood, have been viewed as a culture-bound disorder, rare or absent except in Western cultures, where there is pervasive pressure to diet to obtain a socially desirable weight and/or shape. There is a tradition of self-starvation in some cultures but the motivation of individuals undertaking this ritual is quite different. An intriguing recent study from Ghana questions, however, the Western view of these disorders. First, it says, there are historical descriptions of cases of self-starvation without concerns about weight in cultures in which there is no emphasis on slimness. Secondly, cross-cultural comparison has suggested that the eating disorders do not necessarily follow the accepted Western form. Starvation in these cultures may be an end in itself, often undertaken for purposes of religious devotion. Weight concern as in the usual case of anorexia nervosa may become more common as the degree of Westernisation increases. The Ghana study suggests that anorexia nervosa may take different forms in different cultures and the patients studied there had a form of anorexia nervosa without concerns about weight. Studies examining eating disorders in developing countries seem to have assumed that the psychopathology of anorexia nervosa follows the recognised 'Western' form. The authors of this study suggest that a unifying theme of the diverse cultural presentation of the disorder is morbid self-starvation which may be driven in many ways and that self-starvation may, in fact, be the core feature of anorexia nervosa with the attribution for the self-starvation behaviour varying between cultures. However, there is also evidence that incidence of conventional cases of eating disorders is rising in those parts of the world where the major preoccupation has traditionally been with finding enough food to eat. An interesting phenomenon awaits us if, with growing prosperity and the advances towards globalisation, these disorders became as common in those parts of the world as other psychiatric disorders have usually done. There may also be growing parity between the sexes as roles become blurred as between men and women and the former also start becoming preoccupied with appearance and weight, a feature also believed to be on the increase. This does not make these conditions solely those of social and cultural origins for an intriguing involvement of the brain is found in some of these cases. It is believed, at least in some of these cases, the problem is primarily one concerning body image, that is, of the view that one comes to achieve of one's body, a matter of perception and therefore capable of being traced back to the brain. Social and cultural factors may well provide the raw material for the brain to work on. It has also long been known that complex endocrine changes associated with such symptoms as the loss of menstrual periods, and aberrations in the levels of hormones have also been noted. Whether these are causal phenomena or are effects secondary to the disorder are not always clear. There is a genetic influence that can be seen. Family conflict is often elicited. Childhood trauma, especially involving sexual abuse, has been discovered in a minority of cases.

Bulimia nervosa

A variant of the condition is bulimia nervosa which involves binge-eating which has some similarities to the episodic heavy alcohol intake or dipsomania. There is a history of anorexia nervosa in many who later become bulimic. One of the features in this condition is that normal body weight may be retained, indeed some subjects can be overweight.

Treatment

Treatment of these conditions is far from satisfactory or indeed finding a consensus among therapists. Measures include both practical steps – a regime of controlled re-feeding – and psychological treatment. The latter may involve individual or group psychotherapy and also family therapy. Cognitive behavioural therapy may have some merit and has its advocates. The prognosis is variable dependent as it is on so many factors peculiar to each patient and on account of the poor understanding as yet achieved of these disorders. The severity of the occasional case involving the eating disorders is often underestimated and it is believed that 5 per cent of these patients will die, either through starving themselves or by suicide. Severe cases may need to be treated in hospital and specialised units now exist in an attempt to achieve the best possible result.

Chapter 10

DISORDERS OF PERSONALITY AND PSYCHOPATHY

No other condition in all psychiatric practice leads to such confusion, disagreement and dissent as do those conditions making up this category of mental disorder. The essence of personality disorder is a failure on the part of an individual to adjust to the norms and standards of society. Many definitions have been given, though no single one is satisfactory. The ICD-10 defines personality disorder as:

> '... deeply ingrained and enduring behaviour patterns, manifesting themselves as inflexible responses to a broad range of personal and social situations. They represent either extreme or significant deviations from the way the average individual in a given culture perceives, thinks, feels and particularly relates to others. Such behaviour patterns tend to be stable and to encompass multiple domains of behaviour and psychological functioning. They are frequently, but not always, associated with various degrees of subjective distress and problems in social functioning and performance.'

Not surprisingly these difficulties often spill over into the law, in particular the criminal law, but family and child law also consistently encounter these patients, hence our current interest.

10.1 AETIOLOGY

These patients are rule-breakers. They are also abnormal individuals in the statistical sense. Truly the following could be said of them, employing Thoreau's words for the purpose:

> 'If a man does not keep pace with his companions perhaps it is because he hears a different drummer.'

Perhaps in trying to make sense of these patients a good starting point may be the normal personality, the one from which these patients are deemed to deviate. Although personality has long been studied, many gaps still remain in our knowledge. We do know there are significant genetic influences although, as with many conditions or states or attributes, normal, abnormal and pathological, the precise genetic mechanisms elude us. Brain studies have shown from time to time – through abnormal scans, aberrant electroencephalographic and blood flow studies – that there could be some abnormality in function, perhaps even in structure, of various regions of the brain but these studies are far too indefinite and on occasion contradictory to serve any practical explanatory or diagnostic purpose. In any event the manifestations of these disorders are so wide-ranging it seems unlikely there could be one specific lesion. A high level of autonomic nervous system arousal is sometimes posited in these individuals to account for their impulsive actions. Environmental factors, at first sight, hold greater promise for purposes of trying to explain these conditions but, once again, the available studies prove too contradictory – too much or too little parental attention, deprivation in childhood or, on the contrary, being 'spoilt', too comfortable or too spartan an upbringing, too much or too little caring – to have much value in terms of reliability and validity. All that can be said is that those with personality disorder or psychopathy appear able to spring from any kind of soil – social class, parental background, cultures can be of any kind. In other words, those who desire to turn out well-balanced, responsible citizens have little to work with and can almost never predict with any great confidence how young persons will turn out as adult citizens. Personality disorder and psychopathy are usually diagnoses made with hindsight, as the 'back tracking' to detect childhood and adolescent misbehaviour shows. In most cases, of course, children and adolescents outgrow their years of rebellion and are transformed into estimable citizens.

We suspect, nonetheless, that the social as well as the physical environment very probably do play an often decisive part in moulding an individual's personality characteristics. While the definitive personality emerges at maturity – which, with some arbitrariness, for these are not matters of precise chronological calculation, we may set at the age of 18 – many of the characteristics found in adult life are found surprisingly early in life, even possibly in the first few months of life according to closely observant parents. Numerous studies have shown that persistent and pervasive aggressive and disruptive behaviours seen before the age of 11 are strongly associated with persistence of anti-social behaviours through adolescence and into adult life. The risk extends far beyond anti-social behaviours to unstable relationships, unreliable parenting and underachievement in education and at work. Furthermore, children who do not have conduct problems are very unlikely subsequently to develop anti-social personality disorder, which is rare without a history of conduct problems in childhood. The brain obviously plays a crucial role and its own growth, development and maturity appears to underlie the personality the individual comes to present to the world. Therefore, any insult to the brain, while causing also possible intellectual deficiency (see next chapter) may also hinder the normal development of the personality. These injurious factors may include infections such as encephalitis or meningitis, head injuries, environmental toxins (one recalls the recent impassioned debate on whether or not mercury could have an impact on childhood mental development when used as a vehicle for vaccines), the foetal environment itself (subject as it is to maternal health, drugs taken, etc) and more obvious socioeconomic influences such as poor diet and housing. One must say, however, that the vast majority of patients with personality disorder have no discernible cause for their condition and, even when they suggest one of the above factors for their condition, the examiner remains sceptical for the precise role, if any, for any such causative agent is usually far from clear. If all children suffer infections, some of which are bound to be serious, how does one know which of these children has had its personality development adversely affected by the infection it suffered? These imponderables also affect the analysis of the psychological development of children such as the quality of their upbringing, the nature and number of their attachments, etc. Children brought up in dire deprivation may turn out to be well-adjusted adults and with the ground well prepared for success in all spheres of life. Equally well, those whose lives appear to be little more than a non-ending march to and from the criminal courts and prisons may reveal they had every advantage in their upbringing. The subject of personality development therefore remains one for speculation at the present day. However, an audience of lawyers will be able to appreciate the facts in a case which involved personality change in an adult person following head injury. The case was *Meah v McCreamer* [1985] 1 All ER 367, [1986] 1 All ER 943 and the primary legal interest was on the issue of remoteness in tort. The plaintiff (as these used to be called) was an estimable member of society who, however, foolishly accepted a lift from a drunken driver who proceeded to cause an accident. This passenger suffered head injury. What is of peculiar interest was what the consequences of the claimant's head injury turned out to be. He suffered a calamitous personality change which led him to committing a series of vicious sexual assaults one of which led him into being imprisoned for life. It was held he could recover for this 'loss of amenity' (subject to a reduction for contributory negligence) and that his criminal actions following head injury were reasonably foreseeable. Another man, aged in his forties, involved in both personal injury and childcare litigation, on similar facts turned from being a dutiful partner and devoted father into a drunken lout who came to lose all he had following a series of violent assaults. Fortunately, his aggression abated with time and the court could entertain a claim to his right to have renewed contact with his child with some equanimity.

10.2 GENERAL FEATURES

Some points may be made in trying to break down the kind of compendious definition of personality disorder such as the one given above.

1. The abnormal behaviour pattern is persistent and enduring, in other words it is not episodic as may happen with most forms of formal psychiatric illness. Even in saying that we must utter a word of caution for chronic illness such as some forms of schizophrenia or depressive illness may itself lead to personality change which may be difficult to distinguish from the disease process although the history may suggest normal development up to the first onset of the illness.

2. Personality disorders are mental disorders in their own right but these are to be seen separate from formal mental illness such as depressive illness to which many personality disordered individuals are subject. Similarly, the alcohol and illicit drug misuse these individuals frequently indulge in may found a diagnosis of mental disorder in their own right and must be kept separate from personality disorder.

3. The crux of the problem is the element of 'rule-breaking' in relation to the norms and standards of society. This lack of harmony with their surroundings and the inability to conform may be due to several elements in their psychological functioning, for example, their poor impulse control, their often high levels of anxiety and arousal, their ways of thinking and perceiving, their view of another person, etc.

4. It follows the abnormal behaviour pattern may be pervasive and may lead to maladaptive responses in many areas of personal and social behaviour.

5. Although the diagnosis is not to be made until maturity is reached, at least in chronological terms, problems of adjustment and conduct are invariably seen in childhood and adolescence and persist into adult life.

6. The condition is usually associated with significant problems in the social and occupational spheres.

7. The disorder may lead to significant personal distress although this may happen only later in its course and may not always be detected.

10.3 CLASSIFICATION

Given the state of current knowledge, personality disorder is only amenable to description and the classification of subtypes – themselves subject to change over the course of years as diagnostic methods become refined – is based on clusters of descriptive features. Many subtypes are recognised and we consider briefly here only those commonly seen in the practice of family and child law.

Dependent

One such type is the *dependent* personality disorder referring to an individual who encourages or allows others to make most of one's important life decisions, subordinates one's own needs to the wishes and demands of others, has a feeling of helplessness, is insecure on account of fearing desertion and requires excessive amounts of advice and reassurance from others. It has an association with borderline personality disorder and the aetiology is thought to be the outcome of early social processes within the family environment.

Anxious

Closely related to the *dependent* type is the *anxious (avoidant)* type who has persistent and pervasive feelings of anxiety and tension, believes they are socially inept, physically unattractive and inferior to others, is over sensitive to being criticised or rejected in social situations, unwilling to become involved in situations unless certain of acceptance, leads a restricted lifestyle in order to have security and avoids social or occupational activities that involve significant interpersonal contact because of fear of criticism, disapproval or rejection. It is also associated with phobic disorders, specifically social phobia which has similar clinical features.

Histrionic

The *histrionic* type of personality disorder involves an individual given to self-dramatisation and exaggerated expression of emotion, who is suggestible and easily influenced by others, is shallow with changeable emotions, is continually craving excitement, appreciation of others and the need to be the centre of attraction, is inappropriately seductive in appearance or dress and is unduly concerned with physical appearance, is egocentric, self-indulgent and manipulative. Although traditionally believed to be commoner in women, more recent studies show the gender ratio to be 50-50. It is more commonly found in divorced and separated persons and is associated with parasuicidal behaviour. It is associated also with women who suffer unexplained medical conditions and in men with substance misuse.

Paranoid

The *paranoid* personality type is excessively sensitive to setbacks and rebuffs, has a tendency to bear grudges persistently, is suspicious and with a tendency to distort experiences through misconstruction of the words and actions of others, is combative and tenacious in regard to personal rights, has a tendency to experience excessive self-importance and is given to suspecting conspiracies in regard to personal matters as well as in the world at large. It is more commonly found in males and persons of a lower social class, and also more common among relations of patients with schizophrenia. It exists with anti-social personality disorder and is associated with violent crime.

Schizoid

The *schizoid* subtype is more prevalent in offender populations. It has been suggested that this category may be better classified as a neurodevelopmental disorder than a personality disorder, possibly within the spectrum of autistic disorders.

Obsessive-compulsive

The *obsessive-compulsive* type finds grouped within it 'high functioning' individuals, more commonly white males who are highly educated, married and employed. It has an association with anxiety states.

An important subcategory for the actions of the patients within this type may have significant implications for the practice of family and child law is the *emotionally unstable* type. This kind of personality is governed by his impulses without any considerations of consequences or repercussions. The ability to plan ahead is much reduced and there may be outbursts or explosions of anger sometimes leading to violence. These individuals may be unduly provoked when they are thwarted. There are two variants of this subcategory. One is the *impulsive* type characterised by emotional instability and lack of impulse control. Outbursts of violence or threatening behaviour are commonly found here. The other is the *borderline* type which is also characterised by emotional instability, with disturbed behaviour, a chronic feeling of emptiness within and with a liability to become involved in intense and unstable relationships which are associated with repeated emotional crises which lead to violence (whether directed against oneself or others). It is not unknown for this – and perhaps subtypes such as the paranoid personality – to tip over fleetingly into displaying the features of psychosis including delusions, hallucinations and loss of insight and a sense of reality. It is said to be more prevalent in younger age groups (19–34), white females, associated also with a poor work history and single marital status and also more common in urban areas. It is further associated with substance misuse, phobic and anxiety states and has a 9 per cent suicide rate. It is associated in forensic samples with anti-social personality disorder. There is also an association with depressive illness. It is most severe in individuals aged in their mid-twenties with improvement noted in those aged in their late thirties.

10.4 PSYCHOPATHY

Psychopathy may be referred to as the 'turbo-charged' version of personality disorder. It has achieved notoriety and invariably attracts a bad press. The highest in the land may be caught up in its coils as is exemplified by the Government's seeming inability to know how to deal with some of the more violent members of this group and hence no new Mental Health Act can be seen on the horizon. Traditional classificatory systems used to mark these patients as being inadequate, creative or aggressive. Sociopath is the favoured term in the USA where intensive studies have been undertaken on them with little enlightenment forthcoming. It is believed there is a prevalence of psychopathy of 2 to 3 per cent in most Western societies and it is four to five times more common in men than in women. The highest prevalence is in the 25–44 age group. It is associated with school drop out, homelessness and raised mortality in early adult life. Prevalence is raised in inner-city areas and is lower in rural populations. It has a high association with substance misuse. The symptoms of anti-social personality disorder or psychopathy diminish in middle age but about 20 per cent of sufferers are still said to meet the criteria for diagnosis at the age of 45 years.

Most of the remarks addressed above to personality disordered individuals will also find application to those suffering from psychopathy. The condition remains a matter for observation and classification with little by way of any objective measurement as yet feasible. Some of the features seen in these individuals include a marked unconcern for the feelings of others, a gross and persistent attitude of irresponsibility in terms of the 'rule-breaking' mentioned above, an incapacity to maintain any enduring relationships, a very low tolerance to frustration and boredom with a corresponding low threshold for unleashing aggression and violence, an inability to learn from experience including punishment (whether officially or informally meted out to them), a marked inability to accept responsibility, a tendency to blame others and the possession of a dogged capacity for rationalisation of the usually deplorable acts they have been engaged in.

As with the personality disorders, the causes of psychopathy remain largely mysterious. It is a condition found in every culture and society and even where, say, aggression and assertiveness are more socially acceptable than in cultures where restraint and moderation are the preferred approach to life it is noteworthy how denizens of the former societies can still point to individuals who have overstepped an even higher threshold. A rule-breaker remains a rule-breaker even when the rules may appear to have been adjusted to accommodate his like.

While it has been said already that personality disorder (and psychopathy) can only be diagnosed after maturity, once personality has been deemed to be fully formed, when such diagnoses are being considered it is still believed to be necessary to 'track back', so to speak, and look at the picture that was obtained in childhood and adolescence of the individual concerned. When that is done, it is invariably the case that behavioural disorders are discovered to have been manifested at an early stage in life. Precursors of an anti-social lifestyle are said to include anti-social behaviour in childhood, impulsivity, school failure, anti-social family, poor parenting and economic deprivation. Turning points away from an anti-social lifestyle include finding employment, getting married, moving to a better area for residence and joining the army. Weak bonds to society and individuals, self-centredness, low empathy and lack of religious belief are all associated with substance misuse and an anti-social lifestyle. Early contact with the police, truancy, school misconduct and divorce are significant predictors of premature death. There is often a history of such activities as truanting, fighting, lying, bullying, insubordination, indiscipline, thieving and other features of juvenile delinquency to be found. In other words, personality disorders and psychopathy do not appear to arise *de novo* in adult life but have already laid down patterns early in childhood. All aspects of social and personal life come to be affected in these individuals and often they may leave behind a trail of destruction. Relationships – personal as well as with officialdom – are usually superficial, brittle and unstable. Repeated marriages, along with illegitimate children from numerous extra-marital relationships, are not uncommon. The occupational record is equally chequered with much difficulty shown in relationships with colleagues and superiors and much disruption in the work place as these individuals have a genius for creating chaos. Confrontations, in a repeated pattern, with the law are commonplace as these individuals often have what the law has called 'abnormally aggressive' and 'seriously irresponsible' attitudes leading to involvement with the criminal law following assaults on the person as well as property and, on occasion, for acts of dishonesty. Resort is readily had to abuse of alcohol and indulgence in illicit substances. Their career appears to be one of an individual looking back on the ruins of one relationship and contemplating the next. In early middle age it is customary for these individuals to show some signs of settling down, the convictions and spells of incarceration ease and a *modus vivendi* appears to have been reached with the world. It is often suggested that by that age these individuals could be running out of the animal energy that sustained their destructive and disruptive careers and that some measure of stability is often restored although some individuals may proceed to cause havoc in their lives and those of others right through life.

The older classification into inadequate, aggressive and creative psychopaths had some merit in helping to understand the life and works of these patients. The inadequate individual is the one commonly found to have a poor interpersonal and occupational record. The aggressive individual is the one who had entangled himself with the criminal law and the penal services. The creative individual becomes the renowned businessman or artist in occupations where 'rule-breaking' is the norm, where, in fact, success and progress is not possible if existing rules are not broken, although fulfilment or stability in their personal lives do not regularly match the material or artistic success they come to achieve, a matter readily explored by a study of the biographies of many gifted individuals.

10.5 MANAGEMENT

Treatment of these conditions remains problematical. The Butler Committee (1975) concluded:

> '… the great weight of evidence presented to us tends to support the conclusion that psychopaths are not, in general, treatable, at least in medical terms.'

Three decades later that sentiment remains, by and large, true. There is no specific drug treatment available for these conditions as such, although therapeutic drugs may be useful in dealing with the symptoms of formal psychiatric disorder these patients, like anyone else, may develop. It is often glibly asserted that psychological approaches by way of psychotherapy – individual, group or even institutional – may produce significant results. The results, in fact, are almost uniformly poor within any timescales envisaged by family and child law. Specialist institutions such as the Cassel Hospital have claimed reasonably positive results in cases of personality disorder. Specialist psychosocial treatment for personality disorder, they say, can show appreciable and reliable improvement in symptomatology, social adjustment and global assessment of mental health over a 36-month follow-up period. Improvement is said also to continue after discharge, a proportion of patients showing stable and durable change 2 years after termination of treatment. A phased programme that included a community-based stage of treatment was found to yield more stable improvement than a purely hospital-based programme, as shown by the greater reduction in self-mutilation, attempts at suicide and readmission rates. There is at present a co-operative venture involving the prison department, the Home Office and the Department of Health in a number of locations to see how the most irresponsible of psychopaths – the most dangerously violent – can be dealt with, if at all, therapeutically. No studies have yet emerged to show any promise and the Government's plan to replace MHA 1983 had to be put on hold (and now has been abandoned) as no treatment or management compatible with personal liberty in a civilised society can yet be formulated to deal with these individuals. Secure units and special hospitals remain the institutions for those individuals with these conditions who seriously transgress the criminal law. As far as timescales normally envisaged in family and child practice are concerned, any real treatment of psychopathy is, it is safe to say, not in the realm of practical politics.

No special mention needs to be made of the ways by which these individuals come to attract the attention of practitioners in family and child law. It is easy enough to imagine how the roles and responsibilities of spouses, partners and parents can be compromised in the case of individuals who have personality disorders or psychopathy.

Chapter 11

LEARNING DISABILITIES AND DEVELOPMENTAL DISORDERS

11.1 LEARNING DISABILITIES

The term learning disabilities has been some time evolving. At various periods in recent history the terms mental retardation, mental subnormality, mental handicap or mental impairment have all been employed to describe this phenomenon and some of these terms still find favour with official sources such as the International Classification of Disorders (ICD) (1992, mental retardation) or MHA 1983 (mental impairment). At an earlier period in history the terms used included those such as idiocy, imbecility and feeblemindedness, which nowadays are considered to be too pejorative. The primary problem in this disorder has long been considered to be one of an intellectual shortfall although the more enlightened attitudes of today also give proper attention to the more social and emotional aspects of the processes of learning whose deficiency is now believed to be the core handicap. The ICD defines these conditions as being characterised by 'arrested or incomplete development of the mind, which is especially characterised by impairment of skills manifested during the developmental period, which contributes to the overall level of intelligence'. Intelligence, therefore, still remains a central issue with learning disabilities. The conventional measure of this is the IQ (intelligence quotient) test. Intelligence in the ordinary populations is said to have a normal distribution by which is meant that with a modal score of 100, and a standard deviation of 15, two standard deviations from the mode in either direction would cover 95 per cent of the population. In other words, all but 5 per cent of the public would score between 70 and 130 on an IQ test. A borderline score is about 70, mild learning disabilities would cover scores between 50 and 70, moderate learning disabilities will be found between 35 and 50, severe and profound learning disabilities involve lower scores. The practical difference between those with higher scores – involving the vast majority of patients with learning disabilities – and the lower scores is that the former can hope to live in the community with some support while the latter may come to require institutional care of some kind.

The disorders leading to learning disabilities show clear evidence of both genetic and environmental influences. As a general rule, the more severely afflicted tend to have a known genetic cause for their condition while the mildly disabled have no obvious genetic causation but are believed to be affected to a greater or lesser extent by sociocultural influences. There are obvious exceptions to this rule for severe brain damage due to a clear environmental cause, for example, trauma or infection can lead to grave affliction while a condition such as Down's syndrome can lead to variable levels of intellectual difficulties.

The causes, where known, of learning disabilities are numerous. An example already given involving chromosomal abnormality is Down's syndrome. Genetic disorders include phenylketonuria (involving the metabolism of phenylalanine). Other causes include maternal infections in the course of pregnancy (eg rubella) or other complications of pregnancy and it is also believed the maternal consumption of alcohol, tobacco or prescribed drugs could be important, though as yet unquantifiable, causal factors. Birth injury and childhood infection such as meningitis are well-established causes as are later head injuries. One area whose causative potential is as yet little understood involves the role of adverse social and cultural factors such as poor diet and material deprivation. How these elements affect the developing brain remains unclear for there are children developing in conditions of extreme poverty and privation who yet emerge, as far as can be ascertained, normally into the world with their intellectual inheritance intact. In fact, mild forms of learning disabilities – the forms usually associated with socioeconomic factors – are probably constant the world over in their prevalence. In many undeveloped rural communities learning disabilities, as commonly understood, may not even be seen to be an obvious handicap whereas in complex developed societies it is only all too clear that such an affected individual may be at substantial disadvantage in coping with ordinary existence. Therein lies a paradox which may repay closer study.

For historical reasons the study of learning disabilities has fallen, in the medical sense, to the specialist psychiatrist. It is a condition which is distinct from formal mental illness although associations between learning disabilities and other mental disorders are not uncommon. These conditions may first attract the attention of those involved with the education of the individual or those called upon to deal with the behavioural problems of childhood at which stage problems involving conduct may at first mask the intellectual deficits that may also be present.

As the modern term 'learning disabilities' suggests, the disabilities of individuals suffering from this condition go well beyond intellectual difficulties and may also include those problems associated with social and educational functioning in a wider sense. The assessment of the needs of these patients is a complex exercise and may involve a variety of agencies including the educational services, the local authority and the health authority. The modern trend is to have these patients functioning as far as possible in the community with appropriate support, which may include supported lodgings. The days of traditional institutionalisation are long over, the older institutions now believed to have significantly added to the handicaps suffered by these patients by adding secondary disabilities due to the institutions themselves. Even when some form of residential care may become necessary, emphasis is placed on encouraging independence and fostering self-sufficiency among these individuals.

Learning disabilities, of whatever origins, always arise in childhood. A distinction needs to be made between these conditions and dementia, where intellectual impairment is acquired in adult life.

Patients with intellectual difficulties may impact on the work of practitioners in family and child law in obvious ways as a result of their disabilities. An important consideration in dealing with these patients is appreciating the need to evaluate their capacity to engage in litigation, a subject which has been discussed in Part I of this book.

11.2 OTHER DEVELOPMENTAL DISORDERS – CHILDHOOD AUTISM

Intellectual deficits as found in the learning disabilities are due to one form (though involving many varieties) of developmental disorder. Another form could preferentially lead to impairment in personality development resulting in the personality disorders and psychopathy which we dealt with in the previous chapter. Here we take up a form of developmental disorder which leads to problems of behaviour, emotion and social interaction called the autistic spectrum disorders. These conditions have been prominent in the public mind in recent years on account of the controversy surrounding the triple MMR vaccine (against measles, mumps and rubella) administered in childhood. It was being alleged in some quarters, with little or no scientific foundation in fact, that the MMR vaccine had led to an increase in the incidence of these forms of autistic disorder. This was plainly not the case but it is still legitimate to ask whether the seeming increase in the incidence of these disorders is real or apparent. There is no conclusive answer forthcoming as yet. It has been suggested that it is the increased awareness of the condition among the general public as well as among the professionals along with more refined diagnostic methods that had caused the apparent rise in numbers. Disorders that had previously been considered as being the usual forms of behavioural problems in childhood were now being dignified, it was said, by the diagnosis of autistic spectrum disorder. As so often happens – with ADHD when medication became available for its treatment, bipolar or manic-depressive disorder when lithium treatment first became established – the advent of new therapeutic possibilities raises awareness and leads to a reconsideration of previous diagnoses. In those situations there may be a tendency to overdiagnose some conditions that might previously have been underdiagnosed. The curious feature with the autistic spectrum disorders is that there is as yet no specific treatment available and the greater awareness (and possible overdiagnosis) therefore did not have any therapeutic impetus behind it. For once the pharmaceutical companies could not be convincingly blamed for attempting to raise awareness of a condition so as to promote and be able to sell their therapeutic products.

Childhood autism has been known to exist for a long time and was officially described in 1943. It is a condition of childhood and is recognised before the child is 3 years of age. It has a male preponderance in its prevalence. It afflicts all social classes and the earlier suggestion that it had a preferential higher social class distribution is now known to be false. In fact, this previous assertion was cruel in its further implication that it was 'cold' parents – mostly professionals, some academics – who, by their somehow repressed methods of child rearing, had caused the condition to arise. Looked at now, this suggestions sounds as absurd as it was offensive. There is little doubt that the condition – or the spectrum of disorders – is likely to be shown to be caused by brain dysfunction, the brain being in some way disrupted in its normal development.

The cardinal features of the condition include a solitariness or aloofness found in the child, what is referred to as 'autistic aloneness'. Intimacy is difficult to achieve with these children who appear from early on to have an impaired capacity to form social relationships. These children can be so unresponsive that deafness or learning disabilities may at first be suspected. They lack the playfulness usually associated with children. The second feature is an impaired ability to communicate. This may be manifested by delayed speech, sometimes in a complete failure to talk. Speech, when it appears, is of poor quality and may be repetitive and incorrect in form and content. Comprehension of speech is also poor and language skills such as reading are imperfectly acquired, even then often in a mechanical way with little or no understanding. There is poor eye contact and non-verbal communication is also affected. The third diagnostic feature is the desire for sameness shown by the child with rituals and routines adopted with repetitive patterns of behaviour which, when thwarted, can lead to much distress being caused. There is a mechanical element to play and social communication with little imaginative creativity or fantasy, which reflects the rigidity in the thought processes of the child as well as in its behaviour.

These abnormalities are associated with other intellectual and behavioural deficiencies. Many autistic children are also intellectually impaired and have the kind of learning disabilities previously described. However, the range of intellectual ability is variable and some autistic children are of normal abilities and in some cases celebrated examples of isolated areas of high accomplishment emerge. These areas of excellence usually involve mathematical or artistic abilities, for example, being capable of undertaking prodigious feats of calculation which are usually in the province of advanced computers, accomplishing astonishing feats of memory, rising to incredible precision in drawing architectural structures after a mere glance at the building, etc. These being isolated oases of high performance in an otherwise barren desert of serious disabilities, the term *idiot savant* has come to be applied to these perversely gifted individuals.

Abnormal movements are not uncommonly seen and severe behavioural problems,, including self-mutilation, may be observed. Epileptic seizures are found in a minority of cases.

There is evidence of some genetic influence although the impact of the environmental component in causation is suspected to be far greater in most cases. There is no specific treatment available for the condition and the best results are achieved through the deployment of specialised educational techniques. In fact, it has been said the only worthwhile advance in the management of autistic conditions in the past two generations has come by way of improved educational techniques. Residential care may have to be considered in the most severe cases of behaviour disorder. As might be expected, the prognosis is often poor, another indication that intractable forces in the brain are behind the condition. It is probably rare to see an individual suffering from the average case of childhood autistic disorder growing up to become a passably normal member of society.

11.3 ASPERGER'S SYNDROME

Childhood autism exists at one end of the scale in the disorders of the autistic spectrum. Many atypical or less well-defined cases of autism inhabit the rest of the spectrum which leads to, at this other end, Asperger's syndrome.

This is also a condition that seems to have caught the public imagination. Any mental abnormality in an otherwise reasonably successful individual appears capable of being attributed to Asperger's syndrome, as anyone with experience of family and child law, not to mention other branches of the law, knows. A galaxy of persons are now included among the suspects, in some cases posthumously with the help of tendentiously written (or interpreted) biographical studies. In fact, it is an uncommon form of disorder at the other end of the scale from childhood autism. There is no shortfall of intelligence (in fact, the opposite is usually true, as the public's view shows) and no difficulties with ordinary communication. The diagnosis turns on difficulties these individuals have in social and interpersonal interaction.

In view of the widespread misunderstanding of the condition it is well worth considering the diagnostic criteria. These suggest the following as being required: first, there may be marked impairment of nonverbal behaviour such as involving eye contact, facial expression, bodily posture and gestures; failure to develop appropriate social peer relationships; a lack of social or emotional reciprocity; possessing restricted and repetitive stereotyped patterns of behaviour, interests and activities such as involvement with routines and rituals; the disturbance must cause clinically significant impairment in social, occupational or other important areas of functioning; there is no clinically significant general delay in language; there is no clinically significant delay in cognitive development or in the development of age-appropriate self-help skills, adaptive behaviour (other than social intercation) and curiosity about the environment on childhood, and that criteria are not met for another pervasive development disorder or schizophrenia.

As is evident, there are strict criteria to be met before a diagnosis of the condition is arrived at. There is no place, it would appear, for casual suggestion that an individual could be suffering from the disorder. In one case, the estranged female partner of a 35-year-old man suggested in private law childcare proceedings that he could be suffering from Asperger's syndrome. On examination, the only findings were that he was highly qualified, was rather concerned with household security (he lived in North London in an area notorious for crime and was following police advice given to householders) and was somewhat of a stickler about things and detail. He had been to university which, when the relationship had run into difficulties, had been a point apparently used by the female partner's father as a possible foundation for the diagnosis (inevitably the man occupied a higher social position than the woman's family). A second case involved a 20-year-old woman, a mother in childcare proceedings, who had developed a schizophrenia-like illness and had suffered numerous breakdowns over the course of years. She was known to abuse illicit substances extensively and was non-compliant with medication. The urgent clinical question was whether or not she had true schizophrenic illness with all the implications for having the condition (see previous discussion on schizophrenia) or this was a drug-induced schizophreniform state. However, it became known that she had a half-brother who had severe childhood autism. Asperger's syndrome, as being suffered by her, became a preoccupation during the proceedings.

Chapter 12

SPECIAL SITUATIONS AND UNUSUAL DISORDERS

Some psychiatric conditions, although they could be accommodated within the diagnostic categories already considered, would benefit by separate treatment. One of these conditions is post-partum psychiatric disorder. This refers to mental disorders suffered in the period following childbirth. These conditions, at any rate in their clinical aspect, are indistinguishable from mental disorders suffered at any other time but for many reasons, including their importance in medico-legal situations, they will be taken up separately here.

The distinction to be made between physiology and pathology applies here as it does in all clinical psychiatric, indeed all medical, practice. Physiological states – such as unhappiness, uncomplicated grief reactions, psychological shock – are deemed normal responses. Up to 70 per cent of women suffer some changes in mood in the post-partum period, say within the first 6 weeks. These are the well-recognised 'maternity blues' with an onset normally in the first week following childbirth. Apart from this mood change in the direction of depression, there could also be anxiety, irritability and insomnia. Some negative feelings in respect of the newborn may be the result. These changes in the mood state are normal and do not require any active treatment. All that is usually required is reassurance (it seems to be commoner after the first episode of childbirth) and support. As with the distinction to be made between normal unhappiness and a clinically significant depressive illness, the differences between 'maternity blues' and post-partum depressive illness appears to be quantitative, the psychotic depressive state being rare, however.

12.1 POST-PARTUM DEPRESSIVE ILLNESS

This is a clinically recognised condition, meaning it satisfies the criteria required for a depressive illness to be diagnosed with the only additional element being it happens to be found in the post-partum period. This period is variously defined, but up to 6 months is usually allowed although most cases of depressive illness appear to have their onset within the first 3 months. The full significance of the clinical picture and, hence, the diagnosis could be missed because the symptoms come to be attributed to 'maternity blues' or a mother's natural anxiety especially in the care of a first-born child. Tiredness and exhaustion following childbirth could also mask the clinical picture. Otherwise the clinical picture is as it is found in depressive illness afflicting women, and for that matter men, at other times. The treatment is also broadly similar although there is an additional urgency brought about by the need to ensure mother and baby can bond without too much disruption in their relationship. More severe cases are treated in 'mother and baby' units which are dedicated to treating mother and holding baby so that the processes of bonding continue even as the mother receives treatment. The prognosis, as with modern treatment of any depressive illness, is generally good.

12.2 POST-PARTUM OR PUERPERAL PSYCHOSIS

Like depressive illness, the psychoses may also make an appearance in the post-partum period. The first months following birth are the time when women appear to be most at risk and a significant proportion of these (up to 25 per cent) give a history of previous mental illness. Women with bipolar disorder are at particularly high risk of puerperal psychosis, with episodes following 25–50 per cent of deliveries. In addition to a history of bipolar disorder, other important risk factors include having experienced a previous episode of puerperal psychosis, having a first degree relation who has experienced an episode of puerperal psychosis and having a first degree relation with bipolar disorder. It is, however, a far less common condition than depressive illness in the post-partum period. The onset can be fairly sudden and acute with features of schizophrenia, a schizo-affective disorder, mania or psychotic depression all being possible. There is little or nothing that is distinctive in the symptoms seen in this period as opposed to a condition presenting at other times. There is obviously greater urgency with treatment and it is usual for admission to be sought to a 'mother and baby' unit. Some care has to be taken with medication as the mother may continue to breast-feed and many drugs are known to be transmitted through breast milk. Treatment through modern drugs – and the judicious use of ECT in appropriate cases in the past – is generally successful and a good result may be anticipated. The prognosis is as good as in the non-puerperal case and when there is a protracted or chronic course run by the illness the adverse factors determining this are as for any other illness. Nothing specifically pathogenic or conducive to a poor prognosis has been conclusively shown to exist in the post-partum period in itself. However, as stated, women with a prior history of mental disorder are more vulnerable to mental illness of all kinds in the post-partum period and, if they have suffered one bout of post-partum mental illness, it is usual to predict they could be at higher risk after any subsequent childbirth.

The aetiology of the post-partum psychiatric disorders remains unclear. The obvious potential causative factors are the significant hormonal and chemical changes that occur during pregnancy and persist into the post-partum period.

But these changes are common to all women in this condition and no convincing endocrine or biochemical changes have been established between those women who fall ill and those who do not. The prior history of the mental illness and the persisting risk in any future post-partum period has been noted already. Emphasis has been laid on psychosocial factors such as marital or relationship difficulties, ambivalence towards the pregnancy and the newly born child, and more general factors such as housing and financial worries. In fact, considering the available evidence as a whole, one must conclude the post-partum period (and the preceding pregnancy) probably act as a stressful life event to susceptible women. The fact that childbirth may generally be a desirable event in the minds of most women is not a particularly relevant consideration; a much looked forward to move of house is known to be one of the most powerful adverse stressors to individuals. Prevention makes use of the fact of prior vulnerability in those who have suffered previous mental ill health. Careful monitoring during pregnancy and in the puerperium should be able to prevent the onset of more severe illness and disability.

Practitioners in family and child law are occasionally drawn into situations involving these cases. A mother previously having difficulty looking after a newborn may be deemed to be at risk after any subsequent pregnancy. Liaison between local and health authorities may mean information comes to be shared more sensibly. Prejudice is, however, to be avoided. Although there is evidence that a mother who falls ill once is at higher risk of becoming ill again in the course of a subsequent puerperium, it can never be the case that a mother's childcare abilities should be deemed automatically to be, or at risk of becoming, impaired. In fact, the degree of illness and disability may vary widely and each situation needs careful consideration and analysis in its own right.

12.3 CULTURAL INFLUENCES

With so many communities now displaced from their places of origin, it is widely accepted that diverse cultural influences may be in play when mental illness presents itself for examination and study. The subject is vast and here only the common influences with some impact on family and child law will be taken up. Also, only those possible influences of psychiatric (ie medical) interest will be considered. Some further remarks will be made on the possible cultural aspects of aggression and violence when this matter is touched on in the next chapter.

Mental illness, like all disease conditions, is universal and the signs and symptoms of disorders, at any rate in their technical aspects, are now increasingly studied according to standard criteria. It is, therefore, in the interpretation of these signs and symptoms that the challenge of culture-bound influences resides. We have already remarked on the cultural influences operating in any study of delusions in the chapter on psychotic disorders. A delusion, it will be recalled, is not merely a false belief that is unshakably held despite evidence to the contrary, it is also a belief which is out of keeping with the social and cultural beliefs of the patient. Thus, one finds persisting in many cultures beliefs in such phenomena as witchcraft and 'the evil eye' and an individual from such a culture may express a view that neighbours or family or some person in or outside his culture has evil designs on him, has taken steps to put such designs into practice, that this person should be thwarted lest he succeed in his aim for illness or misfortune due to the machinations of such an individual may otherwise come to afflict him. If within the culture of such an individual such beliefs are commonplace it may not amount to a persecutory delusion and, therefore, is not a symptom of mental illness. Careful analysis of the facts, apart from the possession of a sound working knowledge of the culture in question, is required before one comes to this conclusion for persecutory delusions can, of course, arise in such an individual in the course of schizophrenia or some other psychotic condition. The test, as we have seen before, is to see how any persecutory beliefs an individual possesses might have originated, what form the finished product has attained and, most importantly, what the interpretation or explanation given by family members or others in the community is for this phenomenon. As a rule of thumb, anything deemed abnormal within the family or the community is more suggestive of a true delusion than any belief accepted with equanimity by others within that community.

A 26-year-old woman from Rwanda, who had suffered horrific experiences including acts of multiple rape in the course of the war in that country, became involved in childcare proceedings in England after the child conceived as a result of a rape and born to her showed serious disabilities. It transpired she held strong cultural views on those who might continue to harm her and these beliefs were based on her experience of tribal rivalries. She had also spent time in Uganda where many of her compatriots had been displaced with her. Seeking asylum in Britain, she had also made contact with an evangelical church. She naturally sought comfort among the black community in Britain but her specifications for association with members of the black community were rather strict – she was prepared to trust and work with black Americans and those whose origins had been in the Caribbean or the West Indies but she continued to have the liveliest suspicion of any person originating from Africa.

An 18-year-old girl, of Bangladeshi origins but brought up from infancy in Britain, also became involved in childcare proceedings on account of her very young child. The girl's lifestyle, notwithstanding the strict constraints of her native culture and the location she found herself in (which was predominantly Muslim) as a teenager and adolescent, could have been, on first impression, that of a certain type of native young girl of today – she drank alcohol and got drunk, she freely abused illicit substances and engaged in casual and, for a while, underage sex. Closer inspection showed, however, a more serious disturbance of conduct along with some psychotic features such as auditory hallucinations. In fact, there appeared to be much disruption to a still evolving personality in her case and although it was probably too early yet to arrive at a diagnosis of personality disorder the signs of such a condition were suggestive. What was, however, even more interesting from the clinical point of view, was her belief that her troubles – in particular the symptoms of mental disorder – had been brought about through consuming foodstuffs given to her by the 'the many enemies of the family'. She now took extreme care to examine the provenance of any food she consumed and shunned food that had been sent to her family from abroad. Thus, the outlook and attitudes of a thoroughly modern (if somewhat disturbed) young girl, whose behaviour was to all intents and purposes those of many denizens in the West, could co-exist with beliefs which are commonplace within the Bangladeshi culture. That is why her auditory hallucinations were clearly recognised as being features of a mental disorder but her persecutory ideas had not been.

Where psychotic illness is concerned the presence of some recognised symptoms of illness may be found in some cultures while being absent in others. Moreover, symptoms of illness may also show a change over a period of time. Until about a half century ago there was present, universally as far as one can judge these matters, a symptom of schizophrenia called catatonia. This involved both the phenomena of mutism (mute by visitation of God, in medico-legal parlance) and stupor, that is a severe psychomotor retardation. So common was this condition that a subcategory of schizophrenia called catatonic schizophrenia came to be recognised. Over some generations this condition has shown a dramatic decline in incidence in the nations of the West so much so that the diagnosis (which is still in existence in the ICD-10 Classification of Mental Disorders) is largely made only in the developing parts of the world. This also means the condition may still be found in immigrant communities in the West. Why this decline should have taken place so selectively remains something of a mystery although there have been suggestions that an infectious process might be involved – a virus, perhaps, that mutated into innocuousness in some parts of the world. Whatever the explanation, catatonia remains a condition whereby a physical symptom appears now to be determined by a cultural influence of a more tangible kind.

In a similar vein, the influence of known infection, especially in the causation of acute confusional states, including delirium, which could have been acquired in the cultures of origin is not to be disregarded when it comes to the evaluation of mental disorder in migrants. Other physical illnesses, now rare in the West, as possible causes of mental disorder should also be borne in mind when dealing with these patients.

In the chapter dealing with depressive illness we noted the need to consider the patterns of presentation of depressive illness in various cultures. In those patients originating especially from the cultures of Asia and Africa it is customary for them to emphasise the physical aspects of symptoms (such as the insomnia or the aches and pains associated with depressive illness) and deny or play down the psychical element such as the low mood or the reduced capacity to enjoy oneself. It is usual to ascribe this emphasis on the physical to the stigma still believed to prevail in many parts of the world against mental disorders. Notwithstanding this, it is important to recognise this cultural bias for it has a bearing on the issue of the kind of insight the patient possesses in respect of his disorder. In evaluating the presence of insight it is usual to seek evidence that the patient recognises that he is suffering from a mental or psychological problem. It can be readily appreciated that in a patient from these cultures denial of psychological causation or manifestation of disorder is not necessarily a sign of lack of insight as the term is understood. Further, given the apparent prominence of physical symptoms as reported by these patients, there is also the risk of overinvestigation in the pursuit of supposed physical causes of the disorder. Unnecessary radiological or laboratory investigations are to be deprecated in the management of psychiatric disorder as they tend to reinforce the impression the patient may already have, that what underlies his feeling of being ill is possibly something grave which could be identified if more energetic (and expensive) investigation were only undertaken. One runs the risk of converting someone suffering from a straightforward disorder, such as a depressive illness, into someone with a somatoform disorder or hypochondria.

This leads us naturally into considering the hysterical or conversion/dissociative disorders which were briefly dealt with in the chapter on the neuroses. The grosser manifestations – once very common and which helped to make the reputations of Freud and other psychoanalysts – are now rare in the West. However, the more florid examples of this condition – paralysis, blindness, trance states, etc – are still to be found from time to time in persons from communities drawn from the developing world. Hysterical conditions are believed to be due to a neurotic reaction to stress which may be perceived or only unconsciously expressed. In many cultures gross mental disturbance in the form of psychosis – reactive or stress-related – may also be found. These are usually short-lived episodes of illness proximately related to stressful events, reasonably easily treated through symptom relief by anti-psychotic agents and the treatment does not need to be prolonged. The prognosis of these conditions does not depend on any underlying disease process (as may occur with schizophrenia or the bipolar affective disorders) as such but in the capacity the individual possesses to deal with and cope with future stressful events.

We have dealt here with disease conditions seen in ordinary clinical psychiatric practice and which may be influenced by cultural practices and beliefs. There is no scope in a work of this kind to deal with the many other cultural influences working on spouses, partners and parents which the practitioner in family and child law may come across. Forced marriages are one example of a non-medical kind. The physical chastisement of children, which may be culturally appropriate, may bring parents into conflict with

English law. Strict and inappropriate rules (at any rate to Western eyes) may also bring conflict between parents and their children. In themselves these are not examples of mental disorder which require assessment of the usual kind to establish. It cannot be stressed too often that the diagnosis of disorder is not to be made on unusual or uncommon forms of behaviour alone.

12.4 SOME UNUSUAL PSYCHIATRIC DISORDERS

There are many culture-bound, as opposed to culturally influenced, psychiatric disorders which are of little relevance to everyday psychiatric practice in the West. We mention here only *amok* which has entered the language by way of such phrases as 'running amok'. This is a condition occasionally manifested in South East Asia and which is marked by extravagant behaviour in the face of stressful events and which may lead to homicidal or suicidal acts being committed unless the patient is restrained, usually with the help of a traditional healer.

We are more interested here in a few otherwise uncommon disorders which nevertheless may have an impact on family and child practice. The first of these is morbid jealousy.

12.5 MORBID JEALOUSY

This is referred to also as the Othello syndrome. The main symptom involves a state in which the patient may show a variation between demonstrating excessive suspicion of a spouse or partner's fidelity (males are more commonly afflicted) to possessing full blown delusions, having symptoms in other words which make up a psychotic condition. There is often present an inadequacy in the personality of the sufferer even before the illness sets in and there is also an association with abuse of alcohol. The behaviours engaged in may be unreasonable, even extreme or bizarre. There is a relentless pursuit of the truth the patient has become convinced of, namely that the spouse or partner has been unfaithful and all that is necessary for the evidence to emerge is to leave no stone unturned in looking for that proof. Investigation, interrogation and cross-examination may reach extraordinary levels with spying on movements, checking credit card slips or telephone bills, following the spouse wherever they go, and examining their underwear and bed linen for evidence of sexual activity. Violence is not uncommon and it is one of the psychiatric disorders where in a small minority of cases the killing of a spouse or partner becomes a rather more predictable eventuality than in the usual run of psychiatric cases. Treatment is difficult for the interference of the personality is usually strong and the best results are probably obtained when morbid jealousy is a symptom of another condition such as schizophrenia, depressive illness or alcohol misuse rather than as a free-standing paranoid illness in its own right. The protection of the spouse or partner may become a matter of urgency and affords the family lawyer one of those occasions when, by expressing his views in court and outside (to the patient's GP, for instance), he may actually play a part in saving a life.

12.6 EROTOMANIA

Another condition, once believed to be a rare curiosity, has come into prominence on account of an association, at least in a few cases, with the phenomenon called 'stalking'. In its traditional form – called erotomania or De Clerambault's syndrome – spinsters of a certain age used to be affected. The spinster would become deluded that a man, usually of exalted social status or distinguished standing, was in love with her. She would proceed to arrange her life accordingly and could remain chaste and faithful while waiting for him to come definitively into her life. At this stage things remain fairly innocent but the behaviour could extend to harassment and pursuit which could lead to social, personal and professional embarrassment for the victim (some male doctors have been hauled up before the GMC following a complaint by a spurned female patient suffering from this disorder that there had been an improper relationship between them). The criminal law could also become implicated. Injunctions, their breaches and ensuing incarceration are not unknown. Treatment is rarely straightforward unless, as in the case of morbid jealousy, the delusional belief is a symptom of another psychotic illness amenable to treatment when there is a reasonable prospect of success although relapses are common. The freestanding psychosis is a form of paranoid disorder or a persistent delusional disorder. More recently, the phenomenon of stalking, with a male preponderance, has become recognised although few of these individuals involved in it have any recognised mental disorder in them. There is no conclusive explanation for the phenomenon though it could be suggested that the easy familiarity with the lives of and imagined intimacy with celebrities – one recalls the unprecedented and uncharacteristic outpourings of grief that followed the death of Diana, Princess of Wales – makes it appear that anyone, however high, is now accessible to someone, however low. Treatment, if actually merited, is difficult and the law's protection may have to be sought by the victim. As far as family practice is concerned, the usual 'stalking' behaviour of the common-or-garden variety involves a former spouse or partner whose continuing attention may cause distress and even illness in the victim.

12.7 MUNCHAUSEN'S SYNDROME

This topic has made several sensational appearances in family and child law, especially by way of its alleged variant, Munchausen's syndrome by proxy, and therefore it seems appropriate to make passing reference to it in these pages. The syndrome in its classical form owes its name to an eighteenth-century figure. Baron von Munchhausen (sic) (1720–1797) was a real enough person, a German soldier descended from ancient Hanoverian nobility. He served in military campaigns and was noted for his ridiculously exaggerated exploits. A collection of stories was attributed to him. However, much of the final form of the stories was due to the work of Erich Raspe (1737–1794), a scholar and curator of gems and medals at a museum. Accused of stealing and selling the medals Munchhausen fled Germany for England. Here he engaged in further swindling and had to flee, in turn, to Ireland where he died.

The symptoms displayed in the classical form of the disorder have as much foundation as the baron's stories but display a more humdrum character, which, paradoxically, succeeds in fooling doctors. Young men are preponderantly affected. They show the features of pathological lying, exaggeration (or manufacture) of symptoms and the presentation at various hospitals, especially in their casualty departments. Their symptoms may be described with such skill that extensive investigations may follow. The features of an acute abdominal emergency may be so convincingly described that they may come to have numerous operations and they walk about sporting 'crisscross' patterns on their abdomen as stigmata of their adventures. Apart from the lying there is often also the skilful acting complete with the necessary props, for example, simulation of bleeding, self-injury with swallowed objects and the convincing portrayal of physical and mental illness. They are deemed nuisance patients for they waste so much resource (while also putting themselves at risk of iatrogenic illness or injury) and their details may be transmitted across the land so as to alert hospitals to their existence and possible attendance at their doors.

The syndrome is probably best understood as a form of severe personality disorder although a hysterical basis cannot be ruled out (see case described below). A severe personality disorder is probably the most likely explanation also for the variant Munchausen syndrome by proxy which has achieved such notoriety that the diagnosis has been discredited. In this situation a parent (most usually the mother) repeatedly seeks medical intervention for a child by making up symptoms of disease or by deliberately inducing same in the child by any means including causing injury. In other words the child is being made an instrument of the parent's psychopathology. Gross disorder of mental functioning may be seen in such parents. A 30-year-old woman with a young child – hence their involvement in childcare proceedings – not only made up symptoms of illness for herself and her child but also consistently denied usually impeccable sources of factual information – the details on her birth certificate, marriage certificate, pictures of her wedding, letters written about the child by doctors and other documents in similar vein. She would not accept her recorded age or that for the child even when these had been established through official documentation. When the paternity of a second child was brought into question, she tampered with a sample being taken for DNA analysis and very nearly earned a conviction for attempting to pervert the course of justice. The diagnostic category most closely fitting her behaviour appeared to be mixed dissociative disorders (F 44.7 of the ICD-10). The condition, whether in its classical form or its variant, is untreatable for practical purposes.

A recent notorious case which made public headlines was that involving Beverley Allitt (the full facts of the case involving Benjamin Geen, a nurse in Oxford just lately convicted in similar circumstances, are awaited) who was convicted in May 1993 and sentenced to 13 life sentences for murder, attempted murder and serious assault. She was a nurse aged 24 who craved approval, attention and sympathy from colleagues and senior staff by raising alarms and helping to save the lives of child patients whose lives she had placed in jeopardy through her own actions. She had shown no remorse, indulged in pathological lying and attention-seeking behaviour and had sought to be a member of the medical resuscitation team. It turned out she had herself made 24 visits to the casualty department of a local hospital in the course of a 3-year period. She had been treated for various self-inflicted injuries and had made false complaints of pregnancy, gastric ulcer and brain tumour. She also alleged she had been sexually assaulted at knifepoint and also had had treatment for anorexia nervosa.

Chapter 13

VIOLENT BEHAVIOUR AND RISK ASSESSMENT

In this chapter we shall consider aggressive conduct as it is directed against the self (suicidal behaviour and deliberate self-harm) as well as against other persons and property. The special case of sexual violence is also taken up. These behaviours form the basis for the risk assessment exercise which involves all psychiatric practice and especially informs the practice of family and child law.

13.1 SUICIDAL BEHAVIOUR

A distinction is to be made between suicidal behaviour (including attempts) and behaviour leading to deliberate self-harm. Suicidal behaviour is distinguished by the presence of intent as a mental state required for the act or omission involved. What intent is may be explored by means of the proposals put forward by the Law Commission (*A New Homicide Act for England and Wales*? Law Com No 177 (2005)), which is a proposed attempt statutorily to define what is at present a common law concept. By this proposed definition a person acts intentionally with respect to a result when he acts either:

1.   in order to bring it about; or

2.   knowing that it is/will be virtually certain to occur; or

3.   knowing that it would be virtually certain to occur if he were to succeed in his purpose of causing some other result,

with the proviso that a person is not to be deemed to have intended any result which it was his specific purpose to avoid.

In practice, whether there is suicidal intent is to be determined by the stated views of the individual if these are available (usually conveyed orally or by the writing of a 'suicide note') and the surrounding behaviour of the individual which may perhaps be best illustrated by way of an example.

A 40-year-old single mother could no longer cope with the increasingly disturbed behaviour of her 14-year-old son who was later diagnosed to be suffering from one of the autistic spectrum disorders. She planned to kill herself. She left notes, also made elaborate plans for the future care of her 10-year-old daughter, settled her affairs and asked in a note for her possessions including her jewellery to be passed onto the daughter. Suicidal intent was therefore clear in this case but it may not be so clearly observed in many other cases, a fact explaining the reluctance of some coroners to bring in a verdict of suicide in the absence of incontrovertible evidence of intent being present. Contrary to popular notion, the fact of death or near death through dangerous behaviour does not necessarily distinguish between intentional behaviour and merely reckless action. It is perfectly possible to die following an impulsive act if the means employed are dangerous enough, for example, swallowing a sufficient dosage of paracetamol tablets if they are to hand. Some tragic consequences have resulted even in situations where the victim probably did not intend to die but the circumstances were against her (females more commonly engage in reckless rather than intentional acts of self-harm). Even an apparently trivial consideration such as the day of the week when the act takes place may make a difference as to whether an individual lives or dies. If, say, towards the end of the week, when the supply of paracetamol tablets in the household drug cupboard is running low, an impulsive act takes place, it may well lead to the individual surviving. If the act had taken place, on the contrary, at the weekend, say, when the supply has been replenished after the week's shopping has been done, enough tablets may be available to make death the outcome as sufficient poison would then have been ingested. Recent legislation restricts the amount of paracetamol available for sale in packages; therefore stockpiling may be evidence of intent, for the reckless self-harmer usually merely swallows what is to hand. Pure chance may also otherwise determine the end result. A 40-year-old chartered accountant, beset by many problems and facing possible indictment on a charge of mortgage fraud, decided to end his life through gassing himself by means of his car's exhaust fumes. The turmoil in his mind was such that he had failed to ensure the car had sufficient fuel in its tank for this purpose. The engine accordingly cut out in due course in the isolated woodland spot he had chosen for his deed and he was rescued by some sightseers. He was left with severe, uncorrectable brain damage which virtually completely destroyed his memory.

Risk factors for suicidal behaviour include male sex, unemployment, a single state, psychiatric disorder (especially depressive illness, schizophrenia, anorexia nervosa or abuse of alcohol and/or illicit drugs), chronic physical disability, recent bereavement and personality malfunction. Some 50 per cent of successful suicides have previously made an attempt to end their life.

In the assessment of suicidal risk the examination of the mental state appears to be the most important element. The presence of any psychiatric disorder (and not merely the conditions mentioned above) increases risk. A depressed mood – which may be found as a symptom in any psychiatric disorder – associated with feelings of pessimism, despair and worthlessness will elevate risk. The psychotic disorders are generally believed to carry a lower risk although, as already noted, an appreciable number of schizophrenic patients proceed to kill themselves. Auditory hallucinations may impel a patient to take his life by ordering him to do so. Suicidal ideation is an important sign to elicit in the mental state examination. There is a gradation in those thoughts and we shall consider them in an ascending order of risk. The most innocuous are fleeting thoughts that life may not be worth living. This is followed by momentary notions where actual suicide is contemplated. Next comes recurrent and persistent thoughts of putting an end to one's life. At the extreme end actual planning of the kind we have described is found. It has been shown that suicide attempts among patients with major depressive disorders are strongly associated with the presence and severity of depressive symptoms and predicted by lack of a partner, previous suicidal attempts and the time spent in being depressed. Suicidal thoughts must be actively sought and it is a false sense of propriety and delicacy to decide not to intrude into private matters or even be fearful of putting such thoughts into an innocent mind. The purpose of the inquiry is to be able to arm oneself with the information which may dictate the necessary responses to be made including, where the conditions merit it, compulsory hospital admission under MHA 1983. The actual treatment to be given is, of course, dictated by the underlying disorder when it is treatable. Social measures are very useful in the long term, even those involved in giving such simple information as the availability of the Samaritans organisation. Treatment, even in a hospital setting, does not always provide the necessary security for it is well known that the recovery phase in a depressive illness is a particularly dangerous period for further suicidal attempts. (It is a curious coincidence but historians who have studied revolutions and other social upheavals have long commented that the greatest risk to existing regimes is not when things are at their darkest but when matters are beginning to look up after a dire period, when the lights at the end of the tunnel turn out to be those, in fact, of an oncoming train. It is said that while there had been grave food shortages in France in the years preceding, the storming of the Bastille which heralded the revolution took place in a year when there was promise of an unusually good harvest.) Be that as it may, the explanation usually given in respect of depressive illness is that the marked psychomotor retardation found in the acute stages of the illness is selectively eased with treatment, with improved physical activity coming before psychological uplift so that the patient previously physically incapable of carrying out a suicidal act now has the means as well as a still persisting intention, a case of the flesh becoming stronger while the spirit remains weak.

13.2 DELIBERATE SELF-HARM (DSH)

This is to be distinguished from attempted suicide which, as with any attempt, is marked by the possession of intent. In fact, the behaviour seen in DSH is usually characterised as reckless, for the individual knows that some harm may befall him if he proceeds with the actions he is about to take but he continues with it nonetheless. It should be remembered that mental states, in both the medical and legal sense, can change and vary, and recklessness may give way in time to intentional behaviour. In fact, it is known that in the 12 months following an act of DSH there is increased incidence of both further acts of DSH as well as acts of completed suicide. While death may follow an unintentional act in ways described before, there is some evidence that the perpetrator of DSH might also have had some time before the intention to take his life.

Deliberate self-harm is a fairly recent phenomenon which, at one stage in the 1960s and 1970s, threatened to attain epidemic proportions. It is difficult to find many examples in the historical literature of deliberate self-harm unrelated to hysterical states (except, of course, as acts of mutilatory malingering to avoid going to war) while attempted suicide was, of course, not uncommon. Why this should be so is unclear although the identity of the perpetrators of self-harm – mostly adolescent and young women of lower social origins than is associated with suicidal behaviour – may furnish a clue. Perhaps it results from social emancipation from previously fairly tightly regulated lives. Whatever the cause may be, the methods used in DSH now involve prescribed and off prescription drugs (which account for some 90 per cent of cases of DSH) and some form of self-mutilation which involves (usually) superficial cutting of parts of the body, chiefly the limbs.

The causes of this behaviour are not uniform. While a significant number of these individuals exhibit features of personality disorder (or behaviour disorder if younger than the age of deemed maturity), quite a few have no discernible psychiatric abnormality at all. The most common factor in the act is a precipitating event preceding the act which has caused distress or is perceived as threatening. As many of these acts are impulsive – done in 'moments of madness', as it is commonly described – it is difficult sometimes to identify any persisting personal or social difficulty but there is not uncommonly a pervasive or smouldering feelings of unhappiness or dissatisfaction – neither of which is, of course, a psychiatric symptom – which is waiting for some stimulus or spark to set it off by way of an act of self-harm. Alcohol is commonly involved as a disinhibiting agent.

The assessment of DSH is as for suicidal behaviour, for no conclusions can be arrived at as to whether intent is or was present or the act followed recklessness without proper assessment. It is now routine for psychiatric assessments to take place in Accident and Emergency departments of hospitals to which the patient is taken in the first instance following an overdose. Transfer to a psychiatric unit takes place when there is an underlying disorder detectable or when there is uncertainty about the clinical picture and the patient is believed to be at risk of repeating such behaviour. Treatment is, as with suicidal behaviour, for any underlying psychiatric condition if one exists. Social and personal problems – some of it amenable to advice and practical help such as rehousing or debt management – is often more appropriate than formal psychiatric treatment. The risk of further DSH and suicidal behaviour is always present and the most useful duty of the attending psychiatrist is to detect the presence of some treatable condition in the individual who has engaged in DSH. It has been shown that those patients who display an escalating severity of self-poisoning episodes are at high risk of completed suicide.

13.3 AGGRESSION TURNED OUTWARDS

Violent behaviour is a complex subject and its roots go beyond the psychiatric, yet it is the professional in this field who is often asked to evaluate violent behaviour as part of a risk assessment.

13.4 VIOLENCE ASSOCIATED WITH MENTAL DISORDER

When formal mental illness can be identified, an understanding of the psychiatric origin of cases of violent behaviour may be achieved without too much difficulty. Psychotic violence is not uncommon and conditions such as schizophrenia and mania may feature high in such violence although overall, despite popular prejudice, violence associated with mental disorders is comparatively rare. Perhaps reassuringly – for it confirms what has long been suspected by informed persons – a recent study from New Zealand has reported that homicides by the mentally ill has not increased as a rate and also that people in close relationship with the perpetrator, rather than strangers, are most at risk of being the victim. In schizophrenia the violence may be associated with underlying symptoms such as delusions (persecutory delusions may cause a patient to protect himself against his imagined tormentors) or hallucinations (voices may urge the patient to act violently) though violence may also remain an unexplained feature, indeed lead to the first presentation, of the condition. In the days when it used to be commonly seen, catatonic excitement (when the patient had roused himself or was roused from stupor) used to be a particularly frightening phenomenon and hard to control. Among states of psychotic violence one may also class the condition of delirium or acute confusional states in which lashing out on the part of the patient is not uncommonly seen.

Affective disorder

The affective disorders may also lead to violence. Depressive illness, contrary to popular belief, is not all about slowed down physical and mental functions. There is an appreciable risk of violence in this condition, most often directed against the self as in suicidal behaviour, but other aggressive, even homicidal, features are not unknown. One particular form of violence associated with depressive illness is murder followed by suicide, cases occasionally featured in the media, when a depressed individual kills one or more persons, usually those who have had an intimate relationship with him, before turning on himself, perhaps by using the same weapon. These tragedies are not uncommon especially where the father has been in dispute with the mother over their children who are then killed by the father before he kills himself. It is, of course, by no means the case that depression – in the form of illness – has been suffered in all these instances and there are, in addition, numerous other contributory factors usually involved, but the features of an affective illness are not uncommonly reported in such individuals before the act.

Systemic disorder

Systemic disorder is a possible cause of violent behaviour. Head injury, in particular where it involves personality change, as in the case of *Meah* discussed previously, could be a potent cause of such aggression. Brain tumours may present themselves with aggressive conduct. Epilepsy – especially in the post-fit state – is another cause, and what used to be called 'postepileptic furore' used to match catatonic excitement in its scope for and degree of violence. A well-known physical state involved with violent and other uncharacteristic bouts of behaviour involves the hypoglycaemic state which follows overcorrected diabetes mellitus, usually after the patient has taken his insulin or oral medication but has then failed to keep up his blood sugar levels by eating sufficiently or at regular intervals.

Personality disorder

By far the most common psychiatric condition associated with violent behaviour is personality disorder including its most severe form called psychopathy. Aggression in these individuals is commonly attributed to poor impulse control and lack of restraint though it has to be said their lack of remorse or feelings of guilt may also contribute by means of the absence of personal or social 'brakes' which are so vital for harmonious life in any community. Personality disorder is also commonly associated with the abuse of alcohol and illicit substances though an underlying psychiatric disorder is not required for these substances to act as instruments of violence. Alcohol is widely known to precipitate violence, though sophisticated analysts of the phenomenon accept that there are crucial personal, social and cultural factors also influencing the behaviour when alcohol fuels violence. The disinhibiting effects of alcohol often require some other factor such as the comforting presence of a like-minded mob before appreciable violence is precipitated. The rampaging behaviour of football hooligans is due to both drink and the mob influence. A clear distinction has to be drawn in such cases between public violence and private violence involving individuals who might have been caught up in acts involving the former. Many public exponents of such violence may be peaceable individuals in private. A 35-year-old father, a notorious football hooligan with many convictions and 'away match' bans, wished to have contact with his young child. The public violence he had indulged in had been undertaken under the influence of alcohol and at other times he had also abused cannabis among other illicit substances. Yet, there was no evidence of any violence on his part in private, especially against the child or any other children or, indeed, other individuals. Other cultural factors may also be found operating. In some ethnic minority populations there is perceived to be a greater degree of violence in association with mental disorder. Black patients in high-security psychiatric hospitals are overrepresented eightfold. Unmet needs are more common among black than white patients in these hospitals. Higher prevalence rates of mental illness, particularly schizophrenia, have been found for black Caribbean patients than for white patients. Higher rates of compulsory admission have also been reported and also higher rates of contact with the police and forensic services and with intensive care facilities.

Drugs

Along with alcohol – a lawful and freely available substance – one must consider the possible role of prescribed drugs in the precipitation of violence. We have already referred to the possibility that the newer antidepressant drugs, the SSRI agents such as fluoxetine (Prozac), could precipitate violence in some predisposed individuals. Diazepam (Valium) is widely known to be and is taken as a sedative and anxiolytic drug. Yet, it could paradoxically release aggression and violence as happened on the facts of *R v Hardie* [1984] 3 All ER 848. The appellant's relationship with his girlfriend had broken down. He became upset and consumed several tablets of Valium which, in fact, had been prescribed for his girlfriend for use as a sedative. Under the influence of this drug he started a fire. On a charge of arson he submitted he had had no mens rea. The trial judge refused him on the ground of voluntary self-administration of the drug. The Court of Appeal allowed his appeal on the grounds of misdirection to the jury, noting that Valium is a drug 'wholly different in kind from drugs which are liable to cause unpredictability or aggressiveness'. This paradoxical disinhibiting effect is, of course, a cause of violence due to alcohol or any other normally sedative or anxiety-relieving agent. In these cases a close study needs to be made of the individual propensities of the patient concerned and the manner in which he has behaved on previous occasions when he has been under the influence of these drugs.

Similar considerations apply to cannabis, usually also taken for its sedative or calming properties but which, in some individuals and in large quantities, is capable of precipitating violence or aggravating aggressive conduct. That cannabis is not entirely innocuous as previously believed – and the focus of campaigners demanding its decriminalisation – is now accepted for there appears to be a significant minority of individuals with a predisposition who may be turned towards violence – and also into suffering psychotic conditions – by the consumption of this drug. The position with the amphetamines, cocaine and many other illicit substances is much clearer for violence is to be expected in certain cases following their use. These stimulant drugs cause an apparent increase in energy along with surging self-confidence and self-esteem which could spill over very easily into aggression especially in the atmosphere and circumstances in which these drugs are usually taken. In the course of illicit use the purity of these substances can also by no means be guaranteed and, in those circumstances, there is a wholly new dimension to be considered – for the contaminants themselves may be capable of causing aggressive behaviour. Paradoxically, on occasions when there are no contaminants and the drug is taken in pure form, there could also be aggressive behaviour on account of the unwonted effects of the pure substance. It is easy now to see how the analysis of violence attributable to these drugs and their impact on different individuals is a subject fraught with complexity and uncertainty. While the general principles are clear enough it cannot usually be said with any great conviction, as far as any individual is concerned, that any drug or group of drugs, by their actions alone, will cause particular effects or could have been responsible for specific past behaviours.

13.5 VIOLENCE UNASSOCIATED WITH MENTAL DISORDER

When mental disorder is not part of the picture, the analysis of violent behaviour becomes even more difficult. One searches for any available rules that can be applied in these circumstances. Of all the available rules there is one of especial value that has survived the test of time when it comes to predicting the risk of future violent conduct; and that rule involves a history of previous violent conduct which is a strong predictor of future violence. This behaviour has been tested in relation to previous history of offending. One study showed that 14 per cent of those with a previous conviction for violence, 40 per cent of those with two previous convictions, 44 per cent of those with three previous convictions and 55 per cent of those with four previous convictions were likely to have a further conviction for violence. Overall, violence is also still commoner in men than in women, although it is said that teenage and adolescent girls are catching up with their male peers in that age group. A man who has behaved violently on one occasion is more likely to behave in such a way on a future occasion than one who has no history of violent behaviour. That is a general truth which is subject to qualification. As we have seen with the football hooligan whose case was mentioned previously, violent behaviour can be situation-specific. The hooligan can be predicted to behave violently at football matches in the future, especially when he is under the influence of alcohol and illicit substances and when he is surrounded by like-minded supporters. But it is by no means certain he could be expected to behave violently in other circumstances. In fact, there was little evidence this particular individual behaved aggressively elsewhere; a point made in childcare proceedings in his favour where he had applied to have supervised contact with his young daughter. This illustrates a key point – the precise circumstances of previous episodes of violence need to be studied as well as the situation for which risk is being assessed. The facts required for this analysis include, among other detail, the identity of previous victims, their gender, the particular circumstances (eg whether the individual and victim were previously acquainted and, if so, at what level of intimacy), the role played by alcohol and/or illicit and prescribed drugs and the outcome of the violence including any convictions and the penalties that came to be applied. These are the objective facts. A subjective account should also be obtained from the individual who is being assessed. This is both fair to him and may also help to correct any disputed facts but it may also indicate the attitude he has towards violent behaviour in general and the previous victims in particular. A lack of remorse or regret is taken to be a reliable indicator of future violence and any attitude that is specific (eg hostility to a spouse or partner) or more general (eg against women) is often a dangerous sign.

The role of alcohol and illicit substances has already been touched upon. A rule can be given at a fairly low level of generality that future indulgence in these substances will probably lead to a repetition of acts of violent behaviour but the facts must still be analysed with care for even substance-induced violence can be situation-specific (eg domestic violence).

Violent behaviour, if one is to believe what psychologists and anthropologists say, should be commonplace but it is, in fact, an uncommon phenomenon in most civilised societies, though the levels may not be any less worrying for that. Man is supposed to be an aggressive animal. He would not have succeeded in evolutionary terms if he had not been assertive and ruthless in his dealings with the environment. In fact, social and cultural rules that have been developed and are inculcated in children from a young age may be seen to be attempts designed to curtail this aggression so as to enable life to go on in tolerable tranquillity among members of a social community. This restraint is meant to apply to all members who are expected to curb their aggressive thoughts and impulses. These are surprisingly common to experience, and are found in the most unlikely of individuals, but are relatively uncommonly acted upon. It follows that anything that interferes with normal impulse control in respect of aggression will conduce to violence. Poor impulse control is a feature of personality disorder and psychopathy, and it is the usual finding in clinical psychiatric practice that a crucial element in future risk assessment is an evaluation of the individual's personality. Impulse control is also associated with the expression of anger and reactions to stressful and provoking stimuli. Anger is well recognised to be a source of violence and anger management is the approach usually suggested to deal with excessive and inappropriate anger. Anger management deals with the problem at the behavioural level and a close analysis is still required of factors such as personality and the misuse of alcohol and illicit substances.

Another factor often suggested to function as a protective influence against habitual violent behaviour is the degree of socialisation achieved by individuals. This phenomenon is related to the successful incorporation of social rules. The thinking here is that a person who has been properly integrated into the requirements of society, and in whom the rules of society have been embedded into those centres of the brain which govern socially appropriate behaviour by suppressing impulses and emotions, achieves proper social integration. Such individuals are less likely to resort to violence either because they can successfully master their impulses or they have otherwise learned to take the co-operative and lawful route to achieving their needs and desires and do not have to resort to the 'coerced transactions' (as the economic philosophers characterise robbery) when individuals have failed to use the marketplace for transactions but have turned instead to force to achieve their ends. The lesson to be learned for purposes of risk assessment is that a poorly socialised individual may pose a higher risk of future violence than one who is normally socialised and in whom a solitary act of aggression may be attributed to aberrant behaviour on one occasion. Social isolation with poor social networks, a lonely existence and solitary interests are believed to indicate the former propensity.

Violence, of course, occurs against persons or property. The interaction between assailant and his victim has attracted enormous interest in recent years. At one level, it could be said there is always some interaction, however minimal in degree, between attacker and victim even when a victim might only have found himself, as is said, in the 'wrong place at the wrong time'. We are here, however, concerned with more substantial levels of contact and in the relationship that has existed between attacker and victim as that is the relevant interest in family and child practice. The features present in the victim must also be studied, wherever possible, with care. The age of the victim is of importance for while most assailants and their victims are young men, the selective and purposeful targeting of victims of a certain age, for example, at the extremes of age, the elderly and the very young, may give a clue as to the prospects for future violent conduct. The gender of the victim is an obvious consideration. The personality of the victim, whether it also underlies some mental disorder, may be as important to take account of as that of the assailant. One must seek to find out, especially in situations where recurrent violence has taken place, whether the victim himself is aggressive, unduly anxious or overly dependent on a potential assailant, for these features are often associated with individuals who tend to become victims, especially in the domestic context. We shall consider some of the more specific features of this condition when we later take up domestic violence but the attitude of the victim is always important to evaluate. If recurrent violence has taken place, involving one set of assailant and victim, has the victim complained and supported previous proceedings? If not, why not? It is an obvious inference that if an assailant knows he can get away with violence he will be more prone to violence or aggressive conduct, for even the most impulsive of persons usually has some idea of self-preservation and normally has little wish to entangle himself unnecessarily with the criminal law. The role of mental disorder and the misuse of alcohol and illicit substances in the victim may also be material considerations. It follows that in the ideal situation the assailant and any identifiable future victim should both be assessed although the absence of resources (and possibly consent) do not usually permit this endeavour.

13.6 SOME CONCLUSIONS FROM FORENSIC PSYCHIATRY

Studies in forensic psychiatric practice may be usefully summarised in terms of risk factors influencing reoffending.

1. The mental disorder itself and its lack of recognition by professionals. In a study at the Rampton Hospital of those mentally ill patients who had committed homicide it was found that all these patients had been mentally disordered at the time of committing the offence but only some 25 per cent of them were receiving treatment. Premature discharge from hospital adds to the risk. Repetition of violent acts may be determined by the situation in which a mentally disordered offender finds himself in and the emotional demands that are made on him. It is vital before discharge from hospital to ensure that the offender's psychological resources are sufficient to cope with the vagaries of life in the community.

2. The tendency to engage in impulsive anti-social acts on little or no provocation is another pointer towards increased risk. If aggressive anti-social tendencies co-exist with mental illness or other disorder the risk may increase.

3. The nature of the index offence may give clues as to future risk especially if the victim had been specifically targeted, for example, as being a member of a particular age group (eg the elderly or children) *or of a particular gender*. This may indicate a habitual pattern of serious anti-social behaviour. Random killings by individuals suffering from schizophrenia or other psychotic disorders involving strangers may indicate continuing risk to the public. Incidents prior to the index offence, which if they had not involved prosecution might not have revealed the full facts, could be important. In the notorious *Zito* case, Mr Jonathan Zito had been stabbed to death at a London Underground station by Christopher Clunis who had a history of paranoid schizophrenia and of violence. It transpired at the official inquiry into this case that Clunis had stabbed a fellow resident in a hostel some 5 months before his attack on Mr Zito but had not been prosecuted, a matter which came to be criticised.

4. The uncertainty of the clinical prognosis, especially where there are multiple diagnoses, for example, mental illness with learning disabilities, mental illness associated with a personality disorder, may increase the risk or, at any rate, make it even less predictable.

5. Persisting lack of remorse or continuing denial in the face of overwhelming evidence may be a sign of high risk. This will be enhanced if the clinical condition associated with previous violence – persecutory symptoms, morbid jealousy – persist. A declared intention of future violence in the midst of an unsettled mental state is obviously of considerable concern.

6. The continuing presence of sadistic fantasies even after incarceration and attempts at treatment may be indicative of high risk of reoffending.

7. A history of misuse of alcohol and/or illicit substances, even if the behaviour is in abeyance on incarceration, may be a sign of risk if it is believed the patient may resume his patterns of substance abuse, especially on release from custody.

8. A paradoxical situation involves the offender, often a psychopath, who learns to work the system, appears to be most amenable and succeeds in fooling the professionals evaluating his progress. He may pose a serious risk if only because it is never wholly possible properly to assess future risk to be posed in the community by an individual who is being evaluated in an artificial situation of containment. Good behaviour in an institution does not necessarily mean it will be translated to conditions in the world outside.

While the assessment of future risk of violence remains essentially a clinical procedure at present, a rating scale has been put forward in the form of HCR-20 Violence Risk Assessment Scheme and may come to find more widespread acceptance in the future. This instrument contains 20 items organised around three scales: historical data (10 items), clinical evidence (five items) and risk (five items). The 10 historical items include history of violence, age at first violence, relationship history, employment history, history of substance misuse, previous mental illness, psychopathy, early maladjustment, personality disorder and previous conditional release failure. The five clinical evidence items include lack of insight, negative attitudes, symptomatology, lack of behavioural stability and lack of treatability. The five risk items are concerned with forecasting the patient's future social, living and treatment circumstances, as well as anticipating the patient's reactions to those conditions. This includes lack of plan feasibility, access to destabilisers, lack of support, future non-compliance and stress.

13.7 DOMESTIC VIOLENCE

Domestic violence belongs to a special category of aggressive behaviour and may be deemed to be a subspecies. Many of the points already made in regard to violence in general are applicable when studying this special case from a psychiatric point of view. However, some preliminary points may be made in respect of this issue. First, while all criminal statistics are far from reliable, domestic violence is probably in a league of its own for unreliability. We have to resort to anecdotal evidence and personal professional experience when writing about this issue but it seems true to say domestic violence is far from uncommon. It is found in the most unlikely of situations, no age and neither sex is preferentially favoured among victims, and it cuts across every social class and every community. Social and, especially, cultural factors play a decisive role in determining the level of domestic violence that is found within any given community. There are some communities now established in Britain where cultural practices inform behaviour that leads to domestic violence which, in fact, may not even be recognised as such. Much bewilderment and even offence may be caused to these individuals by investigating such behaviour which, in some communities, may be seen as the norm. Chastising one's wife or child (the wife also joining in the latter activity) is time-honoured and sanctioned by long-standing cultural practice in some communities. It is one of the challenges faced by the family and child practitioner to deal with such behaviour which comes into conflict with the much more enlightened attitudes which now find reflection in English law. One of the insights to be gained from studying practices which are habitual in migrant communities is that they also offer an understanding of behaviour which may be found in native subcultures, for example, those involving persistent criminal activity especially involving gangs associated with the use also of illicit substances where the constituent populations of those marginal communities may be entirely of native origins. It is a conclusion one draws from studying domestic violence, at any rate from the psychiatric point of view, that aggressive behaviour may stem not only from the actions of individuals but also as a reflection of the dynamics of a particular family or community.

Whether special cultural factors are present or not, one still needs to study the mental states of the members of the family who are involved as victims of violence. Where illness or disorder is present (depressive illness, an anxiety state, perhaps dementia in spouse or partner, or some behavioural disorder involving a child) the provoking factors for violence may be clear enough. But often there may not be overt mental disorder present but rather the presence of personality difficulties or defects in the spouse or partner which tends to make him a readier victim than would have been the case if such an individual had possessed a normal, well-adjusted personality. The remarks made concerning the aggressive, anxious or dependent individuals who may become victims of repeated violence apply *a fortiori* to cases of conflict in the domestic situation. There is also apparent collusion on the part of the victim with the acts of violence being perpetrated against him, who conceals or denies these acts and also shows ambivalent behaviour where criminal proceedings are concerned, making and withdrawing complaints and first supporting and then drawing back from prosecutions. A full assessment of incidents of domestic violence involves the examination of both parties. There are obviously other factors besides those of personal emotions operating in families – financial difficulties, debt, housing problems and physical factors such as disability and age. An individual who is trapped within a domestic setting for whatever reason is at greater risk of continuing violence – physical as well as emotional – than one who has the independence of spirit and body and the means to assert himself and, where necessary, effect an escape. There is high risk of repeated violence in a domestic setting and it has been estimated that there are at least two murders each week involving spouses or partners. Risk involves both parties to different degrees for, in a minority of cases, the abused partner, in a case of the worm turning, may kill the abusing partner. This is the extreme case. Far commoner is the involvement of both parties in routine acts of violence committed on one another. The term 'battered wives' syndrome' has sometimes been applied to the mental state a chronically abused spouse or partner suffers as a result of repeated beatings. The term is obviously a misnomer, for a growing number of husbands or male partners are also found to be victims. Further, it is not as yet a recognised psychiatric syndrome and there must be doubt if a special category is needed for violence occurring in a domestic context as opposed to non-domestic situations. Where murder comes to be charged it could be argued in most instances that the facts could satisfy the partial defences of diminished responsibility or provocation, the domestic circumstances merely forming the backdrop to these partial defences.

Mental disorder in the perpetration of domestic violence is relatively uncommon though recognised psychiatric illnesses such as schizophrenia, depressive or bipolar illness may predispose to violence, especially in the acute phase of psychotic illness. Morbid jealousy is known to produce risk of battery suffered by spouse or partner. By far the most common type of mental disorder involved in these cases is personality disorder where the spouse or partner suffering from this condition acts out his aggressive tendencies in the face of domestic stresses or following no provocation at all. Mental disorder, as said, may also be exhibited by the victim when it takes on a similar presentation. In the absence of obvious mental disorder on the part of the assaulting partner or spouse, one is reduced to looking at a situation of bullying translated to the domestic context, cultural or subcultural factors, and any previous experience the perpetrator has been exposed to, especially childhood physical abuse. Many abused spouses or partners show anxiety (avoidant) or dependent personalities. The inability to escape – for whatever reason, be it emotional or financial – may be a factor in exposing such an individual to further violence. Other factors noted in the literature include immaturity, lack of adaptability and emotional conflict suffered by the abusing spouse or partner. Some victims, by repeatedly returning to situations of violence, are believed to have masochistic tendencies along with feelings of being needed. Aggression may also be provoked when the assailant spouse or partner finds himself unable to satisfy the needs of a spouse or partner for excessive dependence on the other. Some men have sadistic tendencies with sexual connotations in that they do not feel fully potent unless they can establish their authority over a helpless female, in the absence of which they cannot give or receive affection in a manner which is emotionally satisfying to them. There is also an element of learned behaviour which contributes to situations of domestic violence. Some individuals have learned in childhood that violence had helped them to achieve their desires and this tendency to aggression might have been reinforced by parental example. This learned violence is carried over into their own relationships when domination is sought to be created over their spouse or partner. Cultural constraints such as the stigma attaching to the separating party, especially when female, in some communities also exposes the victim to recurrent acts of violence. In many cases one is left musing upon that notorious phrase – 'he or she does it because he or she can' – when trying to explain why a violent spouse or partner appears to be getting away with repeated acts of violence. Single mothers appear in general to make up a vulnerable group. They are significantly more likely to have psychiatric disorders and poor mental health outcomes, particularly anxiety states and substance misuse. Lone mothers are also more likely to have experienced physical and sexual violence and these severe traumatic experiences are more strongly associated with the presence of psychiatric disorders than either single parent status or other sociodemographic characteristics.

The role alcohol and illicit drugs play in the victim may also be a crucial element in situations of continuing violence. If both spouses or partners engage in the misuse of alcohol or illicit substances, they may together also inhabit a subculture from which neither feels free to withdraw. One partner may well be dependent on the other for the supply of substances, and the craving associated with the need for alcohol or illicit drugs may make them more literally dependent on the other to ease them out of a withdrawal state. There are other explanations proffered for why spouses or partners – usually women victims but an increasing number of men caught up in these situations as well – continue to accept violence and abuse but most of these (eg a perverse desire to improve or 'cure' a violent partner) are beyond the scope of ordinary clinical observation and therefore this book.

An individual's personality is formed in the context of his childhood spent within his family and it is well accepted (though not yet provable in any quantifiable fashion) that formative experiences are vital to the shaping of any personality. What could be positive experiences and which are negative are not all known by any means but there is sufficient evidence that childhood experiences of abuse – physical, emotional or sexual – do come to play an important part in the psychological make-up of the adult individual and if such adverse experiences do influence the finished personality in relevant ways the stage may be set for the behaviours determined by such a personality to make an impact on those with whom such an individual comes to have relationships with in adult life. Where children are concerned, such difficulties involving the personality may be transmitted to yet another generation. The saying that the abused become abusers has some truth where, at least, physical violence is concerned.

13.8 DOMESTIC VIOLENCE INVOLVING CHILDREN

The physical abuse of children, which of course involves violence, has been the subject of several studies. What kind of parent is likely to abuse children in this fashion has been subject to research. Some studies have shown that in cases of physical abuse the parents need not belong exclusively to any particular social class, level of educational attainment or occupational group but are to be found everywhere in the community. But other studies have found an association between physical abuse of children and deprived areas which held parents belonging to lower socioeconomic classes and also a higher number of mothers who were of less than average intelligence. These parents also frequently showed personality disorders which involved high levels of emotional conflict and anxiety along with difficulty tolerating frustration and controlling impulsive behaviour. Most, though by no means all, had had a history of unsatisfactory parenting themselves and poor childhood experiences. These individuals were emotionally deprived, felt rejected and their need for a dependent relationship frustrated. Their self-esteem, confidence and capacity for trust were correspondingly low. Many had been punished excessively as children and themselves subjected to physical abuse and they, in turn, tended to repeat the styles of parenting and child control to which they themselves had been subjected. They lacked adequate knowledge of the practicalities involved in childcare and failed also to understand or accept the needs and dependence of immature children.

One study has suggested there may be three styles of family relationships associated with the physical abuse of children.

1. The severely hostile, aggressive parent who appeared to suffer almost continual anger, had uncontrolled outbursts of temper and violence at any irritation or frustration, including those provoked by the child.

2. The passive, inadequate parent who looked desperately for opportunities to be dependent, and competed with the children for the attention and support of the spouse or partner. These parents were highly anxious and frequently became depressed. They were capable of neglect as well as abuse of the child.

3. The rigid, compulsively controlled and orderly parent, who lacked warmth and tended to reject the child. Their own need for success and order made it difficult for them to accept the demands and mess created by the child who was expected to show excellence in behaviour and development to assuage the parents' doubts and fears about their parental ability.

13.9 SEXUAL VIOLENCE

This subject, too, may be regarded as another subspecies of general violence, though, of course, some special factors also apply. The subject is vast and controversial and the observations made here are only those which have some relevance to family and child practice. Marital rape or quasi-marital rape is now to be treated like any other act of rape or sexual assault although evidential problems concerning consent may present difficulties above the usual when trying to get a conviction. Domestic sexual violence is usually present in the context of circumstances where non-sexual violence also takes place. Mental disorder is as uncommon as in any other area of domestic violence although periodic sexual violence against spouse or partner may be a characteristic of manic illness which may feature an increase in levels of libido, energy and aggression. Far more likely are personality factors (involving both parties) and a tendency to bully and intimidate a vulnerable partner. Morbid jealousy, either as a symptom of another psychotic illness or as a paranoid disorder in its own right, may be associated with sexual violence against an allegedly unfaithful spouse or partner along with non-sexual violence. The difference usually observable between domestic and non-domestic sexual violence is that in the latter case personality problems associated with inadequacy and anti-social tendencies may be commoner than in cases involving domestic sexual violence. This is only a general observation but it does appear that persons engaging in domestic sexual violence do so because, in the words of George Bernard Shaw's dictum on marriage, 'there is a maximum of temptation with a maximum of opportunity'. Many individuals, especially men, involved in domestic sexual violence appear to be only too conscious of their rights and, as may readily be appreciated, cultural forces applying in some communities may also especially endow the husband or male partner with rights he feels at liberty to enforce irrespective of the consent of the other party.

13.10 SEXUAL VIOLENCE AGAINST CHILDREN

A distinction needs to be drawn between sexual activity, which is by definition unlawful, carried on with children in a public setting, as opposed to such activities in a domestic atmosphere. Family and child law practitioners are naturally concerned with cases involving the latter type, but it is in general true to say that mental pathology is more likely to be found in those cases involving children in a public setting rather than in a domestic context. Formal illness is not common although any form of disinhibition – which tends to loosen social restraints – may also affect sexual conduct. Thus, with the psychoses, in cases of dementia or head injury, inappropriate sexual activity with children may occur. In fact, it is not unknown for dementia, whether senile or pre-senile, to present with uncharacteristic behaviour which may include sexual misconduct with children. Alcohol and illicit substances also have a tendency to disinhibit normal, socially approved behaviour. Far more likely is a personality problem on the part of the perpetrator which may make normal sexual relationships difficult to achieve. Inadequacy of personality is notoriously common. Paedophilia itself is classified (F 65.4 – ICD-10) as a disorder of sexual preference. In one US study involving child sex offenders it was seen that those who committed new sex offences had previously committed more sex offences, had been admitted to correctional institutions more frequently, were more likely to have been diagnosed as being personality disordered, were more likely to be single and had shown more inappropriate sexual preferences on initial assessment than those who did not reoffend. Behavioural treatment did not seem to affect the rates of recidivism.

Domestic sexual violence against children takes on a different colouring. Mental disorder is still uncommon where parents are concerned as perpetrators although it may exist among acquaintances outside the family committing the abuse. More usually there is a dysfunctional relationship within the family, commonly involving the parents, and the children could be sucked into this maelstrom. There is also the case where the parents are feckless and are also into the abuse of alcohol and illicit substances when the general air of neglect pervading the household is conducive also to sexual abuse of the children. Personality problems are not uncommon and add to the inadequacy most often observed in the dependent personality who (most often the wife or female partner) attracts and sustains the type of partner who may proceed to the abuse of children, hers or perhaps even theirs. It is notorious in the nether world of paedophiliacs that certain men (and some women) are known to prey on vulnerable individuals so as to gain access to their children. The parent with a dependent or inadequate personality may through psychological weakness brought about by their need to be cared for by someone at all costs, however unsatisfactory such an individual may be, sometimes perhaps through the incapacity brought about through misuse of alcohol or illicit substances, may leave the child unprotected. In many cases incidents of domestic sexual abuse are traceable to a poor relationship between the parents and the seeking of revenge against spouse or partner, a tendency to bullying and a failure to control impulses, aggravated on occasion by alcohol and illicit substances in the context also of a rather disordered and structureless life.

A 35-year-old man with a long history of personality inadequacy had been convicted of a sexual assault on his 5-year-old niece. He fully accepted his guilt and did not dispute the facts, merely proffering the explanation that he 'loved' the child. He had poor adjustment generally and was virtually incapable of forming normal adult relationships. In time he fathered a child. This child came to make equivocal complaint of possible sexual interference. The man strongly denied he had been responsible in any way for inappropriate behaviour with the child. His seriously inadequate and abnormal personality, however, was sufficient to put him in the high risk category of sexual offending in respect of children – for his previous behaviour could be deemed reasonably likely to recur – whether his child's allegations were proved to be true or not. Only supervised contact with the child was deemed to be appropriate.

What the long-term effects on a child suffering sexual abuse are remains to be fully established. A recent study clearly demonstrated that childhood sexual abuse is associated with increased rates of a range of mental disorders in childhood and adult life. Male victims of childhood sexual abuse seem as likely as female victims to show subsequent psychopathology. Conduct disorders are significantly more frequently found in both male and female victims of childhood sexual abuse but males have significantly higher rates than females.

APPENDICES

APPENDIX A

SPECIMEN INSTRUCTIONS

In this section we set out some brief case histories – the names are fictional but the facts are derived from real cases – and explore how instructions may be given to the psychiatric expert. One or two preliminary points need to be made. It is not uncommon for instructing solicitors to refer to a party as 'our client' rather than by name. This is unsatisfactory from the expert's point of view. He is required to be independent of the parties and have his eye on his overriding duty to the court and even minor considerations such as this should not be seen to be detracting from his detachment from the fray which, as experience in these matters informs us, is usually far from being non-adversarial. It is also the practice in medicine to dignify the patient – as the spouse, partner or parent is for purposes of a medical examination – by giving him his proper name along with the title to which he is eligible.

Case 1

Miss Mary Smith is aged 27. She lives alone and is a mother of twin children aged 3. Soon after they were born she was admitted to a psychiatric hospital suffering from post-partum depression and remained an in-patient for 3 months. The children at that time had been taken into foster care where they remained for 12 months. Miss Smith is now 6 months into another pregnancy and the Local Authority has expressed concern that she may not be able to cope with the newborn child as well as her older children if she were to fall ill again.

Specimen instructions

1. You are requested to conduct a full psychiatric examination of Miss Mary Smith.
2. Please set out Miss Smith's current psychiatric state giving, where appropriate, the diagnosis if she does suffer at present from a mental illness or mental disorder.
3. If she is at present suffering from a mental illness or mental disorder, please indicate what, if any, treatment or other management may be appropriate for the condition.
4. If treatment or other management is being recommended, please indicate how this is to be provided and what timescales should be anticipated if significant improvement is to be obtained.

5. If she is suffering at present from a mental illness or mental disorder, please indicate the prognosis for the condition, with or without any therapeutic intervention.

6. If Miss Smith is currently in good mental health, please indicate the probability of her suffering a post-partum mental disorder, given that she a previous history of such a condition.

7. As far as your expertise will allow you to do so, please give an opinion on any impairment in her parenting abilities in the event she does fall ill as she previously did.

Case 2

Mr John Brown is a 25-year-old man who is the father of a son aged 3 who lives with its mother, who is separated from Mr Brown. Mr Brown has a history of physical violence and numerous convictions against his son's mother. He is also known to abuse alcohol and illicit drugs. Mr Brown now wishes to have contact with his son whom he has not seen since a few months after its birth. The mother is adamantly opposed to any form of contact taking place.

Specimen instructions

1. Please conduct a full psychiatric examination of Mr John Brown.

2. Does Mr Brown suffer from a mental illness or mental disorder at present?

3. Please give an opinion on Mr Brown's misuse, if any, of alcohol and illicit substances.

4. If mental illness or disorder is present in Mr Brown, with or without any relation to any misuse of alcohol and illicit substances, please indicate what form of treatment may be available to him.

5. If treatment is being recommended, please indicate how Mr Brown may be able to access this and what timescales could be envisaged for this purpose.

6 If Mr Brown is suffering from any mental illness or mental disorder, with or without also an association with the misuse of alcohol and/or illicit substances, please indicate the prognosis with and without treatment taking place.

7. Please comment on any propensity for violence Mr Brown may have and to discuss the possible causes for this.

8. As far as your expertise will allow you to do so, please given an opinion on Mr Brown's ability to have safe and appropriate contact with his son and to indicate what risks could be foreseen if contact were to take place and advise, where appropriate, on how any risks could be minimised.

Case 3

Mr James Archer, aged 23, and Miss Ann Jones, aged 21, live together and have two children aged 2 and one. The Local Authority has had serious concerns about this family over a considerable period of time. There is a suspicion that both parents may be suffering from learning disabilities, that there is domestic violence involving them and also that the children may be suffering from neglect.

Specimen instructions

1. Please conduct full psychiatric examinations of Mr Archer and Miss Jones.

2. Please give an opinion on their current mental states, in particular to indicate if they are suffering from mental illness or mental disorder including learning disabilities.

3. Please give an opinion on the capacity respectively possessed by Mr Archer and/or Miss Jones to participate in litigation, to give proper instructions to their legal advisers and sensibly follow proceedings.

4. Please indicate whether any form of treatment is feasible for any mental illness or mental disorder Mr Archer and/or Miss Jones may be found to be suffering from.

5. If such treatment is recommended, please indicate how the couple may be able to access such treatment and the timescales envisaged for such treatment to produce significant improvement in any condition that one or both may be suffering from.

6. Please give an opinion on the prognosis for any mental illness or mental disorder that either one or both parents may be suffering from, with or without treatment.

7. Please comment, as far as your expertise allows you to do so, on the issue of any domestic violence involving Mr Archer and Miss Jones.

8. As far as your expertise allows you to do so, please give an opinion on how any mental illness or mental disorder that may be suffered by Mr Archer and/or Miss Jones may have an adverse impact on their ability to be safe and satisfactory parents.

Case 4

Miss Joan Simon is a 32-year-old single mother of children aged 6 and 8 who reside with her. Miss Simon suffers from a bipolar affective disorder and has had alternating episodes of mania and depression which have led to hospitalisation in the past when, on occasion, she has had to be compulsorily detained and treated. The children on these occasions of hospitalisation have been cared for by family members. Miss Simon has appeared to be free of illness for a couple of years and now insists she is completely well and will continue to take the prescribed medication. However, in recent months, the Local Authority has become concerned about the quality of care she has been giving the children and fear they are suffering neglect and may come to harm.

Specimen instructions

1. Please conduct a full psychiatric examination on Miss Simon.

2. Please give an opinion on her current psychiatric condition and state if she is suffering from any mental illness or disorder.

3. If she is suffering from any mental illness or disorder, please specify the nature of the condition and state whether or not the drugs she is currently prescribed are appropriate for the condition or not.

4. Please state, as far as you are able to, whether she is compliant with the taking of the prescribed medication and in keeping any scheduled appointments with health care professionals.

5. Is any other/further treatment feasible for Miss Simon?

6. Please give an opinion, in the event Miss Simon is found to be free of any mental illness or disorder, on the probability of mental illness or disorder recurring, given her past psychiatric history.

7. Please give a prognosis for any mental illness or disorder she may be suffering from at present or may suffer from in the foreseeable future.

8. As far as your expertise allows you to do so, please give an opinion on how Miss Simon's mental state at present may impact on her ability to offer safe and appropriate care to her children

9. Please comment on any other relevant psychiatric issue.

Case 5

Mr Peter Voler, aged 33, has a previous conviction for a sexual assault on his 5-year-old niece. He is now the father of a female child aged 3 who has made vague allegations of sexual interference against Mr Voler. Mr Voler and the mother of the child have separated since the time of the allegations. Mr Voler strongly denies these accusations but has had no contact with the child who resides with her mother. Mr Voler has applied to have contact with the child.

Specimen instructions

1. Please conduct a full psychiatric assessment of Mr Voler.

2. Please state whether Mr Voler is suffering from any mental illness or disorder at present.

3. If he is suffering from any mental illness or disorder, please indicate if the condition may be susceptible to any form of treatment and, if so, please state how he may find access to such treatment and the timescales that may be envisaged before significant improvement may be seen in his condition.

4. Please give a prognosis for any mental illness or disorder he may be suffering from, with or without any treatment being undertaken by him.

5. Please explore with Mr Voler the circumstances of his previous conviction and give an opinion on what the implications may be for his future behaviour in this respect.

6. As far as your expertise permits you to do so, please indicate what, if any, risk may be posed by Mr Voler if he were to have contact with his daughter and how any such risk may be reduced.

7. Please comment on any other matter of psychiatric relevance.

Case 6

Miss Jane Collins, aged 40, is a single mother who has had numerous episodes of a psychotic illness. She is the mother of two children aged 6 and 4. Recently the Local Authority has expressed concern that after each bout of illness Miss Collins appears to become less capable of looking after her children and now suspect the children may be at risk of neglect or abuse. Miss Collins insists that she is perfectly capable of caring for her children, there is nothing the matter with her (she attributes her previous bouts of illness to stress) and that she needs no help of any kind.

Specimen instructions

1. Please conduct a full psychiatric examination of Miss Collins.

2. Please state whether at present she appears to be suffering from any mental illness or disorder.

3. If she does suffer from a mental illness or disorder, please state its nature and whether it is susceptible to any form of treatment.

4. Please indicate how Miss Collins may be able to access the necessary treatment and the timescales that may be envisaged before significant improvement becomes apparent.

5. Please give a prognosis for any mental illness or disorder that Miss Collins may be suffering from and, given the past psychiatric history, please indicate the probability of any recurrence of illness or disorder.

6. Please give an opinion as to the capacity possessed by Miss Collins to participate in litigation, to give proper instructions to her legal advisers and sensibly to follow proceedings.

7. As far as your expertise allows you to do so, please state what adverse impact any mental illness or disorder Miss Collins may be suffering from could have on the safe and appropriate care of her children.

8. Please comment on any other matter of psychiatric relevance.

APPENDIX B

HANDBOOK OF BEST PRACTICE IN CHILDREN ACT CASES

****

SECTION 5 – EXPERTS AND THE COURTS

Introduction

60 The guidance in this section applies equally to public and private law cases in which experts are instructed.

61 It is of critical importance to distinguish the respective functions of expert and judge.

(*a*) The expert forms an assessment, and expresses an opinion within the area of his expertise. This may include an opinion on the issues in the case, but the judge decides particular issues in individual cases.

(*b*) It is not for the judge to become involved in medical controversy, except in the rare case where such controversy is an issue in the case.

62 The court depends on the skill, knowledge, and above all, the professional and intellectual integrity of the expert witness.

Leave to instruct experts

The role of the instructing parties

63 Applications for leave to instruct experts should be considered by each party at the earliest possible stage of the proceedings in order to avoid serial applications by different parties seeking to counter opinions from experts which do not support their case. Such applications are likely to be refused – see *H v Cambridgeshire County Council* [1997] 1 FCR 569.

64 Advocates who seek such leave have a positive duty to place all relevant information before the court at the earliest opportunity. Applications are unlikely to succeed unless they specify:

(*a*) the category of expert evidence sought to be adduced;

(*b*) the name of the expert;

(*c*) his availability for reporting, meeting with other experts and attendance at court;

(*d*) the relevance of the expert evidence to the issues in the case;

(*e*) whether evidence can properly be obtained by both parties jointly instructing one expert; and

(*f*) whether expert evidence may properly be adduced by one party only, eg the guardian ad litem.

The role of the court

65 The court has a positive duty to enquire into the information provided by the party or parties seeking leave to instruct an expert.

66 The court should never make a generalised order for leave to disclose papers to an expert. The order should specify:

(*a*) the area of expertise;

(*b*) the issues to be addressed;

(*c*) the identity of the expert;

(*d*) the date by which the letter of instruction is to be sent;

(*e*) the documents to be released to the expert;

(*f*) the date for filing the expert's report with the court;

(*g*) a provision for experts of like discipline to communicate (as discussed below) to agree facts and define issues, together with responsibility for fixing the agenda and chairing the meeting; and

(*h*) the availability of the expert to give oral evidence, if required.

67 Expert reports based solely upon leave to disclose documents in a "paper exercise" are rarely as persuasive as those reports based on interviews and assessment as well as the documentation. *Re C (Expert Evidence: Disclosure Practice)* [1995] 1 FLR 204 provides guidance on experts, in contested cases, meeting in advance of the hearing. It should be a condition of appointment of any expert that he should be required to hold discussions with other experts instructed in the same field of expertise, in advance of the hearing, in order to identify areas of agreement and dispute, which should be incorporated into a schedule for the court. Such discussion should be chaired by a co-ordinator, such as the guardian ad litem if there is consent so to act. In advance of the meeting, the co-ordinator should prepare and circulate to all experts a schedule of issues and questions to be addressed at the meeting. The schedule should be prepared in co-operation with all parties, so that all relevant matters are considered by the experts.

68 Problems may arise when an expert's conclusion is unfavourable to the instructing party's case. The court may need to give consideration as to how that expert's evidence is to be adduced.

Letters of instruction and provision of information to experts

69 The letter of instruction should:

(*a*) define the context in which the opinion is sought;

(*b*) set out specific questions for the expert to address;

(*c*) identify any relevant issues of fact to enable each expert to give an opinion on each set of competing issues;

(*d*) specify any examinations to be permitted;

(*e*) list the documents to be sent to the expert, which should be presented in a sorted bundle and include an agreed chronology and background history; and

(*f*) require, as a condition of appointment, that the expert must, in advance of the hearing, hold discussions with other experts appointed in the same field of expertise, and produce a statement of agreement and disagreement on the issues by a specified date.

70 Always disclose the letter of instruction to the other parties, and invite them to contribute to defining the appropriate issues, relevant documentation, history, and questions to be addressed. Include the resulting letter in the bundle of documents for use in court.

71 Doctors who have clinical experience of a child before the commencement of proceedings should have all clinical material made available for inspection by the court and other experts, eg medical notes, hospital records, x-rays, photographs, and correspondence.

72 It is the instructing solicitor's duty to ensure that an expert who is to give oral evidence is kept up to date with relevant developments in the case.

73 It is the duty of the advocate calling an expert to ensure that the witness, in advance of giving oral evidence, has seen all fresh relevant material, and is aware of new developments.

Duties of experts

74 The role of the expert is to provide independent assistance to the court by way of objective, unbiased opinion, in relation to matters within his expertise. Expert evidence presented to the court must be, and be seen to be, the independent product of the expert, uninfluenced by the instructing party.

75 Acceptance of instructions imposes an obligation to:

(*a*) comply with the court's timetable; and

(*b*) notify the instructing solicitors promptly if there is any risk that the timetable cannot be adhered to.

76 Experts should not hesitate to seek further information and documentation when this is required. Such requests should form part of the court bundle.

77 In his report, an expert should:

(*a*) state the facts or assumptions on which his opinion is based, and not omit to consider material facts which detract from his concluded opinion;

(*b*) make it clear when a particular aspect of the case is outside his expertise;

(*c*) indicate, if appropriate, that his opinion is not properly researched because of insufficient data, and is therefore provisional; and

(*d*) inform the other parties, and, when appropriate, the court if at any time he changes his opinion on a material matter.

78 If an opinion is based, wholly or in part, on research conducted by others, the expert must:

(*a*) set this out clearly in the report;

(*b*) identify the research relied on;

(*c*) state its relevance to the points at issue; and

(*d*) be prepared to justify the opinions expressed.

79 It is unacceptable for any expert in a child case, whose evidence is relevant to the outcome, to give evidence without having read, in advance, the report of the guardian ad litem.

Assisting the experts

80 Legal advisers for the parties should co-operate, at an early stage in the preparation for trial, to ensure availability of the experts to give evidence in a logical sequence.

81 It is helpful to timetable experts, in a difficult case, to give evidence one after another, so that each can listen to the evidence of other experts, and comment on that evidence.

82 Child proceedings are non-adversarial, and it is not necessary that witnesses are called in conventional order.

83 Where it becomes clear that an expert's opinion is uncontentious, and that the expert will not be required to attend court, he must be notified at the

earliest opportunity. Whenever attendance at court is necessary, the court must always try to accommodate the expert by interposing the evidence at a given time.

84 In order that all relevant matters are fully considered at the appropriate time in advance of the hearing, it is essential that advocates who will appear at the hearing are involved at the earliest stage in order to consider how the case should be prepared and progressed.

The Expert Witness Group

85 The Expert Witness Group has been active in developing an "Expert Witness Pack", which it hopes to have published in the autumn of 1997. The pack, which will be available for purchase and will be cited in bibliographies, etc, will include several pro formas and:

(*a*) draft letters of instruction and acceptance;

(*b*) a checklist for both solicitor and expert;

(*c*) guidelines and a model curriculum vitae for expert witnesses; and

(*d*) a model format for experts' reports.

86 Further information about the Expert Witness Group and the Expert Witness Pack may be obtained from: Dr Eileen Vizard, Consultant Child and Adolescent Psychiatrist, Camden and Islington Community Health Services NHS Trust, Simmons House Adolescent Unit, St. Luke's-Woodside Hospital, Woodside Avenue, London N10 3HU (Telephone: 0181 219 1883).

****

APPENDIX C

PROTOCOL FOR JUDICIAL CASE MANAGEMENT IN PUBLIC LAW CHILDREN ACT CASES

****

APPENDIX C: CODE OF GUIDANCE FOR EXPERT WITNESSES IN FAMILY PROCEEDINGS

Objective

The objective of this Code of Guidance is to provide the Court with early information to enable it to determine whether it is necessary and/or practicable to ask an expert to assist the Court:

- To identify, narrow and where possible agree the issues between the parties

- To provide an opinion about a question that is not within the skill and experience of the Court

- To encourage the early identification of questions that need to be answered by an expert

- To encourage disclosure of full and frank information between the parties, the Court and any expert instructed

	Action	Party and Timing
1	**The Duties of Experts**	
1.1	Overriding Duty: An expert in family proceedings has an overriding duty to the Court that takes precedence over any obligation to the person from whom he has received instructions or by whom he is paid.	
1.2	Particular Duties: Among any other duties an expert may have, an expert shall have regard to the following duties:	

Action	Party and Timing
• To assist the Court in accordance with the overriding duty	
• To provide an opinion that is independent of the party or parties instructing the expert	
• To confine an opinion to matters material to the issues between the parties and in relation only to questions that are within the expert's expertise (skill and experience). If a question is put which falls outside that expertise the expert must say so	
• In expressing an opinion take into consideration all of the material facts including any relevant factors arising from diverse cultural or religious contexts at the time the opinion is expressed, indicating the facts, literature and any other material that the expert has relied upon in forming an opinion	
• To indicate whether the opinion is provisional (or qualified, as the case may be) and the reason for the qualification, identifying what further information is required to give an opinion without qualification	
• Inform those instructing the expert without delay of any change in the opinion and the reason for the change	
2 Preparation for the CMC	Solicitor instructing the expert
2.1 Preliminary Enquiries of the Expert: Not later than 10 days before the CMC the solicitor for the party proposing to instruct the expert (or lead solicitor/solicitor for the child if the instruction proposed is joint) shall approach the expert with the following information:	10 days before the CMC
• The nature of the proceedings and the issues likely to require determination by the Court;	
• The questions about which the expert is to be asked to give an opinion (including any diverse cultural or religious contexts)	

Action	Party and Timing	
• When the Court is to be asked to give permission for the instruction (if unusually permission has already been given the date and details of that permission)		
• Whether permission is asked of the Court for the instruction of another expert in the same or any related field (ie to give an opinion on the same or related questions)		
• The volume of reading which the expert will need to undertake		
• Whether or not (in an appropriate case) permission has been applied for or given for the expert to examine the child		
• Whether or not (in an appropriate case) it will be necessary for the expert to conduct interviews (and if so with whom)		
• The likely timetable of legal and social work steps		
• When the expert's opinion is likely to be required		
• Whether and if so what date has been fixed by the Court for any hearing at which the expert may be required to give evidence (in particular the Final Hearing).		
2.2 Expert's Response: Not later than 5 days before the CMC the solicitors intending to instruct the expert shall obtain the following information from the expert:	Solicitor instructing the expert	5 days before the CMC
• That the work required is within the expert's expertise		
• That the expert is available to do the relevant work within the suggested time scale		
• When the expert is available to give evidence, the dates and/or times to avoid, and, where a hearing date has not been fixed, the amount of notice the expert will require to make arrangements to come to Court without undue disruption to their normal clinical routines.		

	Action	Party and Timing	
	• The cost, including hourly and global rates, and likely hours to be spent, of attending at experts/professionals meetings, attending court and writing the report (to include any examinations and interviews).		
2.3	Case Management Questionnaire:	The Party proposing to instruct the expert	not later than 2 days before the CMC

2.3 Case Management Questionnaire:

Any party who proposes to ask the Court for permission to instruct an expert shall not later than 2 days before the CMC (or any hearing at which the application is to be made) file and serve a case management questionnaire setting out the proposal to instruct the expert in the following detail:

- The name, discipline, qualifications and expertise of the expert (by way of CV where possible)

- The expert's availability to undertake the work

- The relevance of the expert evidence sought to be adduced to the issues in the proceedings and the specific questions upon which it is proposed the expert should give an opinion (including the relevance of any diverse cultural or religious contexts)

- The timetable for the report

- The responsibility for instruction

- Whether or not the expert evidence can properly be obtained by the joint instruction of the expert by two or more of the parties

- Whether the expert evidence can properly be obtained by only one party (eg on behalf of the child)

Action	Party and Timing	
• Whether it is necessary for more than one expert in the same discipline to be instructed by more than one party		
• Why the expert evidence proposed cannot be given by social services undertaking a core assessment or by the Guardian in accordance with their different statutory duties		
• The likely cost of the report on both an hourly and global basis		
• The proposed apportionment of costs of jointly instructed experts as between the Local Authority and the publicly funded parties.		
2.4 Draft Order for the CMC: Any party proposing to instruct an expert shall in the draft order submitted at the CMC request the Court to give directions (among any others) as to the following:	Any Party	not later than 2 days before the CMC
• The party who is to be responsible for drafting the letter of instruction and providing the documents to the expert		
• The issues identified by the Court and the questions about which the expert is to give an opinion		
• The timetable within which the report is to be prepared, filed and served		
• The disclosure of the report to the parties and to any other expert		
• The conduct of an experts' discussion		
• The preparation of a statement of agreement and disagreement by the experts following an experts' discussion		
• The attendance of the expert at the Final Hearing unless agreement is reached at or before the PHR about the opinions given by the expert.		

	Action	Party and Timing
3	**Letter of Instruction**	Solicitor instructing the expert within 5 days of the CMC
3.1	The solicitor instructing the expert shall within 5 days of the CMC prepare (agree with the other parties where appropriate) file and serve a letter of instruction to the expert which shall:	

- Set out the context in which the expert's opinion is sought (including any diverse ethnic, cultural, religious or linguistic contexts)

- Define carefully the specific questions the expert is required to answer ensuring

  - that they are within the ambit of the expert's area of expertise and

  - that they do not contain unnecessary or irrelevant detail

  - that the questions addressed to the expert are kept to a manageable number and are clear, focused and direct

  - that the questions reflect what the expert has been requested to do by the Court

- List the documentation provided or provide for the expert an indexed and paginated bundle which shall include:

  - a copy of the order (or those parts of the order) which gives permission for the instruction of the expert immediately the order becomes available

  - an agreed list of essential reading

  - all new documentation when it is filed and regular updates to the list of documents provided or to the index to the paginated bundle

  - a copy of this code of guidance and of the protocol

Action	Party and Timing

- Identify the relevant lay and professional people concerned with the proceedings (eg the treating clinicians) and inform the expert of his/her right to talk to the other professionals provided an accurate record is made of the discussion

- Identify any other expert instructed in the proceedings and advise the expert of his/her right to talk to the other experts provided an accurate record is made of the discussion

- Define the contractual basis upon which the expert is retained and in particular the funding mechanism including how much the expert will be paid (an hourly rate and overall estimate should already have been obtained) when the expert will be paid, and what limitation there might be on the amount the expert can charge for the work which he/she will have to do. There should also be a brief explanation of the 'detailed assessment process' in cases proceeding in the Care Centre or the High Court which are not subject to a high cost case contract

- In default of agreement the format of the letter of instruction shall be determined by the Court, which may determine the issue upon written application with representations from each party.

4 **The Expert's Report**	The Expert in accordance with the Court's timetable
4.1 Content of the Report:	

The expert's report shall be addressed to the Court and shall:

- Give details of the expert's qualifications and experience

- Contain a statement setting out the substance of all material instructions (whether written or oral) summarising the facts stated and instructions given to the expert which are material to the conclusions and opinions expressed in the report

Action	Party and Timing
• Give details of any literature or other research material upon which the expert has relied in giving an opinion	
• State who carried out any test, examination or interview which the expert has used for the report and whether or not the test, examination or interview has been carried out under the expert's supervision.	
• Give details of the qualifications of any person who carried out the test, examination or interview	
• Where there is a range of opinion on the question to be answered by the expert:	
• summarise the range of opinion and	
• give reasons for the opinion expressed	
• Contain a summary of the expert's conclusions and opinions	
• Contain a statement that the expert understands his duty to the Court and has complied with that duty	
• Where appropriate be verified by a statement of truth.	
4.2 Supplementary Questions: Any party wishing to ask supplementary questions of an expert for the purpose of clarifying the expert's report must put those questions in writing to the parties not later than 5 days after receipt of the report. Only those questions that are agreed by the parties or in default of agreement approved by the Court may be put to the expert. The Court may determine the issue upon written application with representations from each party.	Any party within 5 days of the receipt of the report
5 Experts Discussion (Meeting)	The Court at the CMC
5.1 Purpose: The Court will give directions for the experts to meet or communicate: • To identify and narrow the issues in the case.	

Action	Party and Timing	
• To reach agreement on the expert questions		
• To identify the reasons for disagreement on any expert question and to identify what if any action needs to be taken to resolve any outstanding disagreement/question		
• To obtain elucidation or amplification of relevant evidence in order to assist the Court to determine the issues		
• To limit, wherever possible, the need for experts to attend Court to give oral evidence.		
5.2 The Arrangements for a Discussion/Meeting: In accordance with the directions given by the Court at the CMC, the solicitor for the child or such other professional who is given the responsibility by the Court shall make arrangements for there to be a discussion between the experts within 10 days of the filing of the experts reports. The following matters should be considered: • Where permission has been given for the instruction of experts from different disciplines a global discussion may be held relating to those questions that concern all or most of them. • Separate discussions may have to be held among experts from the same or related disciplines but care should be taken to ensure that the discussions complement each other so that related questions are discussed by all relevant experts	Child's Solicitor	within 10 days of the filing of the experts' reports

	Action	Party and Timing
	• 7 days prior to a discussion or meeting the solicitor for the child or other nominated professional should formulate an agenda to include a list of the questions for consideration. This may usefully take the form of a list of questions to be circulated among the other parties in advance. The agenda should comprise all questions that each party wishes the experts to consider. The agenda and list of questions should be sent to each of the experts not later than 2 days before the discussion	
	• The discussion should usually be chaired by the child's solicitor or in exceptional cases where the parties have applied to the Court at the CMC, by an independent professional identified by the parties or the Court. In complex medical cases it may be necessary for the discussion to be jointly chaired by an expert. A minute must be taken of the questions answered by the experts, and a Statement of Agreement and Disagreement must be prepared which should be agreed and signed by each of the experts who participated in the discussion. The statement should be served and filed not later than 5 days after the discussion has taken place	
	• Consideration should be given in each case to whether some or all of the experts participate by telephone conference or video link to ensure that minimum disruption is caused to clinical schedules.	
5.3	Positions of the Parties:	Any Party at the PHR
	Where any party refuses to be bound by an agreement that has been reached at an experts' discussion that party must inform the Court at or before the PHR of the reasons for refusing to accept the agreement.	

Action	Party and Timing

5.4 Professionals Meetings:

In proceedings where the Court gives a direction that a professionals meeting shall take place between the Local Authority and any relevant named professionals for the purpose of providing assistance to the Local Authority in the formulation of plans and proposals for the child, the meeting shall be arranged, chaired and minuted in accordance with directions given by the Court.

6	**Arranging for the Expert to attend Court**	Every Party responsible for the instruction of an expert by the PHR
6.1	Preparation:	

The party who is responsible for the instruction of an expert witness shall ensure:

- That a date and time is fixed for the Court to hear the expert's evidence that is if possible convenient to the expert and that the fixture is made substantially in advance of the Final Hearing and no later than at the PHR (ie no later than 2 weeks before the Final Hearing)

- That if the expert's oral evidence is not required the expert is notified as soon as possible

- That the witness template accurately indicates how long the expert is likely to be giving evidence, in order to avoid the inconvenience of the expert being delayed at Court.

6.2 All parties shall ensure: All Parties   at the PHR

- That where expert witnesses are to be called the advocates attending the PHR have identified at the advocates meeting the issues which the experts are to address

- That wherever possible a logical sequence to the evidence is arranged with experts of the same discipline giving evidence on the same day(s)

Action	Party and Timing
• That at the PHR the Court is informed of any circumstance where all experts agree but a party nevertheless does not accept the agreed opinion so that directions can be given for the proper consideration of the experts' evidence and the parties reasons for not accepting the same	
• That in the exceptional case the Court is informed of the need for a witness summons.	

7	**Post Hearing Action**	Solicitor instructing the expert	within 10 days of the Final Hearing
7.1	Within 10 days of the Final Hearing the solicitor instructing the expert should provide feedback to the expert by way of a letter informing the expert of the outcome of the case, and the use made by the Court of the expert's opinion. Where the Court directs that a copy of the transcript can be sent to the expert, the solicitor instructing the expert should obtain the transcript within 10 days of the Final Hearing.		

****

INDEX